1967

This book may be kept

THE BRIDE OF MESSINA

WILLIAM TELL

DEMETRIUS

FRIEDRICH von SCHILLER

THE BRIDE OF MESSINA

or The Enemy Brothers

A TRAGEDY WITH CHORUSES

WILLIAM TELL

DEMETRIUS

or The Blood Wedding in Moscow

A FRAGMENT

Translated by

CHARLES E. PASSAGE

Associate Professor of Comparative Literature
Brooklyn College of the City University of New York

FREDERICK UNGAR PUBLISHING CO.

NEW YORK

THE BRIDE OF MESSINA

INTRODUCTION

In 1776, when Schiller was seventeen years old, two youthful playwrights submitted tragedies in response to a prize competition announced in the newspapers of the previous year by a couple of Hamburg amateurs of the theatre. Johann Anton Leisewitz, aged twenty-four, offered *Julius of Taranto*, a somber play about a pair of brothers, Julius and Guido, rivals for the love of the beautiful Blanca. Unmitigated gloom drew the final curtain, with Julius murdered by Guido in a fit of jealous rage, with Blanca insane from grief, with Guido stabbed by his outraged father, and with the father renouncing his rule over Taranto to become a Carthusian monk. It was young Schiller's favorite play. Friedrich Maximilian Klinger, also aged twenty-four, offered *The Twins* (Die Zwillinge), the plot of which he adapted, rather conveniently, from his competitor, Leisewitz. Young Guelfo, its hero, was morbidly jealous of his older twin brother, Ferdinando, and suspected that he was himself the elder of the two and therefore wrongfully dispossessed. Ferdinando, for his part, sought by every means to conciliate Guelfo, even to passing over the latter's attempt to rob him of his fiancée, Kamilla. At length Guido murdered Ferdinando, and then, with his hand upon the corpse, wildly vaunted his guilt to his aged father. Whereupon the aged father stabbed him with a dagger.

Both plays patently influenced Schiller's own first drama, *The Robbers* (1781), yet so strongly did their memory linger on in his mind that he continued to cherish the plan of a future drama to be called *The Rival Brothers*. Years later, on March 21, 1799, with *Wallenstein* barely finished, he discussed the cherished project with Goethe. Yet *Mary Stuart* was undertaken next, and then *The Maid of Orleans*. At last, in August of 1802, he set to work seriously on the long deferred play, now newly entitled *The Bride of Messina, or The Hostile Brothers* (Die Braut von Messina, oder Die feindlichen Brüder). Six months later his diary triumphantly chronicled its completion on February 1, 1803. Goethe immediately put the work into rehearsal at the Weimar theatre, where a highly successful première was staged on March 19th. This was the occasion of the Duke's displeasure at the concerted hurrah in which Dr. Schütz of Jena led the contingent of university students in the audience. Successful presentations were given twice more at Weimar, then in other German cities. The published version of June, 1803 was exhausted in its six thousand copies and in three reprintings by the time of Schiller's death in 1805.

The subject had undergone a radical change in the author's mind during those long years of waiting. Perhaps as early as 1789 Schiller had begun to see the story in terms of *Oedipus the King,* and it is certain that he worked out the final version in conscious analogy to the progressive revelations of Sophocles' famous drama. The theme of incest, absent from the "Storm and Stress" plays of Leisewitz and Klinger, was likewise surely drawn from the Sophoclean source. A letter of September 9, 1802, to his friend Körner, reveals that Schiller also had Aeschylean models in mind, doubtless by way of reflex from his reading of four recently published translations of that ancient writer. His governing intention was a modern adaptation of classical Greek drama complete with chorus. The Aristotelian unities were to be observed in a form which the author considered closer to their original purport than French classical theorists had defined them. The time limits of the story do not exceed a day and a night and are well within "a single revolution of the sun;" the locale shifts, as in Aeschylus' *Eumenides* and in Sophocles' *Ajax,* but within a small compass, namely the city of Messina and its environs; the singleness of the action conforms to the most rigid demands of either Greek or Frenchman. Above all, the language was to have the sublime exaltation of ancient Greek tragedy.

The play begins well. The troubled queen speaks a stately prologue to the silently listening elders of the city. The stern and "better" brother, Don Manuel, has a convincing dignity; the rashly passionate but more humanly acceptable younger brother, Don Cesar, has an equal dignity. Their respective choruses of vassals lend each a greater force. The reconciliation of the warring brothers as they stand embraced by either arm of their mother makes a fine stylized tableau, which if its effect is not so much ancient Greek as Baroque—somewhat in the manner of Corneille's *Horace*—is still a fine tableau stylized in the grand manner. It is with what is now called Act II—for Schiller originally intended a continuous text without act or scene division—and the entrance of the heroine-sister that the work starts to become problematic.

The maidenly-passive Beatrice does not readily win twentieth-century sympathy, not even with due allowance made for shifting tides of taste. In *Wallenstein* it had been abundantly clear that Thekla was helpless amid the people who surrounded her and that her happiness was doomed beyond a doubt. With Beatrice we are not so sure. Thekla also rose grandly to her death and displayed no small power of will, once she knew what task was hers to perform. Beatrice, on the other hand, is all girlish simplicity and bewilderment. Her "sinless sin" of slipping off to the Prince of Messina's funeral is a trifle coy. Perfect propriety prompted her withdrawal from the ceremony as soon as she became aware of Don Cesar's desirous eyes upon her, and yet we prefer the more interestingly ambiguous propriety of Emilia Galotti in similar circumstances. We also note the purely literary origin of Schiller's motif in Lessing's drama. We find Beatrice's romance with Don Manuel excessively fairytale-like in its beginning and excessively preoccupied with maidenly dreaminess in its failure to ask a few pertinent names and details. One logical question from the girl would have averted the whole catastrophe, and she, of all characters in the play, had the greatest need to inquire. But she loved quite literally with no questions asked. Hers are the least plausible of the entire tissue of coincidences upon which the play depends. Beatrice is static. She causes disaster, wrings her hands, and does nothing.

No doubt we wrongly ask that Beatrice, or anyone else in this play, should be an individual character. The plot as a whole is the poet's real concern, and the persons are no more than bearers of the plot. The core of the dramatic parable is the mystery of human fate, and it was in order to make his parable starkly clear that the author avoided the entanglements of actual history by setting the action in Norman Sicily of approximately 1060, about which time and place few of us are well informed. There Christian, Moslem, and ancient Greek religions overlap,— according to poets' time-honored license, Schiller says, though some of us feel uneasy about it in this instance. There coincidences follow one upon the other thick and fast, and there Fate plays cat-and-mouse with its human victims.

The success of this play, like the success of Sophocles' *Oedipus,* depends on our catching the eerie sense of Fate's closing in upon men and women in order to destroy them. The goodness and dignity of the characters gain our sympathy; the evil in them makes their destruction credible; their behavior in the face of disaster makes us take pride in mankind. The true dramatic conflict, however, lies not with the warring brothers but rather with the struggle between Man and The Mystery. A certain fascination grips us as we perceive the nature of this unearthly and unequal struggle, and we watch breathlessly as the cupped hands of Destiny materialize under, over, and around the human figures and ineluctably close giant fingers upon their petty forms. Once the play is viewed from this angle, the character of Beatrice is a matter of small importance. Fate has marked all members of this family, both the weak and the strong, for annihilation. We behold them in the hour of their doom.

Step by step, that inexorable Fate advances, pausing upon

each foot to allow the human commentary of the solemn chorus to be heard. It is a unique double chorus, each half consisting of twelve speakers. The academic critics of Schiller's day complained at this non-classical irregularity, though something very like it was attempted at least once in antiquity, by Euripides in *Hippolytus*. The verses are further unGreek in being cast in modern and very simple verse patterns, most frequently tetrameters, by the use of rhymes, and by being grouped arbitrarily rather than in symmetrical strophes and antistrophes. Schiller never intended them to be set to music, though he did intend them to be recited by twelve voices in unison. Even on this point he temporized, however, and for the Vienna performance dispatched a manuscript in which the chorus lines were distributed among the twelve speakers, with only one voice speaking at any one time. The two sets of twelve chorus members inevitably lent themselves to debate and argument, reinforcing the debates and arguments of the principal characters, as well as to picturesque formations on stage and to striking tableaux. As for their commentary, its wisdom is simple to the point of being commonplace, yet no less true and pertinent for all that. Its sincerity is undoubted. Its sombre melancholy is Schiller's own.

The Bride of Messina presents a "Storm and Stress" subject reinterpreted in terms of academic classicism. The very notion is striking, interesting, and original. It is not so very far removed from the notion of Eugene O'Neill when he composed *Mourning Becomes Electra*. Its experimental nature should appeal to enterprising minds in the theatre, and, with direction that embodied a good sense for Baroque grandeur, this play might well yield surprising rewards in stage revival.

THE BRIDE OF MESSINA

NOTE

Schiller's essay, *On the Use of the Chorus in Tragedy,* is here prefixed to the text of the play as has been customary since the time of the original publication.

ON THE USE OF THE CHORUS IN TRAGEDY

A poetic work must justify itself, and if the fact does not speak, words will not help very much. It might, therefore, be quite properly left to the chorus to be its own advocate, if it were just presented in the right way. But the work of tragic poetry is rounded to a whole only by theatrical presentation. The poet provides the words merely, and music and dance must be added to bring them alive. Hence, as long as this powerful sensory concomitant is lacking, it will seem an extraneous item in the economy of the tragedy, an alien presence and a hindrance which merely interrupts the course of the action, destroys the illusion, and leaves the spectator cold. To do justice to the chorus a transition must be made from the actual stage to an *ideal* one. Yet the same must be done wherever a higher thing is to be attained. What art does not have, it must acquire, and the accidental lack of auxiliary means must not limit the creative imagination of the poet. He sets loftiest things as his goal, he strives for an ideal, and practical art must accommodate itself to the circumstances.

The commonly heard assertion is not true, that the public debases art. The artist debases the public, and in all eras where art declined, it fell because of the artists. The public needs nothing but receptivity, and this it has. Audiences come before the curtain with an undefined longing and with a many-sided capacity. They bring with them a capability for highest things; they take delight in what is sensible and right; and if they have begun to content themselves with the bad, they will assuredly cease to demand the excellent when such is offered to them.

3

The poet, one hears it objected, may work toward an ideal, the critic may judge according to ideas, but qualified, limited, practical art rests upon needs. The producer wants to subsist, the actor wants to be seen, the spectator wants to be entertained and moved. He seeks pleasure and he is dissatisfied when exertion is expected of him just when he is looking for recreation and entertainment.

But in treating the theatre more seriously no one is trying to spoil the spectator's pleasure, but rather to ennoble it. It is still a fancy, but a poetic one. All art is devoted to joy, and there is no higher, no more serious endeavor than making human beings happy. That art alone is genuine which provides the highest enjoyment. The highest enjoyment, however, is freedom of the spirit in the vivacious play of all its powers.

From the arts of the imaginative faculties everyone expects a certain liberation from the limitations of reality; he wants to delight in the possible and give free rein to his fancy. The man with the least expectations still wants to forget his business, his everyday life, his individual self; he wants to feel himself in extraordinary situations, to revel in the odd vagaries of chance. If he is of a more serious nature, he wants to find on the stage that moral government of the world which he misses in actual life. Yet he himself knows perfectly well that he is only carrying on a pointless game, that in the last analysis he is only indulging in dreams, and when he comes away again from the stage into the actual world the latter will once again beset him with all its oppressive constriction; he will be the world's victim as before, for that has remained what it was and nothing in him has been altered. Nothing has been gained thereby but a pleasing illusion of the moment, which will vanish upon awakening.

And precisely because only a transitory illusion is the object here, nothing is required but an appearance of truth or the cherished plausibility so willingly substituted for truth.

Genuine art, on the other hand, does not have as its object a mere transitory game. Its serious purpose is not merely to translate the human being into a momentary dream of freedom, but actually to *make* him free. It accomplishes this by awakening a power within him, by using and developing this power to remove to a distance of objectivity the sensory world, which otherwise only weighs us down as raw material and oppresses us as a blind force, to transform the sensory world into a free creation of our spirit, and to control the material world through ideas.

Precisely because genuine art aims at something real and objective, it cannot be satisfied with the mere appearance of truth. Upon truth itself, on the solid bedrock of nature it rears its ideal structure.

But how art can and shall be at once ideal and yet in the profoundest sense real—how it can and shall totally abandon actuality and at the same time conform most exactly to nature—this is what few people understand, this is what makes the view of poetic and plastic works so ambiguous, because the two demands seem to cancel each other completely out in the general opinion.

It usually happens, moreover, that people try to achieve the one at the sacrifice of the other and by so doing miss both. He whom Nature has endowed with a faithful mind and a fervor of sensitivity but denied creative imagination, will be a faithful portrayer of actuality; he will grasp accidental appearances but never grasp the spirit of Nature. He will bring us back the material of the world only, but for that very reason it will not be our work nor the free product of our formative spirit, and hence cannot have the beneficent effect of art, which subsists in freedom. Serious, to be sure, but joyless is the mood with which such an artist or poet sends us away, and we find ourselves painfully thrust back into common and narrow actuality by the very art which was to have set us free. On the other hand, one endowed with a lively fantasy but without soul and character, will not be worried about any truth but will merely play with the world-material, will try merely to surprise us with fantastic and bizarre combinations, and, since his whole activity is only froth and illusion, he will entertain us for the moment but he will not found and construct anything in our spirits. His game, like the other's seriousness, is not poetic. Arbitrary lining up of fantastic pictures one after another is not penetrating into the ideal, and imitative reproduction of actuality is not portrayal of Nature. The two claims contradict each other so little that they are really one and the same, namely that art is true only as it abandons actuality altogether and becomes purely ideal. Nature itself is only an idea of the spirit, an idea which never comes to sensory perception. It lies beneath the veil of phenomena but never emerges itself as a phenomenon. Only to the art of the ideal is it vouchsafed, or rather enjoined as an obligation, to grasp this spirit of the universe and to encompass it within a corporeal form. Art itself cannot bring it to sensory perception, but by its creative force it can bring it to the powers of the imagination and thereby be truer than any actuality and more real than any experience. It follows, then, that the artist cannot use a single element from actuality as he finds it, that his work must be ideal in *all* its parts if it is to have reality as a whole and be in consonance with Nature.

What is true for poetry and art in their totality is also valid for all their genres, and the application of the foregoing may without difficulty be made to tragedy. Here too there has been and still is a long struggle with the vulgar concept of the *natural,* which reduces all poetry and art to naught and destroys them. To plastic art a certain ideality is conceded rather grudgingly, though more for conventional reasons than for essential ones; but from poetry, and particularly from dramatic poetry, people demand *illusion,* which, if it were actually to be produced, would forever be nothing but a sorry imposture. All the externalities in a dramatic representation go counter to this concept: all things are symbols merely of actual things. In the theatre daylight itself is only artificial daylight, architecture is only symbolic architecture, and metrical speech is itself ideal. Yet the action is supposed to be real and the part is supposed to offset the whole. Thus the French, having completely misunderstood the spirit of the ancients, introduced a unity of place and time upon the stage in the most vulgar empirical sense, as though there were a different place from purely ideal space and a different time from the purely consistent line of action.

With the introduction of metrical speech one has already been brought a large step nearer to poetic tragedy. Several lyrical attempts have been successfully realized on the stage, and through their living power poetry has gained many a victory in individual details over the prevailing prejudice. But little is gained by individual details unless the error is dispelled in regard to the whole, and it is not enough to have a thing tolerated as poetic license when it is, after all, the essence of all poetry. The introduction of the chorus would be the final and decisive step— and if it served no other purpose than to declare war openly and honestly on naturalism in art, it would be a living wall that tragedy draws about itself in order to shut itself definitely away from the actual world and preserve for itself its ideal ground and its poetic freedom.

The tragedy of the Greeks developed, as is well known, out of the chorus. But just as it extricated itself from it historically and time-wise, so it can also be said to have risen out of it poetically and spirit-wise, and that without those persistent witnesses and bearers of the action it would have turned into a wholly different sort of poetry. Abolition of the chorus and the contraction of that materially powerful organ into the characterless and tediously recurrent figure of a sorry *confidant* was, then, not so great an improvement of tragedy as the French and their blind adherents imagined.

Ancient tragedy, concerned as it originally was with only gods, heroes, and kings, needed the chorus as a necessary concomitant; it found it in nature, and made use of it because it found it. The actions and fates of the heroes and kings were public in themselves, even more so in that simple, primeval time. Consequently the chorus was more of a natural organ in ancient tragedy and followed from the poetic form of actual life. In modern tragedy it becomes an artificial organ, helping to *bring forth* poetry. The modern poet no longer finds the chorus in nature. He has to create it poetically and introduce it, that is, he has to manipulate an alteration in the story he is treating in order to transpose it back into that childlike time and into that childlike form.

Hence the chorus performs far more essential service for the modern poet than for the ancient one, precisely because it transforms the modern, vulgar world into the ancient poetic one, because it renders useless to him everything that goes counter to poetry and forces him upward toward the simplest, most primeval, and most naive motifs. The palace of the kings is now closed; the judges have retreated from the gates of the city to the interiors of houses; the letter has crowded out the living word; the people themselves, that materially living mass, has become the state,—unless it is acting as raw force,—and hence has become an abstract principle; and the gods have returned to the bosoms of men. The poet must reopen the palaces, he must once again bring the judges forth beneath the open skies, he must establish the gods anew, he must restore everything that is direct and which has been abolished by the artificial arrangements of actual life, he must cast off all artificial contrivances in man and around man which hinder the manifestation of his inner nature and his original character, just as sculptors cast away modern garments and accept nothing of all external surroundings except what renders visible the highest of forms,— human form.

But just as the plastic artist adjusts the fullness of drapery-folds about his figures in order to fill out the spaces of his picture richly and graciously, in order to bind the separate parts firmly together in tranquil masses, in order to invest the human forms ingeniously and at the same time make them manifest, just so the tragic poet interweaves and surrounds his strictly delimited action and the sharp delineations of his characters with a weft of lyrical splendor in which, as in a far-flung purple drapery, the acting personages move free and noble with digni-fied restraint and lofty serenity.

In a higher organization the substance or elemental matter must no longer be visible; the chemical pigment disappears in the subtle tint of living flesh. Yet the substance too has its own splendor and can be taken up, as such, in an artistic form. Then, however, it must earn its place by life and fullness and by harmony, it must validate the forms it surrounds instead of oppressing them with its weight.

In works of plastic art this is readily understandable to everyone. But the same thing is true of poetry, and of tragic poetry, our present subject. Everything that the mind expresses in general is precisely like that which merely rouses the senses, it is no more than substance and raw material in a poetic work, and where it predominates it will inevitably destroy the poetic quality. For the latter is situated just at the point of indifferentiation of ideal and sensory things. Now man is so constituted that he always wishes to proceed from the particular to the general, and so reflection must also have its place in tragedy. If it is to deserve this place, it must win anew through presentation what it lacks in sensory life. For, when the two elements of poetry, the ideal and the sensory, do not operate in intimate alliance they must operate side by side, or else all poetry comes to naught. If the scales do not perfectly balance, equilibrium can be achieved only by vacillation of the two scales.

This is what the chorus does in tragedy. The chorus is not itself an individual but rather a general concept. This concept is represented by a sensorily powerful mass which impresses the senses by its expansive presence. The chorus abandons the narrow circle of the action to discourse on past and future, distant ages and peoples, the entire range of things human, in order to draw the great conclusions of life and to pronounce the teachings of wisdom. But it does this with the full power of the imagination, with a bold lyric freedom that marches with the pace of gods about the high peaks of human affairs—and it does so to the accompaniment of the entire sensual power of rhythm and of music in tone and gesture.

The chorus, therefore, *purifies* the tragic poem by dissociating reflection from the action and by endowing reflection itself with poetic power through this very dissociation. In the same way the plastic artist transforms the vulgar necessity of clothing into charm and beauty by means of a rich drapery.

But just as the painter finds himself compelled to heighten the color-tone of living matter in order to hold his powerful materials in balance, just so the lyric speech of the chorus obligates the poet to elevate the total language of his poem, relatively speaking, and by so doing to intensify the sensory power of expression in general. Only the chorus justifies the poet in this elevation of tone which fills the ear, stretches the mind, and expands the total spirit. This single giant-form in his picture requires him to put all his figures upon cothurni and thereby confer tragic grandeur upon his painting. If the chorus is dispensed with, the speech of his tragedy must decline over-all, or else what is now great and mighty will appear forced and exaggerated. The ancient chorus, if it were once introduced into French tragedy, would expose it in all its insufficiency and destroy it. The same chorus would doubtless bring out the true significance of Shakespearean tragedy.

Just as the chorus brings life to language, so does it bring calm into action—but the beautiful and lofty calm which must be the character of a noble work of art. For the spectator's feelings must retain their freedom even amid the most vehement passion; they must not be the victim of impressions, but rather they must come away serene and clear from the agitations sustained. What common judgment finds objectionable in the chorus, namely, that it dispels the illusion and shatters the emotional power of the effects, is just what serves as its highest recommendation. For it is precisely this blind power of passions that the true artist avoids, it is precisely this illusion that he scorns to arouse. If the blows with which tragedy afflicts our hearts were to follow one upon another uninterruptedly, afflic-tion would prevail over activity. We would be confused amid the subject matter and no longer hover above it. The chorus, by holding the parts separate and by intervening between the passions with its calming observations, gives us back our freedom, which would otherwise be lost in the storm of emotional agitation. The tragic persons likewise have need of this respite, this calm, to collect themselves, for they are not real beings that merely obey the force of the moment and represent mere individuals, but ideal personages and representatives of their class, who pronounce upon the profound in mankind. The presence of the chorus, which, as a judging witness, hears them and restrains the first outbursts of their passion by its intervention, motivates the circumspection with which they act and the dignity with which they speak. In a certain sense they stand on a natural stage because they speak and act before spectators, and by that token they come to speak more becomingly from an artificial stage to an audience.

So much for my authorization to bring the ancient chorus back to the tragic stage. Choruses are, to be sure, also to be found in modern tragedy, but the chorus of Greek tragedy as I have used it here, the chorus of a single, ideal person who bears and accompanies the entire action, is essentially different from those operatic choruses, and when I hear people talking, in connection with Greek tragedy, about choruses instead of about a chorus, I suspect them of not rightly knowing whereof they speak. To the best of my knowledge, the chorus of ancient tragedy has not reappeared upon the stage at any time since its fall.

I have, it is true, divided the chorus in two parts and represented it in conflict with itself, but this is the case only when it participates in the action as a real personage or as a blind mass. As a *chorus* and as an ideal personage it is always at one with itself. I have shifted the settings and had the chorus leave the stage several times; but Aeschylus too, the creator of tragedy, and Sophocles, the supreme master of that art-form, also availed themselves of this liberty.

Another liberty I have permitted myself may be harder to justify. I have represented the Christian religion and Greek mythology as intermingled, and have even suggested Moorish superstition. But the scene of the action is Messina, where these three religions continued to make themselves felt, partly in life, partly in monuments of art, and where they spoke to the senses. Then, too, I regard it as a privilege of poetry to treat the various religions as a collective whole for the powers of the imagination, in which whole everything that bears a unique character or expresses a unique way of feeling, has its place. Beneath the husk of all religions lies religion, the idea of a divinity, and a poet must be allowed to express this in whatever form he finds most convenient and most fitting.

CHARACTERS

DONNA ISABELLA, Princess of Messina
DON MANUEL }
DON CESAR } her sons
BEATRICE
DIEGO
MESSENGERS
THE CHORUS, consisting of the retinues
        of the brothers
THE ELDERS OF MESSINA (mute parts)

The action is represented as taking place in the Sicilian city of Messina at a remote time in history, perhaps around the year 1060.

ACT 1

The scene is a spacious colonnaded hall with en-
tranceways on either side. A great double door at
the rear leads to a chapel.

Enter Donna Isabella in deep mourning; the
elders of Messina are standing around her.

ISABELLA: Obedient to Necessity, and not
  To any impulse of my own, I come,
  You grey and reverend elders of this city,
  Before you from my hushed apartments in
  The women's quarters to unveil my face
  To your male gaze. For it beseems the widow
  With husband lost, life's light and glory gone,
  To hide her black-beshrouded form of night
  Away from the world's eye in quiet walls.
  And yet inexorable and all-prevailing   10
  The moment's voice drives me imperiously
  Forth to the disaccustomed light of day.
    The moon its luminous form has not yet twice
  Renewed since I my princely spouse conducted
  Down to his final resting place, the same
  Who ruled this city with his mighty power,
  Protecting you with his strong arm against
  A world that hemmed you hostilely about.
  He is himself departed, but his spirit
  Lives on in a heroic pair of brave   20
  And glorious sons, this country's pride. You have
  Beheld them growing up in joyous strength
  Among you, yet along with them there has
  Sprung up from unknown and portentous seed
  A dire fraternal hatred that has wrenched
  Asunder childhood's cheerful amity
  And ripened deadly with their serious years.
  I never have enjoyed their harmony.

Yet both alike I nourished at these breasts,
Impartially I show them love and care,   30
And both, I know, show me a filial love.
In this sole impulse are they quite agreed;
A bloody strife divides them in all others.

   While yet their father, fear-inspiring, ruled,
He held their wayward turbulence in check
By the dread justness of his own impartial sternness.
Beneath a single yoke of iron weight
He bent their stubborn spirits to a union.
When bearing arms they might not meet together
Nor pass the night beneath a single roof.   40
Thus with his ordinance severe he checked
The savage outburst of their brutish instincts;
But unreformed down in the heart's recesses
He left their hatred. Strong men spurn the task
Of filling in the quiet welling spring
Because they can by force subdue the torrent.

   What had to come, then came. Once he had closed
His eyes in death and once his potent hand
No longer held them down, their ancient grudge
Broke forth like smothered fury of the fire   50
That kindles in the open air to flames.
I tell you what you all bore witness to:
Messina split in two, the brothers' feud
Severed every sacred bond of Nature,
Thus giving universal strife its watchword;
Sword clashed with sword, the city as a battlefield,
These very halls themselves were stained with blood.

   You saw the State's bonds broken off and severed
But not how my heart broke within my bosom.
You felt the public anguish only, but   60
You did not ask about the mother's anguish.
You came to me and spoke these cruel words:
"You see how your sons' feuding has embroiled
The city in a civil war just when,

Beset by wicked neighbors round about,
It can by unity alone stave off
The foe. You are their mother. See that you
Compose your sons' ensanguined argument.
What do we peace-abiding folk care for
Our rulers' quarrels? Must we be destroyed   70
Because your sons wage frantic mutual war?
We mean to help ourselves and do without them
And choose another master over us
Who can and will achieve our own best welfare!"
Thus you harsh men then spoke, unpitying,
Concerned for yourselves only and your city,
And added yet the weight of public woe
Upon this heart which was already burdened
Enough with cares and with a mother's grief.
I undertook what no one dared to hope for,   80
And with my shattered mother's heart I threw
Myself between the madmen, crying Peace!
Undaunted, eagerly, and tirelessly
I sent word to them, first one then the other,
Till I prevailed with my maternal pleas
That they consent to meet each other in
Messina and in their paternal castle
Without hostility, a thing which had
Not happened since the Prince their father died.

This is the day! I wait from hour to hour   90
To greet the messenger of their approach.
Be ready to receive your rulers then
With reverence such as best beseems their subjects.
Let your thought be of nothing but your duty,
For all else let us be responsible.
Destructive to this land, and to themselves
Destruction-bearing has my sons' feud been;
At one and reconciled, they have the power
To be your shield against the entire world
And to assert their rights—in spite of you!   100

(The elders withdraw silently with their hands on their hearts. She beckons to an old servant who has remained behind.)

Diego!

DIEGO: What is your command, my Princess?

ISABELLA: My trusty servant! Honest heart! Approach!
My sorrows you have shared, my sufferings,
Share now a happy woman's happiness.
Unto your loyal heart I have confided
My bitter-sweet and sacred secret. Now
The moment has arrived when it must be
Brought forth into the light of day. Too long
Have I choked Nature's mighty impulse back
Because an alien will imperiously   110
Exerted its dominion over me.
But now her voice may freely be upraised,
Today my heart shall know its satisfaction.
Let this house now, that long was desolate,
Assemble everyone that I hold dear.
    So let your aged footsteps be directed
Toward that familiar convent precinct which
Has kept a precious treasure safe for me.
You, loyal soul, once took it there for me.
And left it for safe keeping until better days,   120
Performing a sad woman that sad service.
Now to the happy woman happily
Bring back the precious pledge!

(Trumpets are heard in the distance.)

                                O hurry, hurry,
And may Joy make your footsteps young again!
I hear the call of warrior trumpets sounding,
Announcing the arrival of my sons.

(Exit Diego.)

(The music is heard again from the opposite side and coming closer and closer.)

Now all Messina is a-stir. A torrent
Of voices intermingling bears this way.
They come! A mother's heart with mighty pulse
Perceives the force and pull of their approach.   130
Yes, they are coming! O my sons! my sons!

(She hurries out.)

(Enter the chorus.)

(It consists of two semi-choruses that enter simultaneously from opposite directions, one from the rear, the other from down-stage. Each then forms in a row on the side where it entered, after making the circuit of the stage. One semi-chorus is composed of old knights, the other of young knights, each distinguished by its own colors and emblems. When both choruses are aligned opposite each other the march-music stops and the chorus leaders speak.)

FIRST CHORUS (CAJETAN):   Reverent greetings I give you,
Mansion resplendent,
You my ancestral
Cradle of Princes,
Roof upon columns loftily borne.
  Deep in its scabbard
Let the sword rest,
Chained outside of the gates
Let Discord be left, the serpent-haired monster.   140
For inviolable thresholds
Of welcoming houses
Are guarded by Oath, the Erinyes' son,
Most dread of the gods of the underworld realm.
SECOND CHORUS (BOHEMUND):   My heart in its fury seethes in
  my breast,

And my fist is clenched for a fight,
For the form of the foe I detest,
The head of Medusa, is in my sight.
The rage of my blood I barely control.
Ought I to grant him the parley's grace?   150
Or shall I obey the wrath of my soul?
But the Erinys my hand restrains,
Protectress of this place,
And the truce of God that obtains.

FIRST CHORUS (CAJETAN): Wiser restraint
Becomes age better;
I who am reasonable grant the first greeting.

(to the second chorus)

May you be welcome,
You who, with me,
Fraternally sharing   160
Equal emotions,
Honor and reverence
The gods that keep watch
Over this palace.
Now that our Princes parley as friends,
Let us in turn trade words of good-will
Innocently and with tranquil blood,
For the word that gives healing is also good.
But let us once meet on the plain,
Then let there be war betwixt us twain,   170
Let steel test our fortitude.

THE ENTIRE CHORUS: But let us once meet on the plain,
Then let there be war betwixt us twain,
Let steel test our fortitude.

FIRST CHORUS (BERENGAR): You I hate not! Not you are my foe!
One city gave us both our birth.
Those inside are an alien race.
But with Princes in feud and in fray,
Servants perforce must murder and slay,

Law so requires, and tradition's ways.   180
SECOND CHORUS (BOHEMUND): They perhaps know
  Why they so bloodily
  Battle in hatred. It is nothing to me.
  But we fight their wars, we wield the sword;
  He has no valor, no honor has he
  Who will permit of shame to his lord.
THE ENTIRE CHORUS: But we fight their wars, we wield the
    sword;
  He has no valor, no honor has he
  Who will permit of shame to his lord.
ONE OF THE CHORUS (BERENGAR): Listen to what I thought in
    my mind   190
  As I walked at leisure where the roadways wind
  Between the high and billowing wheat,
  Lost in reflection deep and sweet.
    In the frenzy of fighting we have not thought
  To take good counsel or see things plain,
  For rage of blood has made us distraught.
    Are they not ours, these fields of grain?
  These elms overgrown with the clustering vine,
  Are they not children of our own sunshine?
  Could we not in pleasant enjoyment   200
  Spin ourselves innocent, comfortable days
  And merrily win ourselves life's easy ways?
  Why draw our swords in a kind of craze
  For an alien clan and an alien name?
  To this soil of ours they have no claim.
  They came here in a ship of the sea
  Out of the sunset's ruddy glow,
  And we took them in hospitably
  (Our forefathers did, long ago),
  And now we are bondsmen one and all,   210
  Held by this alien clan in thrall.
A SECOND (MANFRED): True! We dwell in a fortunate land
  Which the heaven-encircling sun

With friendly brightness ever beholds,
And we could enjoy it with pleasure unmarred;
Only it cannot be bolted and barred,
And the sea that around us its waves enfolds
Makes us prey to the wanton invasion
Of corsairs impudently roving our shores.
We have a treasure whose preservation   220
Only entices the foreigner's oars.
We are slaves in the very homes we have known,
This country cannot protect its own.
Not where Ceres the golden laughs,
Nor the warden of pastures, peaceable Pan,
But where iron grows in the mountain shafts,
Thence is bred the earth-mastering man.

FIRST CHORUS (CAJETAN):   Among the brief-yeared race of men
Life's goods are given with partiality,
But Nature is just everlastingly.   230
Us she favored with the vital fill
Of vigor forever renewable,
To them was apportioned the force of will
And strength forever indomitable.
Armed with a power so dread, they do
Whatever their hearts incline them to,
Filling the earth with a sound of might;
But after the towering loftiness
Follows the thundrous fall from the height.
　　Hence I will praise my lowliness,   240
Cloaking in weakness my defense.
Those great storm-streams of force immense,
Gathered from endless stones of hail,
Gathered from cloudbursts wild in the gale,
Darkly rush and deadly assail,
Wresting bridges and dikes away,
Thundering on with watery sway,
Nothing exists that can slow or stay
Their sweep. But they were born of an hour;

To seep into sands of desolation   250
Is the end of their fearful course of power,
Nothing attests them but devastation.
Alien conquerors come and go;
We obey them, but remain here below.

*(The rear doors open. Donna Isabella appears between
          her sons, Don Manuel and Don Cesar.)*

BOTH CHORUSES (CAJETAN): Honor and praise
  To her rising yonder
  Like a radiant sun!
  Kneeling I reverence your glorious head.
FIRST CHORUS (CAJETAN): Fair is the gentler
  Light of the moon   260
  Amid the shining of glittering stars;
  Fair is the mother's
  Sweet dignity
  Between the fiery force of her sons;
  Not upon earth
  May her image or likeness be seen.

    High on life's pinnacle
  Placed aloft,
  She completes the circle of the Beautiful;
  With the mother and her sons   270
  The world's fulfillment is splendidly crowned.

    Even the Church, of God though it be,
  Shows nothing more fair on the heavenly throne;
  Nothing more lofty
  Can Art itself show, though of birth divine,
  Than the Mother with her Son.
SECOND CHORUS (BOHEMUND): Out of her womb with joy she
    beholds
  A flowering tree spring up, with branches
  Renewing itself everlastingly.
  For she has given birth to a race   280

To walk the course walked by the Sun
And to give a name to cycling time.
(ROGER): Nations decay,
   Names die in echoes,
   Dismal oblivion
   Spreads noctiferous pinions out
   Covering entire races of men.

   Single heads
Of Princes, however,
Gleam with a glory,   290
And Aurora with rays
Eternal touches them
As the towering peaks of the world.
ISABELLA (*advancing with her sons*):
   Cast down thy gaze, O Queen sublime of Heaven,
   And lay thy hand upon this heart of mine
   Lest overweening pride swell it to bursting;
   A mother's joy exceeds too soon its limits
   When mirrored in the glory of her sons;
   Now for the first time since I gave them birth
   I clasp the fullness of my happiness.   300
   Until today I always had to force
   In twain each joyous impulse of my heart,
   One son had always to be out of mind
   If I wished to enjoy the other's presence.
   O, my maternal love is one love only,
   And my sons were, alas, forever twain!
   O tell me, may I yield without fear now
   To my intoxicated heart's full force?
                  (*to Don Manuel*)
   If I now clasp your brother's hand in friendship,
   Do I not thrust the dagger through your heart?   310
                  (*to Don Cesar*)
   If my eyes dwell upon the sight of *him*,
   Will I be robbing you?—O, I must tremble

Lest the very love itself I show you
Add fiercer fuel to your hatred's flame.

(after gazing questioningly at both of them)

Speak! What may I expect from you? With what
Intention in your hearts have you come here?
Is it that ancient hate, still uncomposed,
That you have brought back to your father's house?
And does War wait outside the palace gates,
Held only for some moments in constraint   320
And champing at its brazen bit to burst
Its fetters in fresh fury just as soon
As you have turned your backs on me and gone?

THE CHORUS (BOHEMUND): Peace or war! The lots still unshown
Lie dark in the lap of the future Unknown.
But before we leave, the lots will decide;
We are ready and armed, whatever betide.

ISABELLA *(gazing around the whole circle):*
And what a frightful spectacle of war!
Why should these men be here? Is it a battle
That they are forming up within these halls?   330
Why then this horde of aliens when a mother
Desires to open her heart to her sons?
Within your mother's bosom do you fear
The snares of treachery and sly betrayal
That you so cautiously protect your backs?
O, these wild bands that follow after you!
These sudden agents of your anger, *they*
Are not your friends. Do not believe that they
From love of you give you the wisest counsel!
How could they harbor cordial feelings toward you,   340
The foreigners, the race of the invader,
Who drove them out of their own native earth
And over them achieved the masterdom?
Believe me! Every man loves to live free
And by the laws that he himself has set;

Rule by another is endured with envy,
And through your might alone and through their fear
Are you served where they gladly would refuse you.
Learn to know this race in all its falseness!
Through glee in your discomfiture they find   350
Their vengeance for your fortune and your greatness.
Their masters' fall, the fall of lofty heads
Is matter for their songs and for their talk
Told and retold again from son to grandson
To while away the length of winter evenings.
The world is hostile, o my sons! and false
Of disposition. Each man loves himself
Alone; uncertain, loose, and changeable
Are all the bonds that Fortune ever wove,—
Caprice disjoins what by Caprice was joined,—   360
Nature alone is honest. She alone
Stands fast on the eternal anchor-bottom
When all things else upon the storm-tossed waves of life
Unsteadily go drifting. Inclination
Gives us a friend, advantage a companion,
But happy he to whom birth gave a brother!
That, Fortune cannot give. That friend is given
To him by birth, and opposite a world
Of war and treachery he stands two-fold.

THE CHORUS (CAJETAN):   Yes, something noble there is in the
    ways   370
Of a queenly ruler's masterly mind,
With clear serenity she surveys
The affairs and actions of human kind.
We are swept onward by clashing strife
Darkling and blind through desolate life.

ISABELLA (*to Don Cesar*):
    You who have drawn your sword against your brother,
    Let your gaze pass about this entire host:
    Where is a form more noble than your brother's?

                        (*to Don Manuel*)

Among all these whom you call friends, where is
One worthy to stand by your brother's side?   380
Each one for his age is a paragon,
Each with the other fails not nor prevails.
Then dare to look into each other's faces!
Insanity of jealousy and envy!
You would have chosen him from thousands as
Your friend, you would have clasped him to your heart
And made him the unique and only one;
But now that sacred Nature has bestowed
Him on you from your very cradle days,
You trample on her gift with proud disdain,   390
Offending thus against your very blood,
To throw yourself away on evil men,
To make allies of foes and foreigners!

DON MANUEL: Hear me, Mother!
DON CESAR: Mother, no! Hear *me!*
ISABELLA: This sorry strife will not be settled by
Mere words. Here Mine and Thine, revenge and guilt
Are not to be distinguished any more.
Who could discern again the sulphur-stream's
Old course that poured down floods of molten fire?   400
All things are of the subterranean fire's
Unholy generation, crusts of lava
Lie heaped above all healthy living things,
And every footstep falls upon destruction.
I lay this one charge only to your hearts!
The evil done by man, when in the years
Of his maturity, to man, I hold
Will hardly be forgiven or atoned.
The man will have his hatred, and no time
Will change his mind that he has once made up.   410
Your grudge, however, takes its origin
In the uncomprehending times of childhood:
Its very age is what should now disarm it.
Think back to what first set you two at odds;

You do not know, and if you once found out,
Your childish grudge would make you blush for shame.
And yet it is that ancient childhood quarrel
Which link by link in an unhappy chain
Has borne this latest enmity of yours.
For all the grievous deeds that have occurred till now   420
Are Vengeance's, Suspicion's children merely.
—And now that you are men and grown, you still
Would go on fighting out this boyish feud?

(taking both their hands)

O my sons! Come! Resolve yourselves to make
A clean slate of your mutual accounts,
For equal is the wrong on both your parts.
Be noble, and annul magnanimously
Both these unpayable and monstrous debts.
Most god-like of all triumphs is forgiveness!
Into your father's tomb cast down the ancient   430
Hatred of your early childhood years!
To love let your new life be dedicated,
To harmony, to reconciliation.

*(She falls back one pace between them, as if to
leave them room to approach each other. Both gaze
at the ground without looking at one another.)*

THE CHORUS (CAJETAN): To your mother's admonition give
   ear,
Words of great weight she speaks indeed!
Put an end to your feud that keeps you in fear,
Or carry it further, if such be your need!
With what is your pleasure I will comply,
You are the master, the servant am I.

ISABELLA *(with suppressed sorrow after having remained silent
   for some time in vain expectation of some speech from the
   brothers)*:
I know of nothing further. I have emptied   440

The quiver of my words, used up my force of pleas.
The one who might control you rests within his grave,
And powerless your mother stands between you.
—Complete your work! You have free power! Obey
The demon who compels you madly onward,
Dishonor then the house—God's sacred altar,
And let this very hall that gave you birth
Become the scene of mutual murder now.
Before your mother's eyes destroy each other
With your own hands, not by the hands of strangers.   450
Attack each other like those Theban brothers,
Hand to hand, and wrestling frantically,
Enclasp each other in a grip of steel!
Exchanging life for life, let him prevail
Who drives the dagger to the other's heart,
Till Death himself can not heal up your quarrel,
So that the very flame, the fire's red pillar,
The rises from your funeral pyre aloft
Will cleave in twain and burn in separate parts,
A ghastly sign of how you died and lived.   460

(Exit.)

*(The brothers go on standing with the
former interval of distance between them.)*

THE CHORUS (CAJETAN): These are but words that she has
  spoken,
  Yet by them my cheerful courage in bud
  In my craggy heart now has been broken;
  I have not shed a kinsman's blood.
  Pure unto Heaven my hands I extend:
  You are brothers! Consider the end!
DON CESAR *(without looking at Don Manuel):*
  You are the older brother; speak first then!
  I yield before the first-born with no shame.
DON MANUEL *(in the same posture):*

Say something kind, and I will gladly follow
The high example that the younger sets. 470
DON CESAR: Not that I look upon myself as being
The weaker party or more culpable—
DON MANUEL: No one who knows Don Cesar deems him timid;
If he felt weaker he would talk more proudly.
DON CESAR: Do you think no less highly of your brother?
DON MANUEL: You are too proud for cringing, I for falsehood.
DON CESAR: Contempt my noble heart will not endure.
But in the fiercest bitterness of battle
You thought about your brother with esteem.
DON MANUEL: You do not wish my death; for that I have 480
Sound proof. A monk once offered you his hand
To murder me; you had the traitor punished.
DON CESAR *(steps a little closer):*
If I had sooner known you were so upright,
Much that has happened would not have occurred.
DON MANUEL: And had I known you had a heart so gracious,
I would have spared our mother many griefs.
DON CESAR: You were described to me as much more haughty.
DON MANUEL: It is the curse of men in lofty places
That base men gain the access to their ears.
DON CESAR *(eagerly):*
Quite true. All blame attaches to our servants! 490
DON MANUEL: They set our hearts at odds in bitter hatred.
DON CESAR: They carried evil rumors back and forth.
DON MANUEL: And poisoned every act with false construction.
DON CESAR: And fostered wounds they should have helped to
heal.
DON MANUEL: And raked the fire they could have well ex-
tinguished.
DON CESAR: We were the ones misled, the ones betrayed!
DON MANUEL: Blind instruments of other persons' passions!
DON CESAR: Can it be true that everyone is faithless—
DON MANUEL: And false! You may believe what Mother says!
DON CESAR: Then I shall clasp my brother's hand in mine— 500

(He holds out his hand to him.)

DON MANUEL *(grasps it eagerly):*
Which is the closest to me in the world.

*(Both stand hand in hand and gaze
at each other for some time in silence.)*

DON CESAR: I look at you, astonished and amazed,
And find our Mother's features in your face.
DON MANUEL: And a resemblance is revealed to me
In you, that yet more deeply touches me.
DON CESAR: Can it be really you who speaks so kindly,
So graciously confronts the younger brother?
DON MANUEL: Can this benign and gentle-tempered youth
Be my malicious and detested brother?

*(Silence again; each stands lost
in contemplation of the other.)*

DON CESAR: You claimed the horses of Arabian breed   510
Out of the property our father left,
And I refused them to the knights you sent me.
DON MANUEL: You cherish them. I think no more about them.
DON CESAR: No, take the steeds, and take the chariot too,
Our father's; take them, take them, I implore you.
DON MANUEL: That I will do, but only if you take
The seaside castle over which we quarrelled.
DON CESAR: I will not take it, but I would be happy
If we could live together there as brothers.
DON MANUEL: So be it! Why should we own separate   520
Establishments, now that our hearts are one?
DON CESAR: Why should we any longer live apart
When we by union shall be each one richer?
DON MANUEL: We are apart no more, we are united.

(He flies to his arms.)

THE FIRST CHORUS (CAJETAN) *(to the second):*   Why should we
stand here as enemies

When our Princes embrace, brother and brother?
Their example I follow and offer you peace;
Are *we* forever to hate one another?
If *they* as blood-brothers take friendship's hand,
We are sons and citizens of one land.   530

(Both choruses embrace.)

(Enter a Messenger.)

THE SECOND CHORUS (BOHEMUND) *(to Don Cesar):*
  I see the messenger returning, Lord,
  Whom you sent out to reconnoitre. Now
  Rejoice, Don Cesar! Good news waits for you,
  For this man's face is radiant with joy.
THE MESSENGER: All hail unto this curse-afflicted city!
  My eye rejoices at the fairest sight.
  My master's sons, my Princes, I behold
  In peaceful colloquy and hand in hand,
  Whom I had left in heat of battle's fury.
DON CESAR: You see love rising from the flames of hatred   540
  Anew like the rejuvenated Phoenix.
THE MESSENGER: To the first joy I now shall add a second.
  My herald's staff is green with budding branches!
DON CESAR *(taking him aside):*
  Disclose to me what news you bring.
THE MESSENGER: One day
  Assembles everything that is delightful.
  The lady who was lost, for whom we searched,
  She has been found, she is not far away.
DON CESAR: She has been found! O tell me where she is!
THE MESSENGER: Here in Messina she is hidden, Lord.
DON MANUEL *(turning to the first semi-chorus):*
  With deeper flush I see my brother's cheeks   550
  A-glow and in his eyes there is a flashing.
  I do not know the cause; the hue is joy's,
  However, and I share in his delight.
DON CESAR *(to the messenger):*

Show me the way!—Farewell, Don Manuel.
In Mother's arms we'll meet again. But now
Affairs of urgency call me away.

(He starts to go.)

DON MANUEL: Do not delay. May Fortune go with you.
DON CESAR   *(reflects and comes back):*
   Don Manuel, the sight of you delights
   Me more than I can say. My premonition
   Says that we shall be bosom friends, and that   560
   The impulse long restrained will rise that much
   More strongly, joyously, toward the new sunlight;
   I shall make up for life that I have lost.
DON MANUEL: The blossom promises the fairest fruit.
DON CESAR: It is not right, I know, and I am much
   To blame for tearing myself from your arms;
   Do not believe that I feel less than you
   Because I cut this festive hour abruptly short.
DON MANUEL   *(with obvious absent-mindedness):*
   Obey the moment's need. All of our lives
   From this day forward shall belong to love.   570
DON CESAR: If I revealed to you what calls me hence—
DON MANUEL: Leave me your heart. Your secret is your own.
DON CESAR: Let no more secrets come between us either.
   The last dark fold shall vanish presently.

(turning to the Chorus)

I now proclaim it so you all may know:
Between me and my well-beloved brother
All strife is at an end. And anyone
Who fans the burned-out embers of our quarrel
Into new fire, I now proclaim to be
My mortal enemy who does me harm   580
And I shall hate him like the gates of hell.
Let no one hope to please me or reap thanks
Reporting evil to me of my brother,

Or speeding with a false officiousness
The bitter arrow of the sudden word.
The word that thoughtlessly springs from rash anger
Does not strike lasting root upon the lips;
But if Suspicion's ear has once received it,
It grows and creeps like an insidious vine
And clings with thousand tendrils to the heart: 590
Thus hopelessly, in infinite confusion,
The best and noblest men are kept apart.

*(He embraces his brother again and leaves, accom-
panied by the Second Chorus.)*

THE CHORUS (CAJETAN): Full of amazement I behold you,
   Lord,
 I hardly recognize you any longer.
With parsimonious speech you barely answer
Your brother's words of love when he sincerely
Makes overtures to you with open heart.
Like someone in a dream you stand here sunken
Within yourself as if your body only
Were present while your soul is far away.   600
To see you so, one might accuse you of
A coldness and a proud, unfriendly spirit;
But I shall not blame you for lack of feeling,
For you gaze cheerfully about you like
A happy man, and smiles play on your features.

DON MANUEL: What can I say? What can I answer? Let
My brother find the words. He is seized by
Surprising new emotion, and he sees
The ancient hatred vanish from his bosom;
In wonderment he feels his heart transformed.   610
I—have brought no more hatred with me now,
I hardly know what made us quarrel so.
For over all the things of earth my soul
Floats high aloft on pinions of sheer joy,
And in the sea of radiance around me

All clouds have disappeared and all the dark
Umbrageous folds of life have been smoothed out.
—I gaze upon these halls, upon these rooms,
And picture to myself the startled joy
Of my surprised and much astonished bride   620
When I conduct her through the portals of
This house as Princess and as mistress here.
She loves the lover only: to the stranger,
The man without a name, she gave herself,
She does not dream I am Don Manuel,
The ruler of Messina, who will twine
The golden circlet round her lovely brow.
How sweet it is to make a loved one happy
With the resplendence of unhoped-for greatness!
I long have treasured up this last delight;   630
Nobility, which is indeed its own
Supreme adornment, may grace Beauty's sight:
The golden crown sets off the precious stone.

THE CHORUS (CAJETAN): I hear you, Lord, unseal your word-
　　less lips
From their long silence for the first time now.
I have long followed you with searching eye,
Aware of some extraordinary secret;
But I did not presume to ask you for
The thing you veiled from me in depths of darkness.
The good cheer of the hunt no more delights you,   640
Nor course of horses, nor the falcon's triumph.
You disappear from your companions' sight
As often as the sun comes down upon
The heaven's edge, and no one of our chorus,
Who once shared with you every peril of
A war or hunt, may share your silent path.
Why have you kept this envious veil about
Your happiness of love until today?
Why should a mighty man conceal his goal?
For fear is distant from your lofty soul.   650

DON MANUEL: Swift-winged is Happiness and hard to bind,
 To be contained within a locked box only.
 The sentinel set over it is Silence,
 And quick is its escape if Garrulousness
 Be over-hasty to pry off the lid.
 But now, so near the goal, I well may break
 My lengthy silence, and I shall do so.
 For with the rays of this next morning's sun
 She will be mine, nor will the Demon's envy
 Have any further power over me.   660
 No longer will I go to her by stealth,
 Nor steal the golden fruit of my delight,
 No longer capture joy in hurrying flight,
 Tomorrow with today will match its wealth;
 Not like the lightning-streaks that flash and pass,
 Devoured by darkness swifter than a look,
 My happiness will flow, a steady brook,
 Or like the sand within the hourglass.
THE CHORUS (CAJETAN):   Tell us her name, Lord, who has
 made you happy
 In secret, so that we may praise your lot   670
 And give due honor to our Prince's bride.
 Tell where you found her, where she was concealed,
 In what resort of silent secrecy.
 For roving far and wide across this island
 Along the tangled pathways of the hunt,
 We have found no trace of your happiness,
 So that I could well be persuaded that
 She is enclosed within a magic cloud.
DON MANUEL: I shall dissolve that magic, for the sun
 Shall look this very day on what was hidden.   680
 Now harken to the tale of what befell me.
 Five moons ago it was, my father's might
 Prevailed yet in this land and still compelled
 The stubborn neck of youth beneath his yoke.
 Fierce joy in weapons was still all I knew,

Along with warrior's pleasure in the hunt.
We had been hunting through the entire day
Along the mountain forest—when it chanced
That in pursuit of a white doe I had
Been carried far beyond your company.   690
The shy beast fled on through the valley turnings,
Through copse and glen and trackless undergrowth;
I saw it ever just a spear-cast distant
Yet could not overtake or bring it down
Until at last beside a garden gate
It vanished. Springing swiftly from my horse,
I press pursuit with brandished spear in hand
Till in amazement I behold the beast
In terror lying at a nun's feet as
She tenderly caressed it with her hand.   700
I stand in wonder, motionless, and stare,
With spear in hand and ready for the throw.
But she, imploring, gazes with great eyes
At me. And there we stand before each other—
How long a time I cannot estimate
For I had lost the sense of time entirely.
Her gaze had fallen deep into my soul
And utterly transformed my heart within me.
—What I then said, or what that lovely girl
Replied, let no one now inquire of me,   710
For all that lies behind me like a dream
Out of the dawn-lit days of early childhood.
I felt the beating of her heart on mine
When consciousness returned again to me.
And then I heard the clear sound of a bell,
It seemed to signify a call to prayer,
And swift as spirits melt and fade away,
She vanished and was seen no more that day.

THE CHORUS (CAJETAN): With fear, O Lord, your story fills
 me now.
A theft of things divine you perpetrated,   720

The bride of Heaven by your sin you desecrated,
For dread and sacred is the cloister's vow.

DON MANUEL: Henceforth I had one road to travel only,
My restless, formless yearning had been sealed,
The meaning of my life had been revealed.
And as the pilgrim travels toward the east
Where he beholds his sun of promise shine,
So did my hope and yearning turn to face
That one resplendent quarter of the sky.
No day rose from the sea and sank again   730
Without uniting two rejoicing lovers.
With silent bond our hearts were interwoven,
And only the all-seeing Air above us
Was trusted witness to our hidden bliss;
No further human service did we need.
Ah, those were golden hours, blessed days!
—No theft from Heaven was my happiness,
For by no vows had her heart yet been bound,
Her heart that gave itself to me forever.

THE CHORUS (CAJETAN):   Her convent, then, was only an
   asylum   740
Of tender youth, and not the grave of life?

DON MANUEL: She was entrusted to the house of God
A sacred pledge to be one day withdrawn.

THE CHORUS (CAJETAN):   But of what blood does she make
   boast to be?
For noble things can come of noble only.

DON MANUEL: She has grown up a mystery to herself,
She does not know her race or fatherland.

THE CHORUS (CAJETAN):   And is there no dark trace to lead
   the way
Back to the unknown sources of her being?

DON MANUEL: The only one who knows her origin   750
Asserts that she was born of noble blood.

THE CHORUS (CAJETAN):   Who is the man? Keep nothing back
   from me,

With knowledge only can I give good counsel.

DON MANUEL: An aged servant comes from time to time,
The only link between her and her mother.

THE CHORUS (CAJETAN):   Have you made no attempt to trace
this man?
Old age is faint of heart and talkative.

DON MANUEL: To yield to curiosity I dared not
That jeopardized my secret happiness.

THE CHORUS (CAJETAN):   What was the tenor of his words,
however,   760
When he came on his visits to the maiden?

DON MANUEL: For some time when all things would be resolved
He always put her off from year to year.

THE CHORUS (CAJETAN):   And this time when all things would
be resolved,
He never designated it more closely?

DON MANUEL: In recent months the old man threatened her
With an impending change of destiny.

THE CHORUS (CAJETAN):   He threatened her, you say? And so
you fear
To bring a light to bear that would not please you?

DON MANUEL: A happy man is fearful of all change;   770
If gain may not be hoped for, loss is dreaded.

THE CHORUS (CAJETAN):   And yet the revelation that you
feared
Might also bear good omens for your love.

DON MANUEL: It could as well destroy my happiness;
So I chose what was safest, to forestall it.

THE CHORUS (CAJETAN):   How so, my Lord? You fill me now
with fear,
And I am apprehensive of rash action.

DON MANUEL: All through these recent months the old man has
Repeatedly let fall mysterious hints
Suggesting that the day was not far off   780
When she would be returned to her own kinsfolk.
But yesterday he made the matter clear,

That with the ray of the next morning's sun—
Which is this very day now in its brightness—
Her fate would be decided finally.
There was no time to lose, and my decision
Was swiftly made and swiftly executed.
Last night I carried off the maiden and
Brought her in secrecy here to Messina.

THE CHORUS (CAJETAN): What a foolhardy, bold act of ab-
duction!   790
—Forgive me, Lord, for my free condemnation!
But such is wiser old men's privilege
When rash youth is forgetful of itself.

DON MANUEL: Close by the convent of the Mercy Sisters,
In the seclusion of a quiet garden
Untrodden by the curious, I took leave
Of her just now to hasten hither for
The reconciliation with my brother.
In anxious fear I left her there alone
Behind, expecting anything but that   800
She should be fetched in glory as a Princess
And be displayed before all of Messina
Upon the lofty pedestal of fame.
For she shall not behold me otherwise
Than in my state and splendor, festively
Surrounded by your knightly retinue.
I will not have Don Manuel's betrothed
Approach my mother, to whom I present her,
As either homeless or a fugitive.
In princely manner as a Princess I   810
Shall lead her into my ancestral seat.

THE CHORUS (CAJETAN): Command us, Lord! We bide your
beck and call.

DON MANUEL: I may have torn myself out of her arms
But my concern will be with her alone.
Now you shall come with me to the bazaar,
Down where the Moors lay out their wares for sale,

All that the East affords both in the way
Of noble cloth and fine embroideries.
Let your selection be, first, comely sandals
To shield and to adorn her dainty feet;   820
Then for her raiment choose the rarest fabrics
Of Indies, brightly gleaming like the snow
Of Etna, which is closest to sheer light,
And like the fragrance of the morning let
It fall about the lines of her young limbs.
Of purple worked with slender threads of gold
Then let the cincture be that girds the tunic
Beneath the modest bosom charmingly.
Select a mantle also, woven of
Shimmering silk and gleaming with pale purple;   830
And at the shoulder clasp it with a golden
Cicada. Bracelets too do not forget,
To circle her fair arms delightfully,
Nor the adornment of fine pearls and coral,
Gifts wondrous from the goddess of the sea.
About her locks entwine a diadem
Made of the costliest of jewels set
Together, where the fiery ruby glowing
Will lace its lightnings with the emerald.
High in her hair adornments let the veil   840
Be fastened, which, like a bright cloud of light,
Will fall full-length about her radiant form.
To make the handiwork complete, then let
The virgin myrtle as a crown be set.

THE CHORUS (CAJETAN): It shall be done, Lord, as you have
    commanded;
    These things may all be found in their perfection
    Among the wares displayed at the bazaar.

DON MANUEL: Select the finest palfrey then, and lead
    It forth out of my stables; let its color
    Be white and gleaming like the sun-god's steeds,   850
    Of purple let the housing be, the reins

And harness richly set with precious gems,
For it shall be the bearer of my queen.
Stand by in readiness yourselves to lead
Your Princess home in pomp and knightly splendor
Amid the jubilation of your trumpets.
To look to all these things I leave you now;
Two of your number I choose as companions,
All others wait for me. What you have heard,
Preserve it in your bosom unrevealed   860
Till I declare your lips may be unsealed.

(Exit, accompanied by two of the Chorus.)

THE CHORUS (CAJETAN):   Tell me, what shall we do with our-
    selves,
Now that our Princes rest from their strife,
To fill up the emptiness of the hours
That endlessly wait the days of our life?
Mankind needs something of hope and of sorrow,
Something as well to fear for the morrow,
In order to bear the existence that weighs
Upon his weary monotonous days,
Something that breathes like a wind that revives   870
And ripples the stagnant pools of our lives.

ONE OF THE CHORUS (MANFRED): Sweet is peace. Like a lovely
    youth
Lying beside a quiet brook
While sporting lambs around him graze
Merrily on meadows where sunlight plays;
Drawing sweet tones from his flute, he lies,
Waking the echo far on the hill,
Or in the shimmer of sunset skies
Lulled to sleep by the murmuring rill.
But War is not without honor also,   880
The mover of human destiny;
I like a life that is full of zest,
I like a rolling and rocking and a floating at rest

On the pitching and tumbling waves of Fortune's sea.
    In peacetime a man will rot away,
Idle repose is the grave of courage.
The law is the friend of the weak,
To make things smooth is all he will seek.
He would have the world all flat and bleak;
But warfare will bring a man's strength to the fore,   890
Making uncommon what was common before,
Putting courage in the coward himself.

A SECOND (BERENGAR): Is Amor's temple not open wide?
Does the world not to Beauty go pilgriming?
There is your fear, and your hope, and your pride!
Whoever delights the eyes is a king!
Love too can bestir our lives and make
The greyish hues bright in its wake.
She beguiles our happy years with dreams,
Daughter of foam of ocean streams,   900
And into the dull and drearily real
She weaves the embroider of golden dreams.

A THIRD (CAJETAN): Let blossoms remain with blossoming
    spring,
Let Beauty bloom! And let it bring
Garlands to locks youthfully green;
It befits the manly age of a man
In service of graver gods to be seen.

THE FIRST ONE (MANFRED): Austere Diana, the friend of the
    chase,
Her to the wildwood let us follow,
Where forests deepen their darkest ways,   910
And topple the antelope from cliff to hollow.
For hunting is warfare in symbol phase,
The sombre war-god's light-hearted bride:
Off we go with the dawn's first beams
When the clangor of horns summons us hence,
Out where the valley mistily gleams,
Up to mountains and down glens where

We may bathe our bodies in the immense
And sweetly refreshing rivers of air.

THE SECOND ONE (BERENGAR):   Or shall we rather pledge our
    devotion   920
To that azure goddess of ceaseless motion
Who mirror-bright and friendly-willed
Bids us forth to her endless embrace?
Shall we a floating palace build
And launch it where waves dance in their grace?
Whoever has furrowed that crystalline field
Of green with the hastening keel of a ship
Reaps without seedtime the harvest yield,
He has married Fortune and owns the world.
For ocean is the realm of hope   930
And the wanton realm of changeful chance.
There rich men to poor men are swiftly changed
And the poorest to Princes there advance.
Just as the thought-swift wind will change
And from every compasspoint be blown,
Just so Fate's shifting lots are thrown
And Fortune's globe turned ceaselessly.
All things are waves where the far winds range,
No possession is held on the sea.

THE THIRD (CAJETAN):   Not in the realm of the waves alone
Over the surging flood of the sea,   941
But also on earth, firm though it be
On ancient, eternal pillars fast,
Fortune falters and does not last,
—This new-made peace gives me small hope,
In it my faith I will not put,
On lava paths of the mountain slope
I would not choose to build my hut.
Far too deeply has hatred set
Its tooth, and deeds too grave have been   950
That one can never forgive nor forget;
Nor has the last outcome yet been seen,

And warning dreams fill me with terror.
My lips shall speak no prophecy,
But this unblessed wedlock seems an error
And I much mislike this mystery,
These devious paths of love I hate
And this convent-plundering reckless deed;
Good things favor ways that are straight
And evil fruit comes of evil seed.   960

BERENGAR: Theft was it also, as we all know,
When the former Prince's bride was brought
To a sinful bride-bed long ago,
For she was the bride his father sought.
And the family's founder, fierce in his wrath,
Poured ghastly curses upon the same,
Strewing that bridebed with seeds of crimes.
Monstrous deeds without a name
Lurk in this house since those black times.

THE CHORUS (CAJETAN):   No, it was not well begun,   970
Nor will it, believe me, end a-right;
For all acts are punished beneath the sun
Where raging fury blinds our sight.
It is no chance, no blind work of fate,
That these brothers in fury destroy each other,
For conceiving of strife and bearing of hate,
That was the curse on the womb of their mother.
—But in silence I shall beshroud the fact;
In silence the gods of vengeance act;
It is time enough to lament mischance   980
When it onward comes in actual advance.

(Exit the Chorus.)

ACT II

The scene is shifted to a garden which opens the prospect to the sea. From an adjoining garden house steps Beatrice. She walks restlessly up and down, peering in all directions. Suddenly she stops short and listens.

BEATRICE: It is not he—it was the winds at play
That in the pine-tree tops their rustlings keep;
The sun already bends its westward way,
With laggard steps I see the hours creep,
And I am seized with shuddering and dismay,
The insubstantial silence void and deep
Appals me. Nothing stirs beneath the air;
He has abandoned me to my despair.

Close by I hear the city raucously   990
With teeming people like weir-waters roar;
Afar I hear the sounding giant sea
That hurtles muted thunder to the shore.
Here all the storms of terror rage at me,
I feel as though I am too small before
This vastness; like a leaf dropped from its place
I drift in an infinity of space.

Why did I leave my tranquil convent nook?
There I lived free of yearning, free of harm!
My heart was quiet as a meadow brook,   1000
Without desire, yet full of comfort warm.
Life's wave has caught me up; with sombre look
The world has seized me in its giant-arm;
Thus I have sundered all my former ties

45

To trust a vow that on slight proof relies.

Where were my senses?
What have I done?
Am I with folly
Distraught and undone?

The virginal veil   1010
I have rent in men's sight,
I have torn down the doors of my holy cell!
Have I been blinded by magic of hell?
I followed the man,
The daring abductor, in blameworthy flight.

O come, my Beloved!
Where do you tarry? Set free, set free
My struggling soul! I am gnawed by remorse,
Grief rends me apart.
By your loving presence console my heart!   1020

And should I not yield myself to the man,
The one man in the world attached to me?
I was rejected, suffered exile's ban,
In tender years a cruel destiny
(I may not lift its darkling veil) began,
From mother's arms it snatched me ruthlessly.
I saw her only once,—or so it seems,—
But vanished is her image like my dreams.

And tranquil in tranquility I grew,
With shadows for companions in life's glare;   1030
Then godlike at the cloister gate I knew
He suddenly appeared and saw me there.
O, my emotions no words can construe!
He came as strangers from strange planets fare,
And swiftly, as if it had been so ever,
The bond was forged which mortals cannot sever.

Forgive me, noble mother whom I lost,

My thrust into the fated Hours' round
To seize my destiny at any cost;
I did not choose it: by it I was found.   1040
No threshold barred but that the god has crossed,
The way to Perseus' tower he has found,
No Spirit's sacrifice is ever lost;
Though it be left on stony cliff-sides bound
Or Atlas' sky-sustaining columns, there
A wingèd steed brings rescue through the air.

To look behind me I no more desire,
I do not yearn for homeland any more;
With love I yield to Love: what higher
Happiness than love is in life's store?   1050
I will content myself with my own lot,
All other joys in life—I know them not.

  I do not know, nor do I wish to see
The authors of my poor mortality
If they, Beloved, would part you from me.
I will remain a riddle, it is true,
I know enough, I live for *you!*

(harkening)

Hark! his well-loved voice I hear!
—No—its echo in my ear,
And the ocean's muffled roar   1060
Where waves break upon the shore.
My Beloved is not in sight
Alas, alas, where does he tarry?
Horror chills me with affright.
Deep and deeper
Sinks the sun. Emptier
The emptiness. Heavier
My heavy heart.—Where does he stay?

(She walks restlessly about.)

Beyond this garden's guarded walls
I no longer dare go forth.   1070
When one day I was so bold
To step within the near-by church,
Horror gripped me in its hold:
For a mighty impulse from
My deepest soul rose up and stirred;
When the Vesper call was heard
To kneel down in that holy place
And to the Holy Maid to pray,
I could not other than obey.

What if a lurking spy had seen me?   1080
The world is full of snares,
Cunning has spread out its net,
Cunning has all paths beset
To take pure goodness unawares.
This I learned with horror when
I ventured from the convent fold
Into alien crowds of men
With courage rash and overbold.
At that solemn funeral rite
Held for our Prince, I dearly paid   1090
For my rash action—in my plight
Some god surely lent me aid—
When that stranger-youth approached me
With his burning eyes of flame
And with looks that struck a terror
To my very depths of soul,
Gazed into my inmost heart.
Icy still that horror lies,
Just recalling, deep therein.
Into my Beloved's eyes   1100
Never, never dare I look,
Conscious of that silent sin.

(startled and listening)

Voices outside!
It is he, my Beloved!
Now no illusion
Deceives my ear.
He comes, still others!
Into his arms!
Clasped to his heart!

> (*She hurries with open arms to the rear of the
> garden. Don Cesar advances to meet her.*)

BEATRICE   (*retreating in terror*):
Alas! What do I see?
> (*At the same moment the Chorus enters.*)
DON CESAR: Have no fear, lovely beauty!   1110

> (*to the Chorus*)

The harsh sight of your weapons terrifies
The tender maiden. Fall back and remain
At a respectful distance.

> (*to Beatrice*)

Have no fear.
I hold sweet modesty and beauty sacred.

> (*The Chorus has stepped back. He comes nearer
> to her and seizes her hand.*)

Where were you? What god's might took you away
And kept you hidden this long while? I have
Been seeking, searching for you; waking, dreaming,
You have been my heart's sole emotion since
The day when at the Prince's funeral rite
I caught my first glimpse of you like an angel   1120
Revealed in radiance. Nor did the power
Remain concealed by which you overcame me.
My glances' fire, the stammering of my lips,
My hand that lay and trembled within yours,

Betrayed it to you—More forthright avowal
The place of solemn majesty precluded.
The service of the Mass called me to prayer,
And now that I had risen from my knees
And my first glances swiftly sought for you,
You had departed, vanished from my eyes;   1130
And yet by magic's all-prevailing potencies
You lured my heart to follow after you.
Since that day I have sought you tirelessly.
At all the church doors, all the palace gates,
In every open, every secret place,
Wherever lovely Innocence can go,
I spread my net of spies abroad and bided
My time; and yet my efforts bore no fruit
Until today at last, by some god guided,
The vigilance of spies was crowned with luck   1140
When you were sighted in the near-by church.

> (*At this Beatrice, who has been standing mean-*
> *while trembling and with averted looks, makes a*
> *movement of fright.*)

I have you once more, and may my spirit flee
My body before I give you up! And now,
That I may seize this chance immediately
And ward the Demon's envy off, I vow
Before all witnesses here present that
You are my spouse, whereof in token I
Extend herewith my chivalrous right hand.

> (*He presents her to the Chorus.*)

I shall not ask your name— From you I want
Yourself alone; all else I disregard.   1150
That your soul like your origin is pure,
This your first glance has vouched for me and certified;
And if your birth were base and vilified
You still would have to be my love for sure:

My freedom and my choice are nullified.

And so that you may know if I am also
The master of my deeds and high enough
In worldly rank to lift up what I love
By strength of arm to equal place with me,
No more is needed but to name my name.   1160
I am Don Cesar. In the city of
Messina there is none above me here.

(*Beatrice shrinks back in horror. He notices it
and continues after a brief while.*)

Your modest silence and astonishment
I praise; shy humbleness is of all charms
The crown, for Beauty is a hidden thing
And it is startled at its own great power.
—I shall go now and leave you to yourself
Till you recover from your own affright,
For new things, even happiness, strike terror.

(*to the Chorus*)

Grant her—for such she is from this time hence—   1170
The homage due to my bride and your Princess,
Apprise her of the greatness of her station.
I shall soon come myself to take her home,
As fits my dignity and as becomes her.

(*Exit.*)

THE CHORUS (BOHEMUND):   We hail you, maiden,
Loveliest Princess!
Yours is the crown,
Yours is the triumph!

As the sustainer
Of this high race,   1180
Of future heroes
The mother in prime, I greet you here!

(ROGER):   Threefold blessing be yours!
  Under signs of favor,
  Favored one, you enter
  A house favored and fostered by gods,
  Where garlands of glory are hung aloft
  And the golden scepter in steady succession
  Passes from grandsire down to the grandson.

(BOHEMUND):   Your gracious entrance   1190
  Will gratify
  The gods of the household,
  The lofty and solemn
  Reverend forebears;
  At the threshold will greet you
  Hebe the ever youthful
  And the golden Victoria,
  The winged goddess
  That hovers upon the hand of the Father
  With pinions eternally poised for triumph.   1200

(ROGER):   Never the crown
  Of beauty shall pass
  Out of the family;
  One Princess dying
  Yields to another
  The girdle of grace
  And the veil of decent chasteness.
  But my eye beholds
  The fairest of sights,
  For I see the bloom of the daughter   1210
  Before the bloom of the mother has faded.

BEATRICE   (rousing from her terror):
  Alas! Into whose hand has
  Misfortune delivered me?
  Of all
  That live,
  Not into this one should I fall!

Now I comprehend the horror,
The uncanny sense of terror
I felt, the shuddersome touch of fate,
Whenever to me the name was named   1220
Borne by this dreaded family
Who hate each other with murderous hate,
Who rage one member with another
With bitterness intemperate.
With horror I have often heard
How the brothers' hatred stirred
With vipers' fury; now my own
Fate sweeps me, wretched one and hopeless,
Into the vortex of this hatred,
Into the whirlpool of disaster!   1230

(She flees into the garden house.)

THE CHORUS (BOHEMUND) :   The favored son of the gods I envy,
The lucky possessor of power!
His share is always what is most precious,
And of all that is prized as costly
And splendid by mortal men,
He chooses the choicest himself.
(ROGER): From the pearls that the fisherman-diver brings up
He selects the purest for himself.
For the ruler they lay the best aside
Of what was won by labor in common;   1240
While followers parcel the rest by lot,
For him the finest is certain.
(BOHEMUND): But one thing of his is most precious of all—
Let him be granted all other prerogatives,
This one I envy him beyond the rest—
That he takes the flower of womanhood home,
The delight of all the other men's eyes,
And possesses her for himself.
(ROGER): With drawn sword the corsair leaps ashore
In the raid that plunders by dark of night,   1250

Men he carries off, and women,
And gluts his raging desires.
But the fairest form he must not touch,
She is the King's possession.
(BOHEMUND): But follow me now to guard the entrance
And threshold of the sacred place,
So no one unhallowed shall penetrate
This secret, and so that our master shall praise us,
Who has committed his highest prized
Of possessions into our keeping.   1260

(The Chorus withdraws at the rear.)

SCENE 2

*The scene shifts to a room in the interior of the
palace. Donna Isabella is standing between Don
Manuel and Don Cesar.*

ISABELLA: Now finally the wished-for day has come,
The festive day for which I long have yearned:
My children's hearts I now behold united
Just as I lightly join their hands together,
And for the first time in the family circle
The mother's heart can open joyously.
Gone is the alien witnesses' harsh host
That thrust between us in its war-array.
No more does weapons' clangor fright my ear,
And as the night-accustomed brood of owls,   1270
Once startled from the fire-consumed old ruin
Where with prescriptive right they long have nested,
Flocks up in dismal flight that darkens daylight
When the inhabitants, returning after
Long exile, now approach with jubilation
To make a lively start at new construction,

So ancient hatred flees with its nocturnal train
Of followers—old hollow-eyed Suspicion
And squint-eyed Jealousy and livid Envy—
Flees muttering out of these gates toward Hell,   1280
And Peace now enters, friendly Trust is with her,
And, smiling, lovely Concord enters also.

(She pauses.)

But it is not enough that this day should
Present a brother to each one of you,
No, it has borne you both a sister also.
—You are amazed? You look at me astonished?
O yes, my sons! The time has come for me
To break my silence and undo the seal
That long has lain upon a guarded secret.
I also bore a daughter to your father,   1290
There lives a younger sister yet of yours,
And her you shall embrace this very day.

DON CESAR: What are you saying, Mother? Do we have
A sister and yet never heard of her?

DON MANUEL: We did hear in our early childhood that
A sister had been born to us; the tale,
However, had it that Death took her from us
While in her very cradle.

ISABELLA: That tale lied.
She is alive!

DON CESAR: Alive! And you kept silent?

ISABELLA: I now shall render an accounting for   1300
My silence. Hear what seed was sown before
That now shall ripen to a joyous harvest.
You were still tender boys when wretched discord
Already set the two of you at odds
And loaded grief upon your parents' hearts.
O may that discord never more recur!
Then to your father there one day befell
A strange and wondrous dream. It seemed to him

As though he saw rise from his nuptial bed
Two laurel trees that densely interlaced   1310
Their branches with each other. And between them
There grew a lily flower. This turned into
A flame, which, seizing on the trees' dense branches
And on the rafters, shot up with a roar
And in its fury swiftly had consumed
The entire house in monstrous tides of fire.

  Inspired with terror by this curious vision,
Your father had recourse to an Arabian
Skilled in star-lore, who was his oracle
More favored by his heart than I approved,   1320
To learn its meaning. The Arabian
Declared that if my womb should bear a daughter,
That daughter would destroy both of his sons
And all his family would be destroyed
By her. I did become the mother of a daughter;
But then your father issued a command
Most cruel, to take the new-born child at once
And cast her in the sea. I thwarted that
Inhuman order and preserved my daughter
Through silent service of a trusted henchman.   1330

DON CESAR: May he be blessed who was thus helpful to you!
O, mother-love will never lack for wisdom!

ISABELLA: Not merely mother-love's imperious voice
Alone impelled me to protect the child.
A dream's strange oracle was to me also
Vouchsafed while my womb was made blessed by
That daughter. I beheld a child, fair as
The gods, at play upon the grass, and from
The forest came a lion bearing in
His blood-stained jaws a fresh-slain prey, which he   1340
Relinquished there before the child with homage.
Then from the air swooped down an eagle, in
His talons hung a quivering deer, which he
Set down before the child with homage there.

Then both of them, the lion and the eagle,
Lay meekly down at the child's feet together.
The dream's significance a monk resolved
For me, a man well loved of God, from whom
Hearts found a comfort in all earthly woes.
He said that I would bear a daughter who   1350
Would join the warring spirits of my sons
Together in the heat of ardent love.
—I kept those words within my inmost heart;
With more trust in the God of Truth than in
The god of lies, I saved the daughter of
God's promise and the pledge of all my hope
Who was to be the instrument of peace,
While your increasing hatred still increased.

DON MANUEL *(embracing his brother):*
Our sister is no longer needed to
Entwine love's bond, but she shall knit it closer.   1360

ISABELLA: So in a hidden place far from my eyes
I caused her to be brought up secretly
By alien hands. And I forbade myself
So much as seeing that beloved face
So dearly longed for, fearing your strict father,
Who, in the restless torment of suspicion
And gnawed by dark and somber-brooding doubt,
Had planted spies to watch my every step.

DON CESAR: But it is now three moons the silent grave
Has held our father. What prevented you   1370
From bringing forth the hidden one to light,
O Mother, and rejoicing all our hearts?

ISABELLA: What else prevented but your wretched quarrel,
Which, raging out of all control, flamed up
On the grave of your father barely dead
And left no room for reconciliation?
How could I set your sister in between
Your wild, drawn swords? Or how could you have heard
Your mother's voice amid so great a storm?

Was I to risk *her,* my dear pledge of peace,   1380
The last and sacred anchor of my hope,
Before your hatred's frenzy prematurely?
You had first to endure each other's sight
As brothers; not till then could I present
Your sister to you as an angel of peace.
I *now* can do so, and I bring her to you.
The old retainer I have sent to fetch her
And hourly I wait for his return,
Who, when he has removed her from her refuge,
Will bring her back to my maternal bosom   1390
And back to the embraces of her brothers.

DON MANUEL: And she is not the only one whom you
Will clasp within your mother-arms today.
Joy makes its entry here at every gate,
This desolated palace will be filled
And will become the seat of flowering grace.
Now to my secret also, Mother, listen.
Now for the sister you have given me
I will bestow on you a second daughter.
Yes, Mother, give your blessing to your son.   1400
This heart of mine has chosen; I have found
The one who shall accompany me through life.
Before the sunlight of this day has sunken
I shall bring you Don Manuel's own spouse.

ISABELLA: Into my arms I will receive her gladly
Who has brought happiness to my first-born.
Joy shall spring forth and bloom beside her paths
And every flower that adorns our life
And every gladness shall reward my son
Who thus gives me a mother's fairest crown.   1410

DON CESAR: Do not expend the total, Mother, of
Your blessing on your first-born son alone!
If love confers a blessing, I too bring you
A daughter worthy of a mother such
As you, who has taught me love's new emotion.

Before the sunlight of this day has sunken
Don Cesar also will bring you his spouse.
DON MANUEL: Almighty Love! Well do they term you, Goddess,
And with full right, the Queen of all men's souls!
All elements are subject unto you,   1420
The hostilely opposed you wed together;
No living thing but that acknowledges
Your rule; you have prevailed above my brother's
Wild will which had remained unconquered ever.

(embracing Don Cesar)

I now believe your heart and I embrace you
In these fraternal arms with hope; no longer
Do I have doubts of you, for you can love.
ISABELLA: A threefold blessing be upon this day
That lifts all troubled cares away at once
From my oppressive-laden heart! I see   1430
My race established on enduring pillars
And with a mind at rest I can gaze down
Into the measureless abyss of time.
Just yesterday I saw myself dressed in
My widow's veil, like one deceased and childless
And all alone in these deserted halls,
While now amid the radiance of their youth
Three lovely daughters will stand at my side.
Show me the happy mother who, of all
The women that have ever borne a child,   1440
Can possibly compare with me in glory!
—But what high Princes' royal daughters shine
In beauty on the borders of this country
Of whom I have not heard report? For surely
My sons cannot have made unworthy choices.
DON MANUEL: Just for today yet, Mother, do not seek
To lift the veil that hides my happiness.
The day will come when all will be resolved.
The bride herself will best announce herself,

But be assured that you will find her worthy.   1450
ISABELLA: I recognize the father's very mind
  And spirit in my first-born son. He always
  Loved to spin webs about himself in secret
  And to withhold his own decisions in
  His inaccessible and firmly guarded mind.
  This brief term of delay I gladly grant;
  But my son Cesar will, I feel quite certain,
  Now name to me the daughter of a king.
DON CESAR: It is not my way, Mother, to conceal
  Myself in mysteries. I bear my spirit   1460
  With openness and frankness like my brow.
  But what you now seek to discover from me,
  Allow me to confess quite frankly, Mother,
  This I have not inquired yet of myself.
  Does one ask whence the sun flames in the sky?
  That which illuminates the world, defines
  Itself; its light attests it comes of light.
  Into the clear eyes of my bride I gazed,
  Before her heart of hearts I stood amazed,
  I know the pearl by lustre and by hue;   1470
  And yet I cannot name her name to you.
ISABELLA: How, my son Cesar? This you must explain!
  Too readily you trusted your initial
  Strong impulse like the prompting of a god.
  A youthfully rash deed I would expect
  From you, but not a deed of childish folly.
  Tell me what swayed your choice.
DON CESAR: Choice, Mother? Choice?
  Is there a choice when man is overtaken
  In fateful hour by the stars' compulsion?
  O, I did not set out to seek a bride,   1480
  Such vanity would never have occurred
  To me indeed amid the house of death;
  For there I found one whom I did not seek.
  To me the empty, chattering race of women

Had been indifferent, insignificant,
For I had seen no second one like you,
Whom I adore as if you were a goddess.
It was my father's solemn funeral rite;
Concealed amid the throng of people, we
Were present, you recall, in unknown garb,   1490
Since you in wisdom had ordained it so
Lest our feud's violence should break out wildly
And mar the pageantry's solemnity.
The great nave of the church was draped in black,
And twenty guardian spirits, each one holding
A torch in hand, were standing round the altar,
Before which in sublime repose the bier
Lay covered by the shroud with its white cross.
And on the shroud the staff of regency
Was laid, together with the princely crown,   1500
The knightly ornament of golden spurs,
The sword upon its diamond-studded belt.
In reverent silence everyone was kneeling
When now unseen down from the lofty choir
The organ lifted up its wondrous sound
And hundred-voiced the singing now began.
Then while the choir continued in its hymn
The coffin and the floor supporting it
Sank slowly down into the world below
But left the covering shroud stretched to its full   1510
To close the hidden opening beneath,
So that the earthly ornament remained
Behind, *not* following him who had descended.
Meanwhile upon the seraph-wings of song
The liberated soul was soaring upward
In search of Heaven and the arms of Mercy.
I now describe all this exactly, Mother,
Reviving it all in your memory
So you may judge of whether in that hour
A worldly wish was present in my heart.   1520

It was that moment of solemnity
Which was selected by the guardian of
My life to touch me with the ray of love.
But *how* it chanced, I seek in vain to know.

ISABELLA: Complete the story! Let me hear the rest!

DON CESAR: Where she had come from, how she found her way
To me, do not inquire to know. But as
I turned my eyes, there she was standing at
My side, and with a dark and wondrous power
Her presence seized upon my inmost being.   1530
It was not the enchantment of her smile,
Nor yet the charm that graced her cheek so well,
Not even her resplendent goddess-form:
It was her inmost life of which I tell
When saying it took me by sudden storm
As magic casts its strong, unfathomed spell.
Without a word our souls seem to have met
Directly, as two spirits might combine,
When her breath was commingled there with mine;   1540
She was a stranger and yet intimate,
And suddenly I clearly saw that none
On earth existed for me save this one.

DON MANUEL   *(interrupting with ardor):*
This is the sacred ray of love divine
That strikes and kindles fire within the soul;
When kindred spirits find a kindred goal
There can be no resistance or design,
Man will not part what Heaven has made whole.
—I praise my brother, I applaud his tale;
What he has told, is my own destiny,   1550
And he has deftly lifted off the veil
From the emotion that stirs dark in me.

ISABELLA: Fate means, I see, to take its own free course
In matters where my children are concerned.
The mighty river plunges from the mountain,
Digs its own channel and makes its own way

With disregard for the appointed path
Which wisdom prudently prescribes for it.
So I submit—What other choice is left me?—
To that divine hand of superior scope   1560
That darkly weaves my family's fate and fame.
My sons' hearts are the warrants of my hope,
Their thoughts are quite as noble as their name.

(Diego appears at the door.)

But look! My faithful servant has returned.
Approach, approach, my upright friend Diego!
Where is my child?—My sons know everything.
There is no secret now. Where is she? Speak!
Hide her no longer, we are quite prepared
To bear this highest joy. Come!

(She starts toward the door with him.)

                                        What is this?
You hesitate? You do not speak a word?   1570
This look of yours forebodes no good for me.
What is the matter? Horror seizes me.
Where is she? Where is Beatrice?

(She starts to go out.)

DON MANUEL *(aside, startled)*:   Beatrice!
DIEGO *(detains her)*:   Wait!
ISABELLA: Where is she? I am dead with fear.
DIEGO: She is
Not with me. I have not brought you your daughter.
ISABELLA: What has befallen? Speak, by all the saints!
DON CESAR: Where is my sister? Tell us, wretched man!
DIEGO: She has been stolen! Carried off by corsairs!
O would that I had never seen this day!
DON MANUEL: Be calm, O Mother!
DON CESAR: Mother, be composed!   1580
Control yourself till you have heard him out!

DIEGO: I quickly started out, as you commanded,
  To go the often traveled road down to
  The convent for this final time. Joy bore
  Me on light wings along.
DON CESAR: Come to the point!
DON MANUEL: Speak!
DIEGO: When I stepped within the convent's well-
  Known precincts, where I often was before,
  And asked impatiently about your daughter,
  I saw the sign of fright in every eye
  And horrified I heard the horrible.   1590

  *(Isabella sinks pale and trembling into
  a chair; Don Manuel occupies himself with her.)*

DON CESAR: And Moors, you say, had carried her away?
  Were these Moors seen? Who will attest the fact?
DIEGO: A Moorish pirate vessel was observed
  At anchor in a bay close by the convent.
DON CESAR: Many sails seek refuge in these bays
  Out of the tempest's rage. Where is the ship?
DIEGO: This morning it was seen far out to sea,
  With full sail making for the furthest distance.
DON CESAR: Has there been news of any other raids?
  Moors are not satisfied with single plunder.   1600
DIEGO: The herds of cattle pastured near at hand
  Were driven off with violence and taken.
DON CESAR: How could the pirates secretly make off
  With this well-guarded girl right in the convent?
DIEGO: The convent garden walls were scaled with ease
  On rungs of ladders of a goodly length.
DON CESAR: How did they break into the inmost cells?
  For strict constraint rules over pious nuns.
DIEGO: She who was not yet bound by any vows
  Was free to walk at leisure in the open.   1610
DON CESAR: Was it her habit to avail herself
  Of this free privilege often? Tell me this.

DIEGO: She often sought the quiet of the garden,
She failed today alone in her return.

DON CESAR *(after reflecting for a time):*
If she was free for pirates to discover,
She also had the freedom to *escape.*

ISABELLA *(stands up):*
It *was* by force! It was an arrant kidnap!
My daughter could not so forget her duty
To follow an abductor willingly.
Don Manuel! Don Cesar! I had planned   1620
To give you both a sister; but I now
Shall have to owe her to your heroes' arms.
Rise up in all your strength, then, now, my sons!
Do not with patience tolerate your sister's
Capture as the prize of pirates. Seize
Your weapons! Fit out ships! Search all along
The length of coast! Across all seas pursue
These robbers! Win your sister back by conquest!

DON CESAR: Farewell! I fly to vengeance, and to find her!

(Exit.)

*(Don Manuel, rousing from profound
abstraction, turns uneasily to Diego.)*

DON MANUEL: When did you say it was she disappeared? 1630
DIEGO: She was not missed until this very morning.

DON MANUEL *(to Donna Isabella):*
And Beatrice is your daughter's name?

ISABELLA: That is her name. But hurry! Ask no questions!
DON MANUEL: Just one thing more, O Mother, let me know—
ISABELLA: Fly into action! Emulate your brother!
DON MANUEL: I conjure you to tell me in what region—

ISABELLA *(forcing him away):*
Behold my tears, behold my mortal anguish!

DON MANUEL: But in what region did you keep her hidden?
ISABELLA: She was not deeper hidden in earth's womb!
DIEGO: O, suddenly a desperate fear assails me.   1640

DON MANUEL: A desperate fear of what? Tell what you know!

DIEGO: That I have been this deed's unwitting cause.

ISABELLA: Unhappy man, reveal what has occurred.

DIEGO: I have withheld this secret from you, Mistress,
To spare concern from your maternal heart.
On that day when the Prince was laid in earth
And everyone, from greed of novelty,
Came thronging to that solemn ceremony,
Your daughter begged me,—for the news had even
Penetrated into convent walls,— 1650
Begged me with never-ending supplication
To be allowed to view that ceremony.
Unhappy man, I let myself be swayed,
Enwrapped her in a solemn dress of mourning,
And thus she went as witness to that rite.
And there, I fear, amid that crowd of people
That came in throngs from every quarter, she
Was glimpsed perhaps by watchful pirate's eyes,
For no cloak could conceal her beauty's splendor.

DON MANUEL (to himself, with relief):
O lucky word that sets my heart at rest! 1660
That is not like her. This mark does not fit.

ISABELLA: Insane old man! So doing you betrayed me!

DIEGO: Mistress, I thought I was doing right.
In such a wish I felt I recognized
The voice of Nature and the call of blood.
I thought it was the work of Heaven itself
That with premonitory hidden impulse
Urged on the daughter to her father's grave.
I sought to give free rein to pious duty,
And thus from good intentions I did wrong. 1670

DON MANUEL (to himself):
Why do I stand in fear and anguished doubt?
I shall find light and certainty at once.

(He starts to leave.)

(Reenter Don Cesar.)

DON CESAR: Don Manuel, I'll follow you directly.
DON MANUEL: Follow me not! Let no one follow me!

(Exit.)

DON CESAR *(gazes after him in astonishment):*
   What ails my brother? Mother, what is wrong?
ISABELLA: I do not recognize him any more.
DON CESAR: You see, my Mother, that I have come back,
   For in my eagerness of zeal I had
   Forgotten to inquire from you a sign
   By which to recognize my vanished sister.   1680
   How shall I find a trace of her till I
   Know from what place the thieves abducted her?
   Name me the convent where she was concealed.
ISABELLA: To Saint Cecilia it is dedicated,
   And past the wooded hills that rise in slow
   Ascent toward Etna it lies hidden like
   A silent dwelling place of souls at rest.
DON CESAR: Be of good cheer! And have faith in your sons!
   I will bring back my sister to you if
   I have to search through all the lands and seas.   1690
   But I am troubled yet by one thing, Mother:
   I left my bride in strangers' hands to guard.
   To you alone can I entrust this prize,
   I'll send her to you, she will meet your eyes;
   Against her loving heart, in her embrace
   You will forget the sorrows of this place.

(Exit.)

ISABELLA: When will the ancient curse be abrogated
   That on this house with weighted burden rests?
   With furious envy never to be sated,
   A cunning demon turns my hopes to jests.   1700
   So close to port, I thought, safe from the deep,
   So trusting in the pledge from Fortune's hand,

I fancied all the tempests lulled to sleep,
I saw the joyous beckoning of land
That brightens in the sunset as it saves;
Then forth from air serene the storm clouds stand
And cast me back into the warring waves.   1707

(She goes into the interior of the house;
Diego follows after her.)

ACT III

*The scene shifts to the garden. Enter the Chorus of
Don Manuel in festive procession, adorned with
wreaths and bearing the bridal gifts previously described. The Chorus of Don Cesar tries to prevent
their entry.*

THE FIRST CHORUS (CAJETAN): It would be wise for you to leave
this place.

THE SECOND CHORUS (BOHEMUND) : I will, when better men
demand the space.

FIRST CHORUS (CAJETAN) : You might discern that you are in
the way.   1710

SECOND CH. (BOHEMUND): But just because it irks you, I will stay.

FIRST CH. (CAJETAN): Here is my place. Who will prevent my
stand?

SECOND CH. (BOHEMUND): That I will do. Here I am in command.

FIRST CH. (CAJETAN): Don Manuel, my lord, here stationed me.

SECOND CH. (BOHEMUND): I stand here on my lord's authority.

FIRST CH. (CAJETAN): To elder brothers younger yield their
strength.

SECOND CH. (BOHEMUND): Those in possession own the world
entire.

FIRST CH. (CAJETAN): Be off, vile man, cede me the field, retire!

SECOND CH. (BOHEMUND): O not till we have measured swords
for length.

FIRST CH. (CAJETAN): Am I to find you on my every path? [1720]

SECOND CH. (BOHEMUND): Wherever I so please I'll face your
wrath.

FIRST CH. (CAJETAN): What business have you here to guard
and spy?

SECOND CH. (BOHEMUND): Or what have you to ask and to deny?

FIRST CH. (CAJETAN): To give you answer is not my affair.

SECOND CH. (BOHEMUND): For you I have no seemly words to spare.

FIRST CH. (CAJETAN): Respect, young man, at least is due my age.

SECOND CH. (BOHEMUND): With bravery I can match you in your rage.

BEATRICE *(rushing out):*
Alas! What do these savage hosts presage?

FIRST CHORUS (CAJETAN) *(to the second Chorus):*
I set you and your haughty mien at naught.

SECOND CHORUS (BOHEMUND): I serve a better master than you thought. 1730

BEATRICE: Alas for me if he should now appear!

FIRST CHORUS (CAJETAN): Don Manuel surpasses him by far.

SECOND CHORUS (BOHEMUND): My master wins the prize in any war.

BEATRICE: Now he will come, this is his wonted hour.

FIRST CHORUS (CAJETAN): If peace were not the rule I'd claim my right.

SECOND CHORUS (BOHEMUND): It is not peace that holds you back, but fright.

BEATRICE: O would he were a thousand miles from sight!

FIRST CHORUS (CAJETAN): It is the law I fear, not your defiance.

SECOND CHORUS (BOHEMUND): Quite properly, it is the coward's reliance.

FIRST CHORUS (CAJETAN): Set on, I follow!

SECOND CHORUS (BOHEMUND): I have my sword out. 1740

BEATRICE *(in the most vehement agitation):*
Their swords are flashing, they have come to blows.
You powers of high Heaven, hold him back!
You hindrances, cast yourselves in his way!
Cast nets about his feet to make him stay,
To make him miss this moment of attack!
O all you angels whom I have implored
To guide him here, deny my supplications
And lead him far to other destinations!

(She hurries in.)

*(As the Choruses are attacking each other
enter Don Manuel.)*

DON MANUEL: What do I see? Hold off!

THE FIRST CHORUS

CAJETAN
BERENGAR   } *(to the second Chorus):*   Come on! Come on!
MANFRED

THE SECOND CHORUS

BOHEMUND
ROGER   } :   Down with the lot of them! Come on!
HIPPOLYT

DON MANUEL *(steps between them with sword drawn):* Hold
    off!   1750

THE FIRST CHORUS (CAJETAN) :   It is the Prince.

THE SECOND CHORUS (BOHEMUND) :   The brother! Keep the
    peace!

DON MANUEL: Upon this grass I strike the man down dead
    Who with so much as quiver of an eyelash
    Prolongs this feud and threatens an opponent.
    Are you all mad? What demon sets you on
    To fan the flame of ancient strife ablaze
    Which has been put aside by us, the Princes,
    And which has been composed for evermore?
    Who started this fight? Speak! I want to know.

THE FIRST CHORUS

CAJETAN
BERENGAR } :   These men were standing here—

THE SECOND CHORUS

ROGER
BOHEMUND } *(interrupting):*   They came—

DON MANUEL *(to the first Chorus):*   *You* speak!   1760

THE FIRST CHORUS (CAJETAN) :   We came, my Prince, to make
    delivery of
    These bridal gifts, as you commanded us.

Arrayed as for a festival, in no wise
Prepared for war, as you can see, we had
Come on our way in peace, with nothing evil
In mind, and trusting in the truce avowed.
And here we found them hostilely drawn up,
Denying us the entry here by force.

DON MANUEL:　You madmen! Is there no asylum safe
Enough from your insane and blinded fury?　　1770
Must your contention burst into the very
Remote and tranquil seat of innocence?

(to the second Chorus)

Step back! Here there are secret matters which
Will not endure your rash and warlike presence.

(as the other hesitates)

Fall back! Your lord so orders you through me,
For we are now one head, one heart, together,
And my command is also his. Be gone!

(to the first Chorus)

Stay here and guard the gate.

THE SECOND CHORUS (BOHEMUND):　　　What shall we do?
The Princes have made peace, that is the truth,
And to intrude unbidden and officious　　　1780
Into the quarrels of such lofty chiefs
Incurs small gratitude and frequent peril.
For when the mighty wearies of a quarrel
He will adroitly cast the gory mantle
Of guilt upon the lesser man who served him
And easily will stand guilt-free himself.
So let the Princes make their quarrels up,
I deem it wiser wisdom to obey.

*(Exit the second Chorus, while the first withdraws
to the rear of the stage. At the same moment Beatrice rushes out and throws herself into Don
Manuel's arms.)*

BEATRICE:　It *is* you. I have you again. Cruel man!

How long, how long you have left me to languish,   1790
Abandoned here and left a prey to fear
And to all terrors. But no more of that!
I have you, and in your beloved arms
Is shelter and protection from all dangers.
Come! They have gone! And our escape is clear,
Away, let us not lose a single instant!

> *(She starts to draw him away with her,*
> *but only now looks at him more closely.)*

What is the matter? You receive me so
Aloof and solemnly, you draw back from
My arms as if you meant to cast me off.
I do not know you. Can this be Don Manuel,   1800
My husband, my beloved?

DON MANUEL: Beatrice!

BEATRICE: No, do not speak! This is no time for words!
Let us escape, and swiftly. Every moment
Is precious—

DON MANUEL: Wait! I want an answer from you.

BEATRICE: Away! before those frantic men return.

DON MANUEL: Wait! Those men will not do us any harm.

BEATRICE: O but they will, you do not know them! Come!

DON MANUEL: Protected by my arm, what can you fear?

BEATRICE: Those men are men of power, O believe me.

DON MANUEL: Beloved, none more powerful than I.   1810

BEATRICE: Would you alone stand up against these many?

DON MANUEL: I all alone! These men you are afraid of—

BEATRICE: You do not know them, nor the lord they serve.

DON MANUEL: They are *my* vassals, and I am their lord.

BEATRICE: You are—a shudder courses through my soul!

DON MANUEL: Learn my name at last now, Beatrice.
For I am not the man I seemed to be,
Nor that poor knight whose name was quite unknown,
Who, loving, sued for your love in return.
My true identity, what I control,   1820

What is my race, all this I kept from you.

BEATRICE: Who are you? You are not Don Manuel?

DON MANUEL: Don Manuel is my name,—but I am also
The highest of that name within this city,
I am Don Manuel, Prince of Messina.

BEATRICE: You are Don Manuel, Don Cesar's brother?

DON MANUEL: Don Cesar is my brother.

BEATRICE: Is your brother?

DON MANUEL: What? Does that frighten you? You know Don
Cesar?
Do you know any others of my blood?

BEATRICE: You are Don Manuel, who lives in hatred   1830
And feud implacable with his own brother?

DON MANUEL: We made our peace today and now are brothers
Not only by our birth, but in our hearts.

BEATRICE: You made your peace today?

DON MANUEL: What is it that
Arouses such alarm in you? Do you
Know more than merely the name of my house?
Do I know your whole secret? Is there nothing
That you have kept suppressed in silence from me?

BEATRICE: What do you mean? What have I to confess?

DON MANUEL: You still have told me nothing of your mother.
                                                          1840

Who is she? Would you recognize her if
I should describe her to you, show her to you?

BEATRICE: You know her—know her and yet kept it from me?

DON MANUEL: If I do know her, woe to you and me!

BEATRICE: O she is kindly as the sun's own light!
I see her now before me, memory
Awakes again, and out of my soul's depths
Lifts that divine form up before me now.
I see her clustering curls of dark brown hair
Enshade the noble form of her white throat.   1850
I see the purely molded arch of brow,
The darkling radiance of her great dark eyes,

I hear the soulful tones of her voice waken
In me—

DON MANUEL: Alas for me! You have described her!

BEATRICE: And I have fled from her! I could desert her
Perhaps the very morning of this day
Which might have brought us back together now!
For you I sacrificed my very mother!

DON MANUEL: Messina's Princess will be mother to you.
I take you to her now. She waits for you.   1860

BEATRICE: Your mother and Don Cesar's? What is this
You say? Take me to her? O never, never!

DON MANUEL: You shudder? What does this aversion mean?
Or can my mother be no stranger to you?

BEATRICE: O wretched and ill-starred discovery!
O would that I had never seen this day!

DON MANUEL: What can distress you, now that you know me
And find the Prince where you had known the stranger?

BEATRICE: O give me back the stranger, I would be
Most blessed on a desert isle with him.   1870

DON CESAR   (offstage):
Stand back! Why is this throng assembled here?

BEATRICE: O Lord! That voice! Where can I hide myself?

DON MANUEL: You recognize that voice? No, you have never
Heard it before and cannot recognize it.

BEATRICE: O let us flee! Come, let us not delay!

DON MANUEL: Why flee? It is my brother's voice, and he
Is looking for me. How did he discover—

BEATRICE: By all of Heaven's holy saints, avoid him!
O do not meet that violent contender
And do not let him find you in this place!   1880

DON MANUEL: Beloved soul, your fright bewilders you.
You did not hear me, we are reconciled!

BEATRICE: O Heaven, send me rescue from this hour!

DON MANUEL: But what suspicion dawns on me? What thought
Takes me with horror? Is it possible—
That voice was not strange to you? Beatrice,

Did you—I shudder at this further question—
Did you—attend my father's funeral rites?

BEATRICE: Alas!

DON MANUEL: You were there?

BEATRICE: O do not be angry!

DON MANUEL: Unhappy girl, you were?

BEATRICE: Yes, I was present. 1890

DON MANUEL: Horror!

BEATRICE: Curiosity compelled me.
Forgive me. I confessed that wish to you;
But with a sudden somberness you left
My plea unanswered, nor did I speak either.
And yet I do not know what evil star
Forced me with irresistible desire.
I had to satisfy my heart's strong impulse.
The aged servant lent me his assistance,
And thus I disobeyed you, and I went.

*(She is clinging to him as Don Cesar
enters, accompanied by the entire Chorus.)*

THE SECOND CHORUS (BOHEMUND) *(to Don Cesar)*:
No, you would not believe us. Now believe   1900
Your eyes!

*(Enter Don Cesar with vehemence and at the sight
of his brother he recoils in horror.)*

DON CESAR: Deceit of Hell! What! In his arms!

(coming closer, to Don Manuel)

Envenomed serpent! This, then, is your love!
For this you lied your reconciliation!
My hatred was the prompting of God's voice!
Descend to Hell, deceitful serpent-soul!

(He stabs him.)

DON MANUEL: I am a dead man—Beatrice—Brother!

> *(He falls and dies. Beatrice falls*
> *fainting beside him.)*

FIRST CHORUS   (CAJETAN):   Murder! Murder! Everyone seize
   weapons!
And let this bloody deed be paid in blood!

> *(All draw their swords.)*

SECOND CHORUS   (BOHEMUND):   Hurrah! The long dissension
   has been ended,
Messina now obeys a single master.   1910

FIRST CHORUS

    CAJETAN

    BERENGAR }:   Vengeance! Vengeance! Kill the murderer!

    MANFRED

A sacrifice to placate him who died!

SECOND CHORUS

    BOHEMUND

    ROGER }:   Have no fear, Lord, we shall be true to you.

    HIPPOLYT

DON CESAR   *(stepping between them with dignity):*
Stand back there! I have slain my enemy
Who had betrayed my honest trusting heart,
Who made fraternal love a snare for me.
This action bears a fearful, ghastly aspect,
But Heaven in its justice passed its judgment.

FIRST CHORUS   (CAJETAN):   Woe to you, Messina! Woe on woe!
This thing of monstrous horror has occurred   1920
Within your walls. And woe upon your mothers
And children, on your old men and your youths!
And woe upon the fruit as yet unborn!

DON CESAR: Too late comes your lament. Lend your aid *here!*

> *(pointing to Beatrice)*

Bring *her* to life again! Remove her quickly

Out of this place of terror and of death.
I cannot stay here any longer. Concern
For my abducted sister calls me hence.
Transport her to my Mother's hall, and say
It is her son Don Cesar who has sent her.   1930

(Exit.)

*(The second Chorus place the swooning Beatrice
on a bench and carry her away. The first Chorus
remains behind with the corpse, around which the
boys who are carrying the bridal gifts also stand in
a half-circle.)*

THE CHORUS (CAJETAN):   Grasp it I cannot, what it may mean,
How it came on and was done with such speed.
True, in my mind I long had foreseen
This spectre of terror stalking the scene,
This spectre of the monstrous deed.
Yet icy dread upon me lies
To see it at hand and actually done,
To see fulfilled before my eyes
What I had beheld in my fear alone.
My blood in my veins stops and congeals   1940
At what this grisly moment reveals.

ONE OF THE CHORUS (MANFRED):   Let the voice of lament be
raised in this time.
Youth of high grace,
Lifeless he lies,
Slain in the flower of his prime,
Deeply enwrapped in the night of death
At the nuptial chamber's very doors.
Yet over him who has no breath
The loud cry of lament outpours.

A SECOND (BERENGAR):   We come, we come,   1950
With pomp and with pride
To receive the bride;
These youths have brought

As bridal gifts these garments rich-wrought;
The feast is prepared, the guests await,
But the bridegroom hears no more; from his sleep
No songs will arouse him early or late,
For the slumber of the dead is deep.

THE WHOLE CHORUS: The slumber of dead men is deep and
  profound.
The voice of his bride will wake him never,   1960
Nor cheery huntsman's horn-call ever,
Senseless and stark he lies on the ground.

A THIRD (CAJETAN): What are the hopes, what are the plans
Constructed by man the non-enduring?
Today you embraced as brothers, as one
Were attuned your hearts, your lips, your sight,
While this very descending sun
Lighted your union with glory of light.
Here now you lie wedded to dust,
Slain by the hands of brotherly trust,   1970
Your bosom cleft by the hideous knife.
What are the hopes, what are the plans
That man, the son of time in its flight,
Erects on the treacherous earth in delight?

THE CHORUS (BERENGAR): To your mother I will carry you
  now,
A burden that brings no happiness!
Let us hew down this cypress, bough on bough,
With the murderous blade of the ax,
To weave its branches into a bier.
Never shall living thing appear   1980
To be borne by this tree that bore such sorrow;
In gracious growth it shall not live,
Nor shall it shade to wayfarers give;
This tree from soil of slaughter has fed:
Be it accursed to serve the dead.

THE FIRST (MANFRED): But woe upon the murderer, woe!
Who now with folly's assurance goes!

Downward in clefts of the earth and down
Your blood still flows, still flows, still flows.
And down in the depths there sit and frown,   1990
Lightless, without either speech or song,
The daughters of Themis who never forget,
Who measure justly, unerringly yet
And pour into vessels of gleaming jet
The potions of vengeance that right a wrong.

THE SECOND (BERENGAR): Out of the sun-illumined earth
As easily fades an action's trace
As facile expression fades from a face.
Yet nothing is lost or disappears
Once the mysterious ordaining years   2000
Have taken it into their darkling womb.
Time is a meadow in ageless bloom,
Nature a living thing indeed,
And all things are fruit and all things are seed.

THE THIRD (CAJETAN): But woe upon the murderer, woe
Upon him who has sown the deathly seed!
One visage it wore before it was done,
Another is worn by the accomplished deed.
Bold is its visage, jaunty, smart,
While feelings of vengeance rage in your heart;   2010
But once it is done, it no more speaks
But stares at you with ashen cheeks.
Against Orestes the Furies hurled
The serpents of the underworld,
To matricide inciting the son.
Feigning justice with skill and art,
They lured him to betray his heart
Until the deathly deed was done,
But once the blow was dealt to the breast
That conceived and bore him and made him blest,   2020
Lo, they turned
Against him himself
Monstrously.

And he recognized the dreaded virgins
Who overtake a slayer and seize him,
Who will never again release him,
Who will gnaw him with serpent fangs forever,
Who will hunt him from ocean to ocean forever,
Even to Delphic sanctuary.   [2029]

> *(Exit the Chorus bearing the corpse*
> *of Don Manuel on a bier.)*

ACT IV

*The colonnaded hall. It is night. The stage is
lighted from above by a great lamp. Enter Donna
Isabella and Diego.*

ISABELLA: Still no news from my sons? I wonder whether   2030
  They have found traces of the vanished girl?
DIEGO: No, Mistress, nothing yet. But rest all hopes
  Upon your sons' assiduousness of effort.
ISABELLA: Diego, how my heart is torn with anguish!
  It lay with me to ward off this misfortune.
DIEGO: Do not impress the thorns of self-reproach
  Upon your heart. Where did you stint precaution?
ISABELLA: If I had but produced her earlier
  As my heart's voice so strongly urged me to!
DIEGO: Your prudence kept you from it, you did wisely;   2040
  The outcome is contained in Heaven's hand.
ISABELLA: This way no joy is pure! My happiness
  Would have been perfect but for this mischance.
DIEGO: The happiness is but delayed, not ruined;
  Take your joy now in your sons' peace and concord.
ISABELLA: I have beheld them in a heart-to-heart
  Embrace—a sight I never saw before.
DIEGO: Nor was it just an empty spectacle,
  For their forthrightness hates a lie's forced falsehood.
ISABELLA: I also see that they are capable   2050
  Of tender feelings and of love; with rapture
  I learn that they respect those whom they love.
  Unbridled freedom they are willing to
  Renounce, their wildly rushing youth does not

82

Refuse the check-rein of the law, their passion
Itself retained a moral quality.
I will confess it to you now, Diego,
That I had waited with anxiety
For that dread moment when the opening flower
Of their emotions should bloom forth. For love   2060
Turns easily to rage in violent natures.
And if in the accumulated tinder
Of their old hatred there should strike the lightning
And hostile flame of jealousy besides—
Just thinking of it makes me shudder—if
Their wills, which never were at one, should clash
For the first time precisely on that point!
But happily that thunder-pregnant cloud
Which hung above me blackly menacing
Has been diverted from me by an angel,   2070
And my heart now breathes freely with relief.
DIEGO: Yes, you may well rejoice in your achievement.
With gentle way and quiet mind you have
Accomplished what the Father could not do
For all his power. Yours is the glory,—but
Your star of fortune also merits praise.
ISABELLA: Success was often with me. Fortune also
Did much. It was no small thing to conceal
A secret of that kind all these long years,
To hide it from my husband who was most   2080
Perceptive, to force back into my heart
The impulse of my blood, which mighty as
The god encased in fire strained at its bonds.
DIEGO: I see Luck's long enduring favor as
A pledge that all will turn out for the best.
ISABELLA: I shall not praise my fortune's stars until
I have beheld the outcome of these deeds.
My daughter's flight reminds me and gives warning
My evil Genius is not lost in slumber.
—Reprove or praise what I have done, Diego,   2090

But from a faithful man I shall hide nothing.
I could not bear to stand here idly by
Just waiting for success and let my sons
Seek busily for traces of my daughter.
I too have acted. And where human skill
Is insufficient, Heaven often counsels.

DIEGO: Disclose what it is fitting I should know.

ISABELLA: A hermit on the heights of Etna dwells,
 A pious anchorite through ageless times
 Known as the Old Man of the Mountain, who, 2100
 By life more close to Heaven than is that
 Of other men's low-moving race, and with
 A spirit clarified in purer aether,
 Looks from the mountain of his piled-up years
 Down on the disentangled maze of life
 Incomprehensibly ensnarled below.
 Not unknown to him is my house's fate,
 And more than once that holy man has made
 Inquiry for us unto Heaven and
 Averted curses from us by his prayers. 2110
 To him I sent a messenger's fresh strength
 That he might give me knowledge of my daughter,
 And I await his news from hour to hour.

DIEGO: Unless my eye deceives me, Mistress, there
 The very man approaches in great haste,
 And praise indeed is due to his swift duty.

(Enter the Messenger.)

ISABELLA: Speak out, and neither dire report nor good
 Keep hidden from me, draw the truth up pure!
 What counsel did the mountain sage provide?

THE MESSENGER: That I was to return here swiftly, was 2120
 His answer, for the lost girl had been found.

ISABELLA: O blessed mouth and joyous word from Heaven,
 Things hoped for you have spoken to me ever!

To which one of my sons was it vouchsafed
To come upon the traces of the lost one?
THE MESSENGER: Your elder son found out the hidden one.
ISABELLA: It is Don Manuel to whom I owe her!
  Oh, he has always been a child of blessing!
  And did you take the consecrated candle
  Which I sent to the old man as a gift   2130
  And which he was to light before his Saint?
  For gifts that otherwise delight men's hearts
  This pious servant of the Lord disdains.
THE MESSENGER: He took the candle from my hand in silence,
  And stepping to the altar where the lamp
  Was burning to his Saint, he lit it quickly
  And with it quickly set on fire the hut
  Where he for ninety years had worshipped God.
ISABELLA: What thing of horror are you telling me?
THE MESSENGER: And with the cry of "Woe!" three times
    repeated   2140
  He then came down the mountain side, but signed
  To me in silence not to follow him,
  And thus I hurried here pursued by horror.
ISABELLA: Into the surging turmoil of fresh doubt
  And into dreadful hesitant confusion
  I am plunged headlong by this contradiction.
  My daughter who was lost has been discovered,
  And by my elder son Don Manuel?
  That glad announcement cannot make me happy
  Accompanied by this most unhappy deed.   2150
THE MESSENGER: Look there behind you, Mistress! You behold
  The hermit's word fulfilled before your eyes.
  I am deceived entirely or else this
  Is your lost daughter for whom you are seeking,
  Accompanied by your two sons' retinues.

    *(Beatrice is brought in on a portable chair by
the second Semi-chorus and is set down at the front
of the stage. She is still without life and motion.)*

THE CHORUS (BOHEMUND): Fulfilling now our master's bidding, we

 Now set this maiden down before your feet.

 Thus, Mistress, he commanded us to do,

 And also to declare to you it is

 Your son Don Cesar who is sending her.   2160

ISABELLA *(has rushed up to her with open arms and now steps back in horror)*:

 O Lord in Heaven! She is pale and lifeless!

THE CHORUS (BOHEMUND): She is alive! She will awake! Give her

 Time to recover from astonishment

 Which still has all her senses in its thrall.

ISABELLA: My child! Child of my sorrows and my cares!

 We meet again, like this! In such a fashion

 You make your entrance in your father's house!

 O let me kindle your life at the flame

 Of mine! I want to clasp you now to my

 Maternal bosom, till, from frost of death   2170

 Thawed free, your warm veins pulse with life again.

(to the Chorus)

 O speak! What ghastly thing has here befallen?

 Where did you find her? How did this poor child

 Get into this deplorable condition?

THE CHORUS (BOHEMUND): Do not learn that from me, my mouth is mute.

 Your son Don Cesar will make all that clear

 To you, for it is he who sends her to you.

ISABELLA: My son Don Manuel, you mean to say?

THE CHORUS (BOHEMUND): Your son Don Cesar has sent her to you.

ISABELLA *(to the Messenger)*:

 It was Don Manuel whom the seer mentioned,   2180

 Is that not true?

THE MESSENGER: Quite true. Those were his words.

ISABELLA: Whichever one, he has rejoiced my heart.
I owe my daughter to him. Blessings on him!
O, must a jealous demon now embitter
The rapture of this dearly longed-for moment!
I must contend against my own delight!
I see my daughter in her father's house,
But she does not see me, does not hear me,
She cannot speak to give an answer to
Her mother's joy. Be opened, lovely eyes!   2190
You hands, take on your warmth! O lifeless bosom,
Be stirred with life and throb again with pleasure!
Diego! This is my own daughter—this
Is the long hidden girl, the rescued one;
I now acknowledge her before the world!

THE CHORUS (BOHEMUND): I fancy I conceive a strange new
     horror
Before me here, and I stand lost in wonder
How this confusion is to be resolved.

ISABELLA *(to the Chorus, who are showing expressions of*
     consternation and embarrassment):
O you are hard, impenetrable hearts!
Back from the brazen armor on your bosoms,   2200
As from some beetling cliffside by the sea,
My heart's delight rebounds upon myself.
In vain among the entire circle here
I search for just one eye that shows emotion.
Where are my sons, so that I may in one eye
Find sympathy; I feel as though I were
Surrounded by the heartless hordes of desert
Wastes and by the monsters of the deep.

DIEGO: Her eyes are opening. She stirs. She lives!

ISABELLA: She lives! Let her first glance light on her mother!
                                                    [2210]

DIEGO: She shudders now and shuts her eyes again.

ISABELLA *(to the Chorus)*:
Fall back! The view of strangers frightens her.

THE CHORUS (BOHEMUND) (*steps back*):
I much prefer not to confront her glance.

DIEGO: With eyes of wonderment she looks at you.

BEATRICE: Where am I? I should recognize these features.

ISABELLA: Slowly consciousness returns to her.

DIEGO: What is she doing? Falling on her knees?

BEATRICE: O my mother's fair angelic face!

ISABELLA: Child of my heart, come into my embrace!

BEATRICE: Behold the guilty girl before your feet.   2220

ISABELLA: I have you again. Let all else be forgotten!

DIEGO: Look at me too. You recognize my features?

BEATRICE: The grey head of my honest old Diego!

ISABELLA: The faithful guardian of your childhood years.

BEATRICE: Then I am in the bosom of my people?

ISABELLA: And nothing else but death shall ever part us.

BEATRICE: You will no more send me away to strangers?

ISABELLA: Nothing shall part us; Fate is satisfied.

BEATRICE (*sinks upon her bosom*):
And do I really find myself upon your heart?
And was it all a dream, what I experienced?   2230
A dreadful and oppressive dream—O Mother!
I saw him fall down dead before my feet!
But how do I come to be here? I do
Not recollect.—But, oh, how fortunate
To have been rescued in your arms. They wanted
To take me to the Princess Mother of
Messina. Rather to my grave!

ISABELLA: My daughter,
Bethink yourself! Messina's Princess—

BEATRICE: Name her
No more! At that unhappy name a frost
Of death spreads through my every limb.

ISABELLA: Listen to me.   2240

BEATRICE: She has two sons who bear a mortal hatred;
Don Manuel, Don Cesar they are called.

ISABELLA: And I am she. Acknowledge your own mother.

BEATRICE: What are you saying? What was that you said?

ISABELLA: I am your mother and Messina's Princess.

BEATRICE: You are Don Manuel's mother and Don Cesar's?

ISABELLA: Your mother also! You have named your brothers!

BEATRICE: Woe unto me! O light most horrible!

ISABELLA: What is the matter? What distresses you
So strangely?

BEATRICE (*gazing wildly around, catches sight of the Chorus*):
    There they are! I know them now. 2250
My dream did not deceive me. Here they are!
And they were present—it is dreadful truth!
Unhappy men, where have you hidden him?

  (*With rapid step she advances upon the Chorus
  who turn away from her. A funeral march is heard
  in the distance.*)

THE CHORUS: Woe! Woe!

ISABELLA: Who has been hidden? What is true?
You are abashed and silent—and you seem
To understand her. In your eyes and in
Your voices' broken tones I read some great
Misfortune that is being kept from me.
What is it? I must know it. Why do you
Fix glances of such terror on the door? 2260
What tones are those I hear resounding there?

THE CHORUS (BOHEMUND): It comes. It will declare itself with
  terror.
Be strong now, Mistress, arm your heart with steel,
And with composure bear what now awaits you,
With manlike soul support the mortal pain.

ISABELLA: What is it that is coming? What awaits me?
—I hear the grim tone of a funeral dirge
Resounding through the house.—Where are my sons?

  (*Enter the first Semi-chorus with the corpse of
  Don Manuel borne on a bier, which they set down*)

on the unoccupied side of the stage. A black pall
is spread over it.)

THE FIRST CHORUS (CAJETAN):   Through streets of cities,   2270
  With Grief in train,
  Strides Disaster.
  It stalks about
  The houses of men,
  Knocking today
  At this door, tomorrow
  Knocking at that one;
  None was ever spared its knells.
  The not-desired
  Tidings of sorrow
  Sooner or later   2280
  It delivers to every
  Threshold where a mortal dwells.

(BERENGAR):   When leaves are shed
  In the circling year,
  When grave-ward are led
  Old men and sere,
  Then Nature obeys
  Her ancient ways,
  She does but mind
  Her eternal habit;
  It is nothing to horrify mankind.   2290

    But learn to expect in life on earth
  The monstrous also in all its power!
  With violent hand
  Murder also dissolves the holiest bond.
  In his Stygian boat
  Death also can gloat
  Over youth's life also in its full flower.

(CAJETAN):   When towering clouds blacken the sky,
  When hollowly the thunder roars,   2300

Then all hearts feel themselves caught by
Destiny's appalling force.
But even from cloudless heights of air
The thunder can strike with its fires ablaze;
Therefore amid your cheerful days
Of Misfortune's treacherous presence beware!
Count not such possessions as gain
As adorn our life all to no use!
Whoever possesses, let him learn to lose,
Whoever is lucky, let him learn pain.   2310
ISABELLA: What is it I am now about to hear?

> (*She takes a step toward the bier, then stops
> hesitant and uncertain.*)

What does this pall conceal? It draws me forward
And draws me back with some cold hand of horror.

> (*to Beatrice, who has cast herself down between
> her and the bier.*)

No, be it what it may, I shall unveil it!

> (*She raises the pall and discovers Dan Manuel's
> corpse.*)

O Powers of Heaven, it is my son!

> (*She stands frozen with terror. Beatrice with a
> cry of grief sinks down beside the bier.*)

THE CHORUS
  CAJETAN ⎞ Unfortunate mother, it is your son!
  BERENGAR ⎬: You have pronounced it, that word of grief,
  MANFRED ⎠ Not from my lips has it flown.
ISABELLA: My son! My Manuel!— O everlasting
  Mercy! Must I find you in this state!   2320
  Were you obliged to buy your sister from
  The pirates' hands with your own life!—Where was
  Your brother that his arm did not protect you?

A curse upon the hand that dug this wound!
A curse on her who bore the evil man
Who has thus slain my son! A curse on his
Whole race and stock!

THE CHORUS: Alas! Woe and alas!

ISABELLA: Is this the way you keep your word to me,
You Powers of Heaven? Is this, *this,* your truth?
O woe to him who trusts you honestly!   2330
What have I hoped for, at what have I trembled,
If this must be the outcome?—You who stand
Around me here in terror, feasting glances
Upon my sorrow, learn to know the lies
With which our seers and our dreams befool us!
Believe who can in speeches of the gods!
When by this daughter I felt motherhood
It chanced one day her father had a dream:
Up from his nuptial bed he saw grow forth
Two laurel trees. Between them grew a lily,   2340
But then this lily was transformed into
A flame that seized the densest branches of those trees
And in its fury spreading swiftly swallowed
The entire house in monstrous floods of fire.
Affrighted by that strange and eerie vision,
The Father asked a taker of bird-omens
And dealer in black magic for the meaning.
The man of magic gave this explanation:
If my womb were delivered of a daughter
She would become the murderess of both   2350
His sons and would annihilate his race.

THE CHORUS

CAJETAN   ⎫: What are you saying, Mistress? Woe! O Woe!
BOHEMUND ⎭

ISABELLA: Therefore her father ordered her be killed.
But I delivered her from that dread fate.
The poor unfortunate! While yet an infant
She was driven from her mother's bosom

So that, once grown, she should not kill her brothers.
And now at pirates' hands her brother dies,
Nor did this innocent effect his slaughter!

THE CHORUS: Alas! Alas! Alas!

ISABELLA: I set no store   2360
Then by that idol-worshiper's advice;
A better hope gave courage to my soul,
For other lips which I considered true
Had prophecied to me about this daughter:
In ardent love she would some day unite
My two sons' hearts. And thus the oracles
Pronounced in contradiction to each other
Both curse and blessing simultaneously
Upon my daughter's head. That innocent
Did not bring down the curse, nor was she granted   2370
The time to bring the blessing to fulfillment.
Those mouths both lied, that spoke to be believed.
The art of seers is emptiness of sight,
They are deceivers or they are deceived.
About the future no truth can you know,
Not if you draw from hellish streams below
Nor if you draw from daysprings of the light.

THE CHORUS (CAJETAN): Stop! What are you saying? Alas
for you!
Tame your tongue's reckless rages!
Oracles *see* and they do come true,   2380
The outcome will vindicate the sages.

ISABELLA: I will not tame my tongue, but rather I
Shall cry aloud as my heart prompts me to.
To what end do we visit holy houses
And raise our pious hands aloft to Heaven?
Good-natured, simple fools, what do we gain
By all our faith? It is impossible
To reach the gods who dwell on high, just as
One cannot shoot an arrow to the moon.
The future is from mortals walled apart   2390

And no prayer penetrates the iron sky.
Let birds fly to the right or to the left,
Let stars stand this or that way in the sky,
There is no sense in Nature's book, the art
Of dreams is dreams, and all the portents lie.

THE SECOND CHORUS (BERENGAR): O cease, unhappy woman!
　　Woe!
You deny the gleaming light of the sun
With eyes of blindness. The gods do live:
Acknowledge their dread prerogative!

BEATRICE: O Mother, Mother, why did you preserve me?　2400
Why did you not abandon me unto
The curse that menaced me before my birth?
O foolish Mother! Why did you imagine
That you were wiser than all-seeing ones
That knit the far and near together and
Gaze on the distant grain-fields of the future?
To your harm and to mine, and all of us,
You have deprived the death-gods of their prey
Which they required, and now they claim it of
Themselves with double and three-fold exaction.　　2410
I do not thank you for the sorry gift,
You rescued me for sorrow and for grief.

THE FIRST CHORUS (CAJETAN)　(*looking toward the door in
　　vehement agitation*):
　　Break open, ye wounds!
Flow now, flow now!
In night-black jets
Gush forth, ye brooks of blood!

(BERENGAR):　　Of iron feet
　I hear the tread,
　Of serpents of hell
　The hissing tones,　　　　　　　　　　　　　2420
　I perceive the step of the Furies!

(CAJETAN):　　Collapse, ye walls!

Sink, O threshold,
Under the tread of those ghastly feet!
Arise, black vapors, from the pit up-drawn
Rolling and dense! Consume the daylight's
Lovely shine!
Protective gods of the house, begone!
Let the avenging goddesses in!

(Enter Don Cesar.
At his coming the Chorus disperses before him in
movements of flight. He is left standing alone in
the middle of the stage).

BEATRICE: Woe, it is he!
ISABELLA *(advances to meet him)*:
               O my son Cesar, must we meet   2430
Again in such a fashion? O look here
And see the villany of a cursed hand.

(She leads him to the corpse.)

(Don Cesar falls back in horror and covers
his face.)

THE FIRST CHORUS (CAJETAN, BERENGAR):
  Break open, ye wounds!
Flow now, flow now!
In night-black jets
Gush forth, ye brooks of blood!
ISABELLA: You shudder and stand rigid. Yes, this is all
That there is left you of your brother now!
There lie my hopes. And it has died a bud,
That tender blossom of your harmony,   2440
And I shall not live to behold fair fruits.
DON CESAR: Take comfort, Mother! We sincerely meant
Our concord. Heaven called for blood, however.
ISABELLA: O I know you loved him. I was overjoyed
To see the fine bonds knitted up between you.
You meant to cherish him within your heart

And amply make up to him for lost years.
This gory murder cut your love off short.
—Now there is nothing left for you but vengeance.

DON CESAR: Come, Mother, come. This is no place for you. 2450
Withdraw, before this most unhappy sight.

(*He starts to lead her away.*)

ISABELLA (*falls upon his neck*):
You still are left. My only son now, you!

BEATRICE: What are you doing, Mother?

DON CESAR: Weep your fill
Against this loyal heart. Your son has not
Been lost to you because his love lives on
Immortally within your Cesar's bosom.

THE FIRST CHORUS

CAJETAN   ⎫ Break open, ye wounds!
BERENGAR   ⎬ Speak in your muteness!
MANFRED   ⎭ :In night-black floods
                         Gush forth, ye brooks of blood!   2460

ISABELLA (*taking the hands of both*):
My children!

DON CESAR: O how it delights me to
Behold her, Mother, clasped in your embrace!
Yes, let her be your daughter now! My sister—

ISABELLA (*interrupts him*):
This rescued girl I owe to you, my son!
You kept your word, and you have sent her to me.

DON CESAR (*astounded*):
Whom, Mother, did you say I sent to you?

ISABELLA: Why, her who stands before you here, your sister.

DON CESAR: She is my sister?

ISABELLA: Who else should she be?

DON CESAR: My sister?

ISABELLA: Whom you sent to me yourself.

DON CESAR: She was *his* sister also?

THE CHORUS: Woe! Alas!   2470

BEATRICE: O Mother mine!

ISABELLA: I am astounded—Speak!

DON CESAR: Then be the day accursed when I was born!

ISABELLA: What ails you?

DON CESAR: Cursed be the womb that bore me!
  And cursed also be that secrecy of yours
  Which has occasioned all this horror! Let
  The thunder fall that will strike down your heart.
  No longer will I hold it back to spare you.
  Know then that it was I who slew my brother,
  I had discovered him in *her* embrace;
  She is the one I love, the one I chose   2480
  To be my bride—but I came on my brother
  In her embrace.—Now you know everything.
  But if she is indeed his and my sister,
  Then I am guilty of a deed of horror
  That no remorse or penance can atone.

THE CHORUS (BOHEMUND): It is spoken now, you have heard it
    at last,
  The worst you know, no more is to relate.
  As the seers pronounced, so has it passed.
  For no one yet has escaped his fate,
  And one who presumes by guile to escape it   2490
  Must labor to complete and shape it.

ISABELLA: What matter is it to me if the gods
  Are liars or if they can prove themselves
  All true? Upon me they have wreaked their utmost.
  I challenge them to strike me yet more harshly
  Than they have stricken me already. One
  Who has no more to lose no longer fears them.
  Murdered here lies my beloved son,
  And from the living one I part forever.
  He is my son no longer. I have nurtured   2500
  A basilisk and fed at my own breast
  Him who has stabbed my better son to death.
  My daughter, come. Here is no place for us.

Unto avenging spirits I consign
This house. It was a crime that brought me here,
It is a crime that drives me from it now.
I entered with aversion, dwelt with fear,
And in despair I leave it. Guiltless I
Endure all this. But let the oracles
Remain in honor, and the gods are saved.   2510

(*Exit, followed by Diego.*)

DON CESAR   (*holding Beatrice back*):
Stay with me, Sister! Do not leave me thus!
Let my mother curse me, let this blood
Cry accusation of me unto Heaven,
Let all the world condemn me, but do you
Not curse me! I could not bear that from you!

(*Beatrice with face averted points to the corpse.*)

It was not your beloved whom I killed.
I slew your *brother* and I slew *my* brother.
—The dead man now is no more near of kin
To you than I am, I who am alive,
And more than he I merit sympathy,   2520
For he departed pure, and I am guilty.

(*Beatrice bursts into vehement tears.*)

Weep then for your brother, I will weep with you,
And what is more, I shall avenge him! But
Do not weep for the lover! I cannot
Endure this preference shown the dead man now.
Let me draw this one final consolation
Out of our sorrow's bottomless abyss,
That he did not stand nearer to your heart
Than I, for our appalling fate makes our
Rights equal as our miseries are equal.   2530
Caught in a single snare, we are destroyed
Together, two dear brothers and a sister,

And share the sad prerogative of tears.
But if I am compelled to think your sorrow
Is more for a beloved than a brother,
Then rage and envy mingle in my grief,
The final comfort in my sadness fails me.
Not joyously, as I could wish, could I
Then make the final offering to his shade.
But I will gently send my soul to him   2540
If I but know that you will gather up
My dust with his within a single urn.

                    (*putting his arm around her
                    with passionately tender eagerness*)

I loved you as I never loved before
When you were no more than a stranger to me.
Because I loved beyond all proper limits
I bear the heavy curse of fratricide,
And my love for you was my only guilt.
You are my sister now, and I demand
Compassion from you as a sacred due.

                    (*He looks at her with inquiring
                    glances and painful expectation,
                    then turns from her with vehemence.*)

No, no, I cannot watch these tears—My courage   2550
Deserts me in the presence of this dead man,
And doubt divides my heart. Leave me in error!
Go weep in some secluded place! And *never*
See me again! I never want to see
Again you or your mother—never—never—!
She never loved me. At long last her heart
Betrayed her there, when sorrow opened it.
Her *better* son she called him! She has practiced
Dissimulation all her life!—And you
Are just as false as she! Do not control   2560

Your feelings! Show your loathing! You shall never
Behold my face again! Farewell forever!

(Exit.)

(She stands indecisive in the struggle of conflicting
emotions, then tears herself away and leaves.)

THE CHORUS (CAJETAN) [*after an interval of silence*]:
Blessed is he who far from strife,
Amid rural meadows undefiled,
Far from the distractions of life
Lies at Nature's breast like a child.
For my heart is heavy in Princes' halls
When from the peak of Fortune's prime
I see how the most exalted falls
In the swiftness of an instant's time.   2570

He too is well-berthed and in admirable shape
Who out of life's stormy surge and swell,
Timely forewarned, has made his escape
Into the cloister's peaceful cell.

He who, with greed for honors obsessed,
Has sluffed off pleasure that satisfies never,
In tranquil heart has lulled to rest
Those wishes that wish and desire forever,

In the maelstrom of life is never caught
By passion's frenzy and fury blind,   2580
In his quiet refuge is never distraught
By the sorry figure of mankind.

Only up to a certain height
Do crime and hardship rise and swell,
As the plague from lofty places takes flight
To roll toward the cities' smokes of hell.

BERENGAR ⎫ In the mountains is freedom! The breath of
BOHEMUND ⎬ : graves
MANFRED ⎭ Does not ascend to the pure aether's waves;

The world is everywhere in perfection
Where man does not bring his torment's infection   2590
THE ENTIRE CHORUS *repeats*: In the mountains etc.

(*Reenter Don Cesar.*)

DON CESAR   (*more calmly*):
I exercise a ruler's right a final time
To lay this well-beloved body in the grave,
Such is the ultimate magnificence of dead men.
Hear then the solemn stern commandment of my will
And as I order you, so do you execute it
Exactly. — Fresh still in your memories must be
Those solemn rites, for they were held no long time since,
With which you brought your Prince's body to the tomb.
The echoes of the funeral dirge have hardly died   2600
Away, and one corpse crowds the other onward to
The grave, so that one torch is lighted from another
And on the steps of stairways the processions of
The mourners may almost encounter one another.
Arrange therefore a solemn rite of burial
Within this palace church which guards my father's dust;
Let all be done without a sound, behind closed doors,
Precisely in accordance with that former time.
THE CHORUS (BOHEMUND): This task shall be performed with
    rapid hands, O Master.
The catafalque still stands just as it was erected,   2610
The monument to those foregoing rites, and no
One has yet laid a hand upon that funeral framework.
DON CESAR: That was no omen of good luck that the grave's
    mouth
Should be left open in the household of the living.
How did it happen that that sorry scaffolding
Was not destroyed as soon as it had done its service?
THE CHORUS (BOHEMUND): The times' necessity and that
    disastrous feud
Which burst in flames just afterward dividing all

Messina, drew our eyes away from the deceased,
And empty and deserted stood that sanctuary.   2620
DON CESAR: To work directly, then, without delay! And let
This midnight task be done before the night is finished!
And may the next sun find a house pure of all crime
And may it shine upon a much more cheerful race.

*(Part of the knights withdraw with
Don Manuel's corpse.)*

THE CHORUS (CAJETAN): Shall I go summon here the pious
    brotherhood
Of monks and have them say the office of the dead
According to the ancient usage of the Church
And sing the dead man to his everlasting rest?
DON CESAR: Let them perform their singing by our grave amid
The shining of the candles for the rest of time;   2630
Today, however, their pure office is not needed,
Murder drives all holy things away.
THE CHORUS (CAJETAN): O make no bloody, violent decisions,
    Master,
Raging against yourself with act of desperation;
For in this world lives no one who can punish you,
And humble penance turns the wrath of Heaven away.
DON CESAR: In this world lives none who can judge and
    punish me,
Hence I myself must do those things upon myself.
I know that Heaven will accept a true remorse,
But bloody murder is atoned by blood alone.   2640
THE CHORUS (CAJETAN): To stem the tide of sorrow beating on
    this house
Would best beseem you, not to add grief unto grief.
DON CESAR: By my death I will break the house's ancient curse.
A willing death alone can break the chain of fate.
THE CHORUS (CAJETAN): You owe yourself as ruler to this
    orphaned country
Since you have robbed us of our other ruler's head.

Don Cesar: I shall first pay my debt unto the gods of death;
Some other god may guard the welfare of the living.

The Chorus (Cajetan): As far as sunlight shines there is hope still, and only
From death is nothing to be gained. Consider well!   2650

Don Cesar: And you consider your own duty as a servant!
Let me obey the fearful spirit that impels me.
No happy man can see into my inmost heart.
If you do not respect the Master in me, still
Fear the criminal on whom the direst curse lies heavy.
Respect the head of an unfortunate,
A head by gods held holy!—Any man who learns
What I now feel and suffer in my heart
Will give no mortal man a reckoning.

> (*Enter Donna Isabella with hesitant steps and
> casts uncertain looks at Don Cesar. Finally she
> comes nearer to him and speaks in a calm tone.*)

Isabella: My eyes were not to have again beheld you,   2660
Such was the vow I swore in midst of grief.
But with the wind pass those decisions which
A mother in unnatural frenzy makes
Against the prompting of her heart. — My son!
A wretched and unhappy rumor drives me
Out of the empty dwelling places of
My grief. — Shall I believe it? Is it true
That one day is to rob me of two sons?

The Chorus (Cajetan): You see him of fixed purpose to
Descend now voluntarily   2670
To the dreary portals of the dead.
So try what the power of blood can do,
And the moving force of a mother's plea.
Of no avail was all I said.

Isabella: I call back all the imprecations which
In the blind madness of despair I hurled
Against your much beloved head. A mother

Cannot curse the offspring of her very body
To whom with such pain she imparted life.
Such sinful prayers are not accorded ear   2680
By Heaven; burdened down with tears they fall
Back down repulsed by that resplendent vault.
Live, my son! I would rather see the slayer of
One child than be compelled to mourn for both.

DON CESAR: You do not realize what you are asking,
Mother, for yourself and me. My place
Can not be with the living. If *you* could
Endure the murderer's God-hated face,
I, Mother, still could not endure the silent
Reproaches of your everlasting grief.   2690

ISABELLA: Reproaches shall not hurt you, no complaint
By word or sign shall cut into your heart.
My grief shall be resolved to gentle sadness,
And by our common mourning we shall weep
For our misfortune and beshroud the crime.

DON CESAR (*takes her hand, in a gentle voice*):
That, Mother, you shall do. So shall it be.
Your grief shall be resolved to gentle sadness—
Then, Mother, when one monument enfolds
The murdered and the murderer together,
When one stone stands above the dust of both,   2700
The curse will be disarmed and you no longer
Will make a difference between your sons.
The tears shed by your beauteous eyes will then
Be spent both for the one and for the other.
Death is an intercessor of great power.
There all the fires of anger are extinguished,
There Hatred is atoned, and lovely Mercy
Stoops down, a weeping sister figure, in
A clinging soft embrace upon the urn.
Do not, therefore, prevent me, Mother, from   2710
Descending that the curse may be atoned.

ISABELLA: Christendom abounds in shrines of grace

In pilgrimage to which a heart in torment
Can find its peace. Many a heavy burden
Has been cast off within Loretto's house,
And from the Holy Sepulchre is wafted
Celestial power that cures the world of sin.
The prayers of pious men are potent also,
With copious store of grace contained in them,
And on the spot where murder once took place   2720
A purifying temple can arise.

DON CESAR: The arrow may be drawn out of the heart
But never will that injured organ heal.
Let him who can, spend his life in remorse
And by slow stages of a savage penance
Remove an everlasting guilt. I can
Not go on living with a broken heart.
I must gaze up with joy toward joyous ones
And with unfettered spirit reach aloft
Into the aether. — Envy turned my life to gall   2730
While we still shared your love quite equally.
Do you think I will bear that preference which
Your sorrow granted to him over me?
Death in his palace which endures forever
Possesses powers of purification
To clarify all mortal things and make
Them purest diamond of unmarred virtue
And to consume the flaws of faulty man.
As far as the stars stand beyond the earth
He will sublimely stand on high above me,   2740
And if our ancient grudge divided us
In life when we were equal brothers, it
Will gnaw away at my heart restlessly
Now that he has foregained eternity
And far beyond all rivalries of earth
Walks like a god in human memory.

ISABELLA: O have I had you summoned to Messina
For nothing but to bury both of you?

I called you here to see you reconciled,
And ruin-bearing Destiny transmutes   2750
All of my hopes into their opposites.

DON CESAR: Do not speak evil, Mother, of the outcome!
All that was promised is to be fulfilled. With hopes
Of making peace we entered through these gates,
And peacefully together we shall rest
Atoned forever in the house of Death.

ISABELLA: Live, my son! and do not leave your mother
Behind and friendless in a land of strangers,
A butt for their harsh-hearted mockery
Because her sons' strength now no longer shields her.   2760

DON CESAR: If heartlessly and cold the whole world mocks you,
Go forth and seek a refuge at our grave
And there invoke your sons' divinity,
For we shall then be gods and we shall hear you,
And like the Heavens' Twins, that constellation
That shines for ships, we shall be close to you
With comfort and confirm your soul with strength.

ISABELLA: Live, my son! Live for your mother's sake!
I cannot bear to lose all that I have.

> (*She throws her arms around him with passionate
> vehemence. He gently disengages himself from her
> and with averted face extends to her his hand.*)

DON CESAR: Farewell.   2770

ISABELLA: Ah, well do I perceive with sorrow that
Your mother has no power over you.
Is there no other voice that can reach to
Your heart more mightily than my voice can?

> (*She goes to the entrance way.*)

Come in, my daughter. If his brother dead
Attracts him so intensely toward the tomb,
Perhaps his sister, his beloved sister

Can with the magic glow of life's fair hopes
Entice him back into the sun's clear light.

(*Enter Beatrice. At sight of her Don Cesar,
profoundly agitated, covers his face*).

DON CESAR: O Mother! Mother! What have you devised? 2780
ISABELLA: (*leads her forward*):
His mother's pleas have been of no avail,
Entreat him, conjure him to go on living!
DON CESAR: So you would test me that way, cunning Mother!
You want to throw me back into the struggle
And make the sunlight dearer still to me
Upon my journey to eternal night?
—There stands Life's lovely angel mightily
Before me, shedding down a thousand flowers,
A thousand golden fruits fragrant with life,
Out of his horn of plenty in a flood; 2790
My heart is opened in the sun's warm ray
And newly wakened in my withered breast
Are hope and love of life and interest.
ISABELLA: Implore him,—he will lend you ear or no one,—
Not to destroy the staff of our support.
BEATRICE: A sacrifice the dead man does require,
And to him, Mother, that shall be vouchsafed,—
But let me be the victim! I was marked
For death before I ever entered life.
The curse that lies upon this house claims *me* 2800
And it is theft from Heaven, this life I live.
I was the one who murdered him, who roused
The sleeping Furies of your feud,—and it
Beseems me best to give peace to his Manes.
THE CHORUS (CAJETAN): O Mother full of sorrows! Down to
death
Your children vie with one another to
Descend and leave you here alone behind
Amid a waste of joyless, loveless life.

BEATRICE: Preserve, my Brother, your beloved head.
   Live for your mother's sake! She needs a son.   2810
   A daughter she found just today, and what
   She did not have before, she can dispense with.
DON CESAR (*with deeply wounded soul*):
   Yes, Mother, we may live or we may die
   So long as she is joined with her beloved!
BEATRICE: What! Are you jealous of your brother's dust?
DON CESAR: He lives a blessed life within your sorrow,
   I shall be dead forever with the dead.
BEATRICE: My Brother!
DON CESAR (*in the tone of the utmost passion*):
                              Sister, do you weep for *me*?
BEATRICE: Live for our mother's sake!
DON CESAR (*releases her hand, stepping back*):
                              For Mother's sake?
BEATRICE (*yields to his embrace*):
   Live for her sake and give your sister comfort.   2820
THE CHORUS (BOHEMUND):   She has won! His sister's moving
   plea
   He could not resist unfeelingly.
   Sorrowing Mother, make room for hope,
   He has chosen to live, you have your son!

   (*At this moment a choir is heard singing, the
   double doors are opened, and inside the church the
   erected catafalque is seen with the coffin surrounded by candelabra.*)

DON CESAR (*turning toward the coffin*):
   No, Brother, I shall not deprive you of
   Your sacrificial victim.—From your coffin
   Your voice more strongly calls than Mother's tears,
   More strongly than the plea of love. In my
   Embrace I hold what can make earthly life
   The equal of a destiny of gods—   2830
   But I, the murderer, should be thus blessed

While unavenged your sacred innocence
Should lie deep in the grave? O never may
The all-just Helmsman of our days allow
Such an allotment to be in His world!
I have seen tears that flowed for me as well,
My heart is satisfied, I follow you.

> (*He plunges a dagger into himself and, dying,
> sinks down beside his sister, who throws herself into
> her mother's arms.*)

THE CHORUS (CAJETAN)   *(after a profound silence):*
I stand here overwhelmed, uncertain whether
To laud or to lament his destiny.
One thing I clearly feel and here aver: 2840
Of all possessions life is not the highest,
The worst of evils is, however, *guilt*.   [2842]

WILLIAM TELL

INTRODUCTION

Schiller's last completed play, *William Tell* (Wilhelm Tell),
owes its existence to a freak of chance. In 1801 the rumor
reached his astonished ears that he was engaged in writing precisely that work when, as a matter of fact, he was busy with
The Maid of Orleans and well aware that his friend Goethe
had been planning since 1797 to write a narrative poem on
the subject of the Swiss legendary hero. As time went on, the
two authors in their close association effected a transfer of
matter and with Goethe's enthusiastic approval Schiller was
to give the subject a dramatic, rather than a narrative, form.
Composition began on August 25, 1803, after extensive re-
searches in Swiss history, for Schiller never visited Switzerland.
Six months sufficed for the task. On February 18, 1804 the
play was finished, and within a month after that, on March
17, 1804, it received its première at Goethe's theatre in Weimar.
Success was overwhelming and instantaneous. Goethe praised
the opening scene as being a whole play in itself, and it must
be granted that Shakespeare himself never composed a more
arresting and functional exposition. The public could not
have enough of the work. For more than a hundred years it
drew audiences to German theatres as no other native or translated play could draw them. As its centenary approached, stat-
istics of the stage show that it was averaging 232 performances
a year, when the most popular of repertory pieces barely reached half that number and when plays by Goethe and Lessing
achieved less than ten revivals per year. Translations gave the
work currency abroad, until to many people in many countries
Schiller was "the author of *William Tell*" and until Tell's

apple-shot became part of the folklore of Western civilization.

As folklore the story began, and folklore it remains, for sober history knows nothing of it, in spite of its specific dating, in spite of its realistic localization, in spite of forged records, in spite of the convictions of native Swiss and untold foreigners that it all happened, and in spite of Tell-sites eagerly sought out by tourists in Switzerland. The political conditions represented in the play are true enough as a generalization but they telescope events of different generations and charge all opposition to Swiss liberties to Emperor Albrecht, who in fact had no or very small quarrels with his Swiss subjects. The conflict of wills and purposes did indeed exist in Albrecht's reign, but that conflict had been centuries in the making and slow centuries were to bring about its resolution.

The German-speaking Alemannic majority of the Swiss people had been subjects of the Holy Roman Empire since Charlemagne's day; the Romance-speaking Burgundian minority had been brought into that empire in 1032. In their several subdivisions by "canton" these people had "immediate" dependency upon the Emperor, which is to say direct allegiance to the Emperor's person, with matters of local government left to the discretion of their own leaders. Less fortunate segments of the multisegmented empire often had "mediate" dependency upon the Emperor, that is they were subject to some locally absolute ruler—King, Duke, Count, Bishop, etc.—who *in turn* owed his own personal allegiance to the Emperor. As for the Emperor himself, he held an elected office, being traditionally chosen upon a predecessor's death by seven Electoral Princes, four temporal and three ecclesiastical, and though effort was repeatedly made to create a hereditary crown, no line of succession was ever established. Able rulers were sometimes successful in prearranging the election of their sons so that dynastic families such as the Hohenstauffens did, sometimes for generations, retain the supreme title. But there were no sure guarantees of such transfer of power and the death of any Emperor inevitably created anxious political hours.

In the thirteenth century the Hapsburg family, hereditary

and absolute Dukes of Austria, gained the reputation of being the most land-hungry rulers within the empire. They exploited every means afforded by the feudal system to acquire a parcel of territory here, a tract of territory there, until hardly an area of the southern German-speaking land was left without an adjoining area under the control of the house of Hapsburg. The Duke of Austria ruled the inhabitants of such lands with absolute authority, and, though his subjects were nominally subjects of the Emperor who was *his* overlord, they had no access to the Emperor except through him. For many years the Swiss had uneasily watched the piecemeal acquisition of lands by the Hapsburgs around and within their own mountain valleys. For safety they clung to their ancient traditions of "immediate" dependency upon the Emperor and in the case of Canton Uri, to an ancient written charter which had explicitly conferred such "immediacy" in 843. Great, then, was their dismay in 1273 when Rudolf of Hapsburg was elected Emperor. Now their foe and their defender were one and the same person. Through Rudolf's reign they remained in uneasy peace. Upon his death they made haste, before his successor could be named, to frame a kind of statement of the rights of their political status. This League of the three "Forest Cantons," Uri, Schwyz, and Unterwalden, in 1291 and its much more emphatic reassertion in 1315 after Swiss victory in actual battle against Hapsburg armies, form boundary dates for a period of tribulations and political uncertainties under four successive Emperors chosen from three different families. Squarely in the middle of this troublesome period falls the action of our play.[1]

As for William Tell and his feat of November 18th (or 19th), 1307, contemporary historians mention no such matter, nor do church records list any person of such a name within a century of the date in question. Austrian records of the period mention no uprising of the Swiss cantons at this time, nor do

[1]For further information see the Historical Reference Table at the end of this Introduction.

they list any governor named Gessler, nor the assassination of any Austrian bailiff; in fact, only native Swiss magistrates held the leading position in the cantons, as far as is known. Nowhere is there mention of Tell until almost 1400, when his story is told in the *Tell Song* and in the *White Book of Sarnen*. Schiller's principal source of information, however, was neither of these, but the *Chronicon Helveticum* of the sixteenth century historian Aegidius Tschudi (1505-1572). This patriotic writer freely admitted that he accepted popular traditions without seeking to verify them in order "to enhance the honor of the (Swiss) Confederation and of every canton in particular," feeling that worthy tales would "cause them no harm whatever."

Famous shots of famous archers, moreover, figure in the folk traditions of widely separated peoples, several such being recorded within Germanic tradition, and of these a remarkably close analogue is to be found in the works of the late mediaeval Danish historian Saxo Grammaticus. There the hero is a soldier named Toko, who once boasted at a banquet that he could hit with his arrow a tiny apple set up as a distant target. Comrades who were jealous of his skill reported his boast to King Harold Bluetooth, who then maliciously ordered the marksman to shoot the apple off the head of his own son. Death was to be the penalty if he missed. Toko faced his test staunchly, but before delivering his successful shot, he selected three arrows from his quiver. When King Harold questioned him about this, he declared the other two arrows were for the tyrannical king in case his first shot missed its mark. Subsequently forced to a second trial, this time at skating, Toko escaped on snowshoes down a steep mountain into the sea, where people thought he perished. He escaped, however, and returned to kill the tyrant from ambush. A plausible hypothesis would explain Tell as the hero of an Alemannic variant of an early German saga, with the story of Toko as a Scandinavian variant of the same unrecorded original.

The inconclusive attempts to etymologize the hero's name could well be passed over in silence, were it not for one curious circumstance. In the face of the tyrant's stern questioning just before the famous shot, Tschudi's chronicle makes the archer reply: "If I were clever, my name would not be Tell," (Wär ich witzig, so hiess ich nit der Tell.) Some pun seems to underlie the statement, and it has been suggested that the missing term is some form of the dialect word *dalen* or *talen*—"to talk nonsense." Schiller felt obliged to parallel, if not to include verbatim, this riposte, hence the puzzling line 1873 of the text: "My name would not be Tell if I were cautious," (Wär' ich besonnen, hiess ich nicht der Tell). Proponents of the *dalen/talen* etymology think that the hero in antecedent forms of the legend was "William the Witless." An alternate etymology making him "William the Arrow," on the basis of Latin *telum*—"weapon, arrow," seems far-fetched.

Schiller attacked his subject with gusto, lavishing upon its canvas bright patches of local color in the form of uniquely Swiss words, elaborate geographical detail, and picturesque Alpine settings. Enlivening incidental music was indispensable to his general plan. Into the work he poured his sincerest feelings about popular liberties, and on this point it is interesting to observe how cautiously qualified his libertarianism is in comparison with the roughriding iconoclasm of his early prose plays, especially *The Robbers*. Schiller had sobered notably since 1781. He seems to have had qualms at this stage of his life and career about portraying political assassination at all and was at great pains to make the deed morally acceptable. No device was left unexploited to justify the Swiss people's cause and to canonize Tell's murder of the tyrant. The latter is accordingly painted in absolute black and the former in absolute white. Then, as though still unsure as to whether the case were severely enough defined within the limits of morality, he confronted the hero in the last Act with a man who had committed precisely the same deed of assassination for the *wrong* reasons: Johannes Parricida is banished by Tell with horror and expelled by the author from among the sinlessly rejoicing population. The scene with Parricida rarely found favor with nine-

teenth-century enthusiasts for the play and was often omitted
from stage performances. Playgoers were convinced of the
rights and wrongs of the situation before that point, they ex-
ulted in wicked Gessler's downfall, and further debates without
action seemed useless to them. The enthusiasts found the work
as a whole abounding in inspiration for liberalism in general,
a veritable poetic credo of their most cherished ideals. To enhance his lofty theme, Schiller made his Swiss people in the
very image of such a rural and uncorrupted society as Rousseau
had taught was the perfect condition of mankind, endowing
them with all the social and private virtues, and giving them
language which was to be grandly simple like the language of
Homer and the Book of Genesis and at the same time as richly
eloquent as Shakespeare's. With his unfailing technical skill
he held firmly together an extraordinarily large cast of characters dispersed about a play that repeatedly shifts locale and
which, in the hands of a less skillful writer, could have become
a hodgepodge. Conciseness further made this drama the shortest
of his major works for the stage.

Great dramatic tact withheld the hero of this panoramic drama,
after his brief initial appearance, until the mid-point of the
action. Not only was the legend sparse as to details about him,
but this hero *must* be noncomplex. A Tell given to finesse of
ideology or conspiracy could not be the man of giant strength
and single purpose who could selflessly destroy the tyrant. Tell
is a simple man who is distressed by his people's sufferings and
does not know what to do; he directly experiences the hateful
fury of Gessler, and then he immediately knows what to do;
once he knows what to do, he does not rest until it is done. For
him there are no subtle pro's and con's. He is all muscle and
morals, innocent of intellectualism. Like the Herakles of Euripides' *Alkestis,* he goes his own way until he sees a wrong harming
a right; then he throws his giant strength against the wrong
and annihilates it. He lacks, of course, the lusty humor of Herakles, and once the direly necessary has been accomplished, a
Christian docility makes him seek only to become once again

a simple man among his fellows. He does not make derring-do a career, he has one and only one adventure. It was no small accomplishment of Schiller's to make such a man the appropriate hero of a five-act drama.

For all its demonstrable excellences, however, *William Tell,* which delighted a whole century, will delight somewhat fewer people today. Persons of artistic discrimination saw its artistic flaws even in its heyday. They saw all along that its emotions were facile, that its psychology was oversimplified, that its language fell short of being Homeric, Biblical, or Shakespearean, and that this play was brass-band music beside the fine symphonies of Schiller's own *Wallenstein, Don Carlos,* and *Mary Stuart,* not to mention the noble music of those plays whose average annual performances around 1900 never reached anything like the figure of 232 per year. But it was not persons of artistic discrimination who made the work the darling of the nineteenth century stage.

Times have changed radically since 1920, to set a fair terminus-date for the play's popularity. Rousseau's ideal of the uncorrupted rural society has lost credence since then. One might almost say it had lost face. Bitter sociological experiences, technological progress, anthropological research, Darwinian, Marxian, Freudian concepts, and a host of other factors have, each in its own way, discredited the very premises upon which the play was constructed. In modern times, sinless populations, whether dwelling in beautiful mountain valleys or elsewhere, have had a way of turning out to be economic liabilities and insoluble political problems. Revolutions too have proven uglier in the carrying out and far less conclusive in their results than this Swiss revolution portrayed by Schiller.

But Schiller cannot be held responsible for either the invention or the discrediting of the Rousseauistic ideal. He *can* be held responsible for the creation of Berta and Rudenz, whom hard-bitten modern taste finds unduly naive. They are just that. Their purpose was, we readily perceive, to represent the aristocracy in a work which wished to portray a nation in

all its classes. A society lacking an aristocracy finds them super-
fluous, but the aristocratic segment of Schiller's audiences were
no doubt gratified to see that society's purification did not de-
pend upon the liquidation of their class. It is the coy eighteenth
century gallantry of this pair that makes them seem artificial.
Dramatic necessities of the play as a whole, moreover, hurried
their story, leaving Berta's role a mere outline and precipitating
Rudenz' change of heart with a speedy ease that is, at the very
least, unusual in real life. The author of *Wallenstein, Don
Carlos,* and *Mary Stuart* must also bear responsibility for indulging in such an extensive array of all-virtuous people, or at
least of characters which seem to have one quality a-piece. If,
however, all these one-quality characters are taken as parts of
one great character, the Swiss people, the procedure becomes not
only understandable but the author is seen as a pioneer experimenter in drama dealing with society rather than with individuals and his shortcomings are the pardonable shortcomings
of a pioneer experimenter. Then Berta and Rudenz, however
sketchily portrayed, are necessary to the action, for the social ideal
provides happiness for all, not the vindictive triumph of one
group over another. Here Schiller's own—and Beethoven's—"Embrace, ye millions!" provides the true key to the author's purposes. Once *this* ideal is understood to be the play's true meaning, our sardonic criticisms of the work falter and die upon our
lips; we wish we could exchange some of our bitter sophistication
for even a portion of that ebullient optimism.

Sobered by such thoughts, we pose wholly different questions.
Why did this work speak its glorious ideal so clearly to several
generations when it speaks so faintly to us? Is history our evil
genius? Are we obtuse? Is our taste corrupt? Was the Tell
legend an inadequate vehicle for the thought? Was the author's
experiment at social drama unguided by examples that his
well-proven dramaturgy could not cope with such content? Or
have changing tides of taste merely submerged—perhaps temporarily—a masterpiece? Debate on these points would be long
and far-ranging, but the weight of aesthetic judgments would

tip the final scales. Before that last decision, however, the play should once be seen in an outdoor summer performance in Switzerland with the actual Alps for backdrops, as the "Passion Play" of joyous eighteenth century optimism.

HISTORICAL REFERENCE TABLE
FOR SWITZERLAND

Prehistoric period	Switzerland inhabited by cave and lake dwellers; subsequently conquered by Celtic Helvetians and Rhaetians.
58 B.C. ff.	Conquest of the Celtic Helvetians and Rhaetians by the Romans.
200-400 A.D.	Conquest of the Romanized Celts by the Germanic Alemanni and Germanic Burgundians.
c. 406	Installation of the Alemanni in the north-eastern part of Switzerland, where their German-speaking descendents now compose c. 70% of the population. (The narrative of the migration as told in lines 1167 ff. is fanciful.)
c. 443-450	Installation of the Burgundians in south-western Switzerland, where their French-speaking and Italian-speaking descendants now compose c. 30% of the population.
768-814	Alemannic Switzerland included in Charlemagne's Frankish empire.
843	Alemannic Switzerland included in the German Empire (Holy Roman Empire) of Ludwig the German, grandson of

Charlemagne, upon the partitioning of Charlemagne's territories.

Ludwig bestowed large parts of Uri on the local inhabitants in hereditary fief whereby they paid rentals directly to the Emperor but retained local self-government.

1032	Burgundian Helvetia added to the Holy Roman Empire.
1218	Emperor Frederick II of Hohenstauffen appointed a member of the Hapsburg family as Imperial governor of Canton Uri, to the alarm of the inhabitants, who were well aware of Hapsburg landhunger.
1231	Heinrich, the rebellious son of Frederick II, granted Uri a formal charter guaranteeing perpetual direct dependency from the Emperor and pledging that Uri should never be enfiefed, sold, or mortgaged to anyone else.
	The Hapsburgs now owned small estates in Uri but much larger estates in adjoining Canton Schwyz.
1240	Canton Schwyz sent some 600 men to support Frederick II in the Battle of Favenza in northern Italy, one of the major conflicts in Frederick's war with the Pope. Their distinguished service at Favenza was rewarded with a charter much like that of Canton Uri. (See line 911 and line 1213 ff.)
1246	Sparsely populated Canton Unterwalden made an alliance of self-defense with Cantons Schwyz and Lucerne during the

wars between the Pope and the Emperor.
(The "old alliance" of line 1156.)

1254-1273   The interregnum: a period of anarchy in
                 the Holy Roman Empire after the down-
                 fall of the Hohenstauffens during which
                 time there was no Emperor.

1273   Rudolf of Hapsburg elected Emperor. He
                 confirmed the charter of Uri, refused to
                 recognize the charter of Schwyz, though
                 he did not interfere with affairs in that
                 canton, and left charterless Unterwalden
                 undisturbed.

1291 (August 1) Within seventeen days of the death of Ru-
                 dolph of Hapsburg, and before his
                 successor could be chosen, the three
                 "Forest Cantons" —Uri, Schwyz, and
                 Unterwalden—made a conservative Lea-
                 gue, asking guarantee of the *status quo,*
                 with independence from Hapsburg Aus-
                 tria but with continued "immediate"
                 dependency upon the Emperor, whoever
                 the new Emperor might be, and requir-
                 ing that none but native Swiss be ap-
                 pointed as chief magistrates in the three
                 cantons.

1292-1298   Emperor Adolf of Nassau, a Hapsburg
                 rival; he was killed in battle in 1298 by
                 Albrecht of Hapsburg, son of Rudolf.

1298-1308   Emperor Albrecht of Hapsburg.
                 This is the tyrannical Emperor of the
                 play, but in actual fact he granted a
                 charter of liberties to Unterwalden—
                 though he refused to confirm the char-

acters of Uri and Schwyz—and maintained good relations with his Swiss subjects. Native magistrates held office in the cantons and no tryannical governors were installed.

1307 (October 28 to November 21)	*The action of Schiller's* WILHELM TELL.
1308-1313	Emperor Henry VII of Luxemberg, a Hapsburg rival.
1313	Death of Emperor Henry VII; new rivalry for the Imperial crown between Ludwig of Bavaria and Friedrich of Hapsburg, son of Emperor Albrecht. The Swiss supported the former, whereupon Friedrich sent his brother Leopold with an army to conquer the dissident Swiss.
1315 (November 15)	Defeat of the Austrians under Leopold by the Swiss in the Battle of Morgarten.
(December 9)	Delegates of the three "Forest Cantons" met at Brunnen and renewed the League of 1291. The Swiss Republic names this date for its beginning.
1332	Five new cantons added to the original three of the Swiss Federation.
1481-1513	Five further cantons added to the Confederation to make a total of thirteen.
1814	The Swiss Constitution adopted for a confederation of twenty-two cantons.

WILLIAM TELL

CHARACTERS

HERMANN GESSLER, Imperial Bailiff in Schwyz and Uri

WERNER, BARON OF ATTINGHAUSEN, Standard-bearer

ULRICH OF RUDENZ, his nephew

Countrymen from Schwyz:
WERNER STAUFFACHER
KONRAD HUNN
ITEL REDING
HANS AUF DER MAUER
JÖRG IM HOFE
ULRICH THE SMITH
JOST VON WEILER

Countrymen from Uri:
WALTER FÜRST
WILLIAM TELL
RÖSSELMANN, the pastor
PETERMANN, the sexton
KUONI, the herdsman
WERNI, the huntsman
RUODI, the fisherman

Countrymen from Unterwalden:
ARNOLD OF MELCHTAL
KONRAD BAUMGARTEN
MEIER OF SARNEN
STRUTH OF WINKELRIED
KLAUS VON DER FLÜE
BURKHARD AM BÜHEL
ARNOLD OF SEWA

GERTRUD, wife of Stauffacher

HEDWIG, Tell's wife, daughter of Fürst

BERTA OF BRUNECK, a wealthy heiress

RUDOLF THE EQUERRY, Gessler's master of the horse

JOHANNES PARRICIDA, Duke of Swabia

A MASTER STONEMASON, JOURNEYMEN, AND LABORERS

HORSEMEN of Gessler and of Landenberg

MANY COUNTRYMEN from the Forest Cantons

Mercenary Soldiers:
HARDHEART
FOLKLOVE

Peasant Women:
ARMGARD
MECHTILD
ELSBETH
HILDEGARD

AN OVERSEER
PUBLIC CRIERS
BROTHERS OF MERCY

Tell's little boys:
WALTER
WILHELM

PFEIFER OF LUCERNE
KUNZ OF GERSAU
JENNI, a fisher boy
SEPPI, a herd boy
STÜSSI, a game keeper
THE BULL OF URI
AN IMPERIAL MESSENGER

Time: October-November, 1307

Place: Various points in the three Forest Cantons of Switzerland: Schwyz, Uri, and Unterwalden

ACT 1

SCENE 1

*The high rocky shore of Lake Lucerne
opposite Canton Schwyz* [*October* 28, 1307]

*The lake forms a bay in the coast; a hut stands
not far from the shore; a fisher lad is rowing about
in a boat. Beyond the lake may be seen the green
meadows, villages, and farmsteads of Schwyz lying
in bright sunshine. To the spectators' left are visible the peaks of the Haken surrounded by clouds;
to the right, in the far distance, snow-capped mountains can be seen. Even before the curtain goes up
there is heard the cowherd's song and also the
melodious tones of the cowbells, which continues
for some time after the curtain has gone up.*

THE FISHER LAD (*sings in his boat*):
    Melody of the cowherd's song
With smiling allure the lake calls the land,
The boy fell asleep upon the green strand;
      A singing he heard then
      Like flute-tones arise,
      Like voices of angels
      In Paradise.
And as he awakens to joys of the blest
The waters are washing over his breast;
      From the depths comes the cry:
      You belong now to me!
      Sweet sleeper, I draw you
      To the depths of the sea.

A SHEPHERD (*on the mountain*):
> *Variation of the cowherd's song*

> You meadows, farewell,
> You fields of the sun!
> The summer is done,
> The herdsman departs.

Back to the mountains we shall come once again
When the cuckoo calls, when the songs begin,
When the earth is new clad in flowered array,
When the snow-rills flow in the sweet month of May.

> You meadows, farewell,
> You fields of the sun!
> The summer is done,
> The herdsman departs.

AN ALPINE HUNTER (*appears opposite on the top of the cliff*):
> *Second Variation*

Peaks thunder, the frail narrow footbridge sways,
No fear feels the archer up dizzy ways;

> Over fields of ice
> He treads undaunted;
> No branches show green there,
> No springtime is flaunted;

And under his feet lies an ocean of cloud
And cities of men are hid in its shroud;

> Through cloud-rifts alone
> May the world be seen,
> And deep under waves
> The fields of green.

> (*The landscape is altered; a muffled roar is heard from the mountains; shadows of clouds hurry across the scene.*
>
> *Ruodi the fisherman comes out of the hut. Werni the huntsman climbs down from the cliff. Kuoni the herdsman comes along with his milk-pail on his shoulder, followed by Seppi, his helper-boy.*)

RUODI: Step lively, Jenni! Beach the skiff! Here comes
  The grey lord of the valley, glaciers boom,
  The Mythenstein is putting on its cap,
  And from the weather-cleft a cold blast comes;   40
  The storm, I think, will strike before we know it.
KUONI: Rain's coming, Ferryman. My sheep are greedy
  For grass, and Watcher here keeps pawing earth.
WERNI: The fish are jumping, and the waterfowl
  Are diving under. Storm is on the way.
KUONI *(to the boy)*:
  See that the cows don't wander off now, Seppi.
SEPPI: I still can tell brown Liesel by her bell.
KUONI: The rest, then, are close by; she goes the furthest.
RUODI: You've got a pretty peal of bells there, Herdsman.
WERNI: And nice cows, too, my friend. Are they your own? 50
KUONI: I'm not that rich—No, they're my gracious lord's—
  Lord Attinghausen's—and given to my keeping.
RUODI: How nice that ribbon looks on that cow's neck.
KUONI: And well she knows that she leads all the rest;
  She would stop eating if I took it off.
RUODI: Ridiculous! A brute beast does not know—
WERNI: That's easy said. But beasts have reason too,
  As we who hunt the chamois are aware:
  When they go out to graze they shrewdly post
  Their sentinel who pricks his ears and warns them   60
  With high-pitched whistling cry when hunters near.
RUODI: *(to the herdsman)*:
  Your herd is heading home now?
KUONI: All the Alp-grass
  Is pastured off.
           A prosperous journey, Herdsman!
KUONI: The same to you! Not all your trips end in
  Return.
RUODI: Here comes a man at breakneck speed.
WERNI: I know him too. It's Baumgart from Alzellen.

  (Enter Konrad Baumgarten rushing in breathless.)

BAUMGARTEN: In God's name, Ferryman, lend me your boat!

RUODI: Come, come, why all the hurry?

BAUMGARTEN: Quick! Untie it!
  You will save me from death! Take me across!

KUONIS   What is the matter, friend?

WERNI: Who's after you?   70

BAUMGARTEN   (to the fisherman):
  O hurry! Hurry! They are at my heels!
  The Bailiff's cavalry are right behind me.
  I am a dead man if they capture me.

RUODI: Why are the cavalry pursuing you?

BAUMGARTEN: First save me, then I will explain it to you.

WERNI: Why, there are blood stains on you. What has
    happened?

BAUMGARTEN: The Emperor's Burggrave who held Castle
    Rossberg—

KUONI: That Wolfenschiessen! Is he pursuing you?

BAUMGARTEN: There's no more harm to come from him. I
    killed him.

ALL   (fall back):
  May God have mercy on you! You did what?   80

BAUMGARTEN: What any free man in my place would do!
  I exercised my family right against
  The violator of my wife and honor.

KUONI: The Burggrave did offense against your honor?

BAUMGARTEN: God and my trusty ax prevented him
  From the fulfillment of his vile desires.

WERNI: You split his head in two then with your ax?

KUONI: O tell us all about it, you have time
  Before he has the boat out from the shore.

BAUMGARTEN: I had been felling timber in the woods   90
  When up in mortal terror runs my wife:
  "The Burggrave was down at my house, he had
  Commanded her to fix a bath for him.
  And then he had desired improper things
  Of her, and she had run away to find me."

Then I ran down there fast, just as I was,
And with my ax I blessed his bath for him.
WERNI: And you did right. No man will blame you for it.
KUONI: The fiend! He got what he deserved! He had
It coming from the Unterwalden people.   100
BAUMGARTEN: The deed got noised about; I am pursued—
And while we talk—God!—time is slipping by—

(*It begins to thunder.*)

KUONI: Quick, Ferryman—take this good man across!
RUODI: It can't be done. There is a bad storm coming.
You'll have to wait.
BAUMGARTEN: Good God! I cannot wait.
The least delay will be the death of me—
KUONI   (*to the fisherman*):
In God's name, try! A neighbor must be helped.
The like could happen to us all, you know.

(*Roaring and thunder.*)

RUODI: The Föhn is blowing now. You see how high
The lake is. I can't buck the storm and waves.   110
BAUMGARTEN   (*embraces his knees*):
So help you God, have pity on me now—
WERNI: It's life and death. Show mercy, Ferryman!
KUONI: He is a father and has wife and children.

(*Peals of thunder one after another.*)

RUODI: What of it? I too have a life to lose,
And wife and child at home, like him. Just see
Those breakers, see it seethe and boil in whirlpools,
And how it stirs the waters to the depths.
I would be glad to rescue this good man,
But you can see it is impossible.
BAUMGARTEN   (*still on his knees*):
Then I must fall into my foeman's hands,   120
And with the shore of rescue close in sight!
Just over there it lies! My eyes can reach it,

My voice can carry sound across to it,
Here is the boat that would take me across,
And I must lie here helpless and despair!

KUONI: Look who comes here!

WERNI: It's William Tell from Bürglen.

(*Enter Tell with his crossbow.*)

TELL: Who is the man who lies here begging help?

KUONI: It's a man from Alzellen; he defended
His honor and he murdered Wolfenschiess,
The King's Burggrave who lived at Castle Rossberg.   130
The Bailiff's cavalry are at his heels.
He wants the ferryman to give him transport,
But he's afraid of the storm and will not cross.

RUODI: Now here is Tell, he also plies the oar,
He'll bear me out if this trip can be ventured.

TELL: If need be, Ferryman, all things may be
Attempted.

(*Violent claps of thunder; the lake
surges up.*)

RUODI: I must leap into the jaws
Of hell? No man in his right mind would do it.

TELL: A man of courage thinks of himself last.
Rely on God and rescue the oppressed.   140

RUODI: Advice is easy in the port of safety.
There is the boat and there the lake. Go try it!

TELL: The lake, but not the governor, may show
Some mercy. Try it, Ferryman!

HERDSMEN AND HUNTSMAN: Save him!

RUODI: Not if it were my very son or brother,
It cannot be. Today is Simon-Judas day,
There roars the lake and wants to have its victim.

TELL: With idle talk here nothing will be done.
The hour urges, this man must be helped.
Well, Ferryman, will you attempt it?

RUODI: No,   150
  Not I!
TELL: In God's name then! Give me the boat.
  I will attempt it with my feeble strength.
KUONI: Ah, doughty Tell!
WERNI: That is the huntsman's way!
BAUMGARTEN: You are my savior and my angel, Tell!
TELL: I'll save you from the Bailiff's power, but
  Another's help must save you from the storm.
  Yet better fall into the hands of God
  Than into man's.

(to the herdsman)

        Console my wife, now, Friend,
  If I should meet with mortal destiny.
  I have done what I could not leave undone.   160

(He jumps into the boat.)

KUONI   (to the fisherman):
  You are a master helmsman, and you would
  Not dare to do what Tell is undertaking?
RUODI: Better men might not take Tell's example.
  There are not two like him in all these mountains.
WERNI   (has climbed the cliff):
  He's pushing off. God help you now, brave swimmer!
  See how the boat is pitching in those waves!
KUONI   (on the shore):
  The swell is passing over it—I can
  Not see it any more. Wait! There it is!
  The man is fighting bravely through the breakers.
SEPPI: Here come the Bailiff's horsemen at a gallop!   170
KUONI: God knows they are! Ah, that was help in need.

(Enter a troop of Landenberg cavalry.)

THE FIRST TROOPER: Produce the murderer you have
    concealed!
THE SECOND: He came this way, it's useless hiding him!

KUONI AND RUODI: Who's that now, Trooper?

THE FIRST TROOPER (*discovers the boat*): Ha! What do I see?

WERNI   (*above*):

You're looking for the man in yonder boat?—
Ride right ahead! With speed you'll catch him yet!

THE SECOND TROOPER: Damnation! He has got away.

THE FIRST TROOPER   (*to the herdsmen and fishermen*):
    And you helped him
Escape. You'll pay for this!—Cut down their herds!
Pull down that hut, set fire, smash everything!

(*They rush off.*)

SEPPI   (*rushes after them*):
    O my poor lambs!

KUONI   (*follows*):   Alas the day! My herds!   180

WERNI: The monsters!

RUODI   (*wrings his hands*): Justice of Almighty Heaven!
When will a savior come into this land?

(*He follows them.*)

SCENE 2

*At Steinen in Schwyz. A linden tree in front of Stauffacher's
house on the high road, near the bridge.*

Enter Werner Stauffacher and Pfeifer of Lucerne in conversation.

PFEIFER: Yes, Master Stauffacher, as I was saying,
Do not take oath to Austria if you
Can help it. Stand firm with the Empire as
Before, and God protect your ancient freedom.

(*He clasps his hand cordially and
starts to go.*)

STAUFFACHER: Do stay until my wife comes back. You are
My guest in Schwyz, as in Lucerne I'm yours.

PFEIFER: Thanks! I must get to Gersau yet today.

—Whatever hard things you have to endure   190
From arrogance and greed of your harsh regents,
Bear it with patience. It can change, and swiftly,
Another emperor may come to the throne.
Once you are Austria's, you're hers forever.

(Exit.)

*(Stauffacher sits down dejectedly on a bench
under the linden tree and is so discovered by Gertrud, his wife, who sits down beside him and observes him for a time in silence.)*

GERTRUD: So grave, my friend? I hardly recognize you.
For several days I have observed in silence
The gloomy broodings furrowing your brow.
A wordless grief is pressing on your heart.
Confide in me; I am your faithful wife
And Í demand my half-share of your sorrows.   200

*(Stauffacher gives her his hand
and remains silent.)*

What lies so heavy on your heart, tell me.
Your industry is blessed, your fortunes thrive,
The barns are full, and all the herds of oxen,
The herd of sleek and well-fed horses has
Been safely brought down from the mountains home
To winter in their comfortable stalls.
Here stands your house, rich as a noble mansion,
New timbered out of handsome solid beams
And squared off true and neatly joined together;
Its many windows give a cheerful shining;   210
It is adorned with colored coats-of-arms
And with wise mottoes which the traveler
Reads as he tarries and admires their meanings.
STAUFFACHER: The house does stand well timbered and
      well joined,
But ah—the ground on which we built it totters.

GERTRUD: My Werner, tell me what you mean by that.

STAUFFACHER: Beneath this linden tree I sat not long ago
In joyous thought of what was well accomplished,
And up from Küssnacht, his high castle, came
The Bailiff riding with his mounted men.   220
Before this house he halted in amazement.
I quickly rose and in respectful fashion,
As it was fitting, I approached the lord
Who represents the Emperor's judicial
Power in this land. "Whose house is this?"
He asked maliciously, for he well knew.
But thinking quickly I made him this answer:
"This house, Lord Bailiff, is my Lord's the Emperor's,
And yours, and mine in fief." And he replied:
"I am the Regent in the Emperor's stead   230
And will not have the peasants building houses
Of their own will and living lives as freely
As if they were the masters in this country.
I shall endeavor to prevent such things."
So saying, he defiantly rode off.
But I was left behind with grieving soul
To ponder on the wicked man's remark.

GERTRUD: My faithful husband and my consort, will
You take some honest counsel from your wife?
I boast of being noble Iberg's daughter,   240
A much-experienced man. We sisters used
To sit and spin our wool in those long evenings
When leaders of the people used to gather
Up at my father's house and read the parchments
Of ancient emperors and deliberate
The country's welfare in calm, reasoned talk.
Attentive, I heard many a wise word there,
What prudent men believe, what good men wish for,
And silently I kept these in my heart.
So listen now and give heed to my words,   250
For I have long known what was troubling you.

The Bailiff bears ill-will toward you, would like
To do you harm, because you thwart his wishes,
So that the men of Schwyz do not submit
To the new Princely House but loyally
Cling steadfast to the Empire as their worthy
Forefathers always did before them.—Is
This not so, Werner? Tell me if I lie.

STAUFFACHER: It is, and that is Gessler's grudge against me.

GERTRUD: He envies you because you live in peace,   260
A free man on your own ancestral land,
For he has none. From Emperor and Empire
You hold this house in fief; you can display it
As well as any Prince displays his lands;
For you acknowledge no lord over you
Except the Lord Supreme of Christendom.
He is a younger son of his house merely,
Owning nothing but his knightly mantle,
And so he sees all honest men's good fortune
Through squinting eyes of envious disfavor.   270
He long ago vowed your destruction—but
You stand unharmed yet.—Are you going to wait
Until he satisfies his evil will?
A wise man thinks ahead.

STAUFFACHER: What should be done?

GERTRUD   (steps closer):
Then here is my advice. You are aware
How here in Schwyz all upright men complain
About this Bailiff's greed and tyranny.
Then have no doubt but that the people yonder
In Unterwalden and in Uri also
Are weary of oppression and this yoke.   280
If Gessler is outrageous here, across
The lake there Landenberg is just as bad.—
There is no fishing boat that comes across
But brings us word of some new mischief and
Outrageous actions of the governors.

Therefore it would be well if several
Of you, of honest purpose, got together
To see how this oppression might be stopped.
Then I feel certain God would not desert you
But would be favorable to the just cause.   290
Do you not have a friend in Uri, tell me,
To whom you could disclose your heart quite frankly?
STAUFFACHER: I know a number of stout-hearted men there
And high, respected men of standing too
Whom I call intimate and trusted friends.

(*He gets up.*)

Wife, what a storm of dangerous ideas
You have aroused within my quiet bosom!
You bring my inmost thoughts into the daylight,
And what I secretly forbade myself
To think, you boldly say with ready tongue.   300
Have you considered well what you advise me?
It is wild discord and the ring of weapons
That you are calling to this tranquil valley.
Should we, a feeble folk of herdsmen, dare
To battle with the master of the world?
They're waiting only for a pretext to
Unleash the savage hordes of military
Might against this poor defenseless country,
Just so that they may rule as conquerors
And with a show of righteous punishment   310
Destroy the ancient patents of our freedom.
GERTRUD: You are men *too*. Know how to wield your axes
And God will help brave men that help themselves.
STAUFFACHER: O Wife, war is a frightful, raging horror.
It strikes the herds and strikes the herdsmen also.
GERTRUD: Man must endure whatever Heaven sends;
A noble heart will not endure injustice.
STAUFFACHER: You like this house that we have just built
new,

But monstrous war will burn it to the ground.

GERTRUD: If my heart were bound fast to earthly goods   320
I would set fire to it with my own hand.

STAUFFACHER: You have faith in humanity. War will
Not spare the tender infant in its cradle.

GERTRUD: In heaven Innocence has intercessors.
—Look forwards, Werner, not behind you now!

STAUFFACHER: We men can die in battle bravely fighting,
But what fate may there lie in store for you?

GERTRUD: The final choice is open to the weakest;
One leap down from this bridge can set me free.

STAUFFACHER   *(falls into her arms)*:
Whoever presses such a heart against   330
His own, can fight with joy for hearth and home
And need not fear the hosts of any king.
I shall set out for Uri right this instant;
Lord Walter Fürst lives there, a friend of mine
Who thinks the same as I about these times.
There too I'll find the noble standard-bearer
Von Attinghaus; though he is of high race,
He loves the people and the ancient ways.
I will take counsel with them both to see
How best we may ward off our country's foes.   340
Farewell! and while I am away, maintain
With your good sense the order of the household.
To pilgrims faring toward the house of God,
To pious monks collecting for their cloisters,
Give generous alms and send them on well cared for.
Stauffacher's house is not concealed. It stands
Out plain beside the high road as a haven
For all the travelers that fare this way.

*(As they walk off toward the rear
enter Wilhelm Tell and Baumgarten
downstage.)*

TELL   *(to Baumgarten)*:

Now you will have no further need of me.
Just go into that house, there Stauffacher lives,   350
Who is a father to all men in need.
—Look, there he is himself. Come, follow me.

(*They walk toward him; the scene changes.*)

SCENE 3

A public square near Altorf.

> *On an elevation at the rear may be seen a fortress under construction, far enough advanced that the shape of the whole building is apparent. The back section is finished, work is going on on the front; the scaffolding is still up, with workmen climbing up and down it. At the peak of the roof hangs the slater. All is movement and work.*

The Overseer. The Master Stonemason. Craftsmen and laborers.

THE OVERSEER   (*drives the craftsmen with his staff*):
No idling now! Step fast! Bring up those stones,
And get that lime and mortar over here!
If the Lord Bailiff comes to have a look
At how the work is going—It's a snail's pace.

(*to two laborers carrying things*)

Do you call that a load? Take twice that much!
O how these time-thieves do short-change their duty.
FIRST CRAFTSMAN: It's hard, though, to be forced to carry stone
For our own fortress-keep and prison.
THE OVERSEER: Why   360
Should you complain? It is a sorry people,
Good for nothing but to milk their cows

And traipse about the mountains doing nothing.

AN OLD MAN (*stops to rest*):
I am exhausted.

THE OVERSEER (*shakes him*): Quick, old man, to work!

FIRST CRAFTSMAN: Don't you have any heart inside you,
driving
That old man that can hardly drag himself
To hard forced labor?

THE MASTER STONEMASON AND CRAFTSMEN: Why, it shrieks
to heaven!

THE OVERSEER: You mind your business, I'll look after
mine!

SECOND CRAFTSMAN: What will they call this fortress we
are building,
Overseer?

THE OVERSEER: It will be called Keep Uri,   370

CRAFTSMEN: Keep Uri!

THE OVERSEER: What is there to laugh about?

SECOND CRAFTSMAN: This little shack will keep all Uri
down?

FIRST CRAFTSMAN: We'll see how many molehills they will
have
To pile like this one, one upon the other,
To make a mountain like the least in Uri!

(*The Overseer walks toward the rear.*)

THE MASTER STONEMASON: I'll throw the hammer in the
deepest lake
That served in putting up this cursed pile!

(*Enter Tell and Stauffacher.*)

STAUFFACHER: To think that I have lived to look at this!

TELL: It is not good to be here. Let's go on.   380

STAUFFACHER: Am I in Uri, in the land of freedom?

THE MASTER STONEMASON: O Sir, if you had ever seen
the cellars

Beneath those towers! Men with quarters *there*
Will never hear the roosters crow again.

STAUFFACHER: My God!

THE MASTER STONEMASON: Just see those bastions and
  those buttresses,

They're built to last for all eternity.

TELL: What hands have built, hands can tear down again.

(*pointing toward the mountains*)

But God has founded yonder house of freedom.

(*A drum is heard. Enter men carrying a hat
upon a pole. A Crier follows them, with women
and children pressing behind in a tumult.*)

FIRST CRAFTSMAN: What is the drum for? Pay attention!

THE MASTER STONEMASON: What

  A carnival procession! What's the hat for?   390

THE CRIER: In the Emperor's name! Hear ye!

CRAFTSMEN: Be quiet! Listen!

THE CRIER: You see this hat before you, men of Uri!

  It will be placed upon a lofty pillar

  On the highest spot in Altorf here,

  And this is what the Bailiff wills and orders:

  Respect shall be paid to this hat as to

  Himself. With bended knee and with bared head

  It shall be reverenced. And by such token

  The King will know who is obedient.

  And any man disdaining this commandment   400

  Shall forfeit life and goods unto the King.

(*The people burst out laughing.
The drum is sounded. They pass on.*)

FIRST CRAFTSMAN: What new unheard of thing the
  Governor

Has thought up now! We reverence a *hat*!

Say, did you ever hear the likes of this?

THE MASTER STONEMASON: Now we should bend the
   knee before a hat!
  Is this a joke of his with sensible people?
FIRST CRAFTSMAN: Why, if it were the Emperor's crown!
   It's only
  The hat of Austria; I saw it hanging
  Above the throne where fiefdoms are assigned.
THE MASTER STONEMASON: The hat of Austria! Watch
   out! It is   410
  A trick to sell us out to Austria!
CRAFTSMEN: No man of honor will endure this shame.
THE MASTER STONEMASON: Let's see what others think
   about this game.

(They retire to the rear.)

TELL   *(to Stauffacher)*:
  You now know what I think. Farewell, Lord Werner.
STAUFFACHER: Where are you going? Don't leave us like
   this.
TELL: My household lacks its father. So, farewell.
STAUFFACHER: My heart is very full from talking with you.
TELL: A heavy heart is not made light by words.
STAUFFACHER: Words might, however, lead us on to action.
TELL: Our only action now is patient silence.   420
STAUFFACHER: Must we endure the unendurable?
TELL: It's the harsh rulers that rule only briefly.
  When out of its abyss the Föhn comes up
  We put all fires out, and our ships make haste
  To seek a haven, and the mighty spirit
  Without a trace walks harmless across the earth.
  Let everyone live quietly at home;
  A peaceful man will be left quite in peace.
STAUFFACHER: You think so?
TELL: Unprovoked snakes do not bite.
  They will grow weary of themselves at last   430
  Once they see how the provinces stay quiet.

STAUFFACHER: We could do much if we just stood together.

TELL: In shipwreck separate men will come out better.

STAUFFACHER: Can you reject the common cause so coldly?

TELL: A man can only count upon himself.

STAUFFACHER: United, weak men also can be mighty.

TELL: A strong man is most mighty when *alone*.

STAUFFACHER: The fatherland, then, cannot count on you
When it is desperate for self-defense?

TELL (*gives him his hand*):
Tell rescues the lost lamb from the abyss   440
And would desert his friends in time of need?
Do as you will, but spare me your transactions.
I am not one to ponder and to choose;
If you want me for some specific actions,
Then call on Tell, and I am yours to use.

(*They leave in opposite directions.*)

(*A sudden tumult begins near the
scaffolding.*)

THE MASTER STONEMASON (*hurries over*):
What is it?

FIRST CRAFTSMAN (*comes forward shouting*):
The slater has just fallen off the roof.

(*Enter Berta and her retinue.*)

BERTA (*rushing in*):
Has he been dashed to pieces? Save him! Hurry!
If help is possible, save him! Here's gold!

(*She throws her jewelry among
the crowd.*)

THE MASTER STONEMASON: Plague take your gold! You
think that everything   450
Is bought with gold. When you have taken fathers
From their children, husbands from their wives,
And caused grief and distress across the world,

Then you think you can make it good with gold.—
Go—We were happy people till you came,
With you came desperation to our midst.
BERTA   (*to the Overseer who returns*):
    Is he alive?

> (*The Overseer gives a sign to the
> contrary.*)

> O wretched castle, built
With curses, curses will inhabit you!

> (*Exit.*)

SCENE 4

Walter Fürst's dwelling.

*Enter Walter Fürst and Arnold von Melchtal
simultaneously from different sides.*

MELCHTAL: Lord Walter Fürst—
WALTER FÜRST: What if someone surprised us!
    Stay where you are. We have spies all around us.   460
MELCHTAL: You bring no news from Unterwalden?
    Nothing
    About my father? I can bear no longer
    This lying idly here as prisoner.
    What have I done that is so criminal
    That I should hide out like a murderer?
    I swung my staff and only broke the finger
    Of that smart rascal who was going to
    Drive off my oxen, my fine team, before
    My eyes, because the Bailiff ordered it.
WALTER FÜRST: You are too rash. It was the Bailiff's page   470
    And he was sent by your superiors;
    You had received a penalty and should,

Harsh as it was, have quietly submitted.

MELCHTAL: I should have countenanced the shameless
    creature's
  Flippant talk: "If peasants want their bread,
  Then let them pull their plows themselves in harness!"
  It cut me to the heart to see that boy
  Unharnessing those splendid animals.
  They bellowed low as though they had a sense
  Of something wrong, and struck out with their horns.   480
  And then a righteous anger overwhelmed me,
  I lost control and hit the messenger.

WALTER FÜRST: When we can hardly master our own hearts,
  How is rash youth to practice self-restraint?

MELCHTAL: I'm only worried for my father's sake.
  He needs care badly and his son is far
  Away. The Bailiff has a grudge against him
  Because he has steadfastly fought for freedom.
  They will harass the old man for that reason
  And there is no one to shield him from outrage.   490
  So come what may, I must go over there.

WALTER FÜRST: Wait and possess yourself in patience here
  Till news comes to us from your forest home.
  I hear a knock—Go in there—It may be
  The Bailiff's messenger—Go in there—Here
  In Uri you are not safe from the arm
  Of Landenberg; the tyrants help each other.

MELCHTAL: They're teaching us what *we* should do.

WALTER FÜRST: Go in there!
  I'll call you when it's safe out here again.

          (Melchtal goes inside.)

  The hapless fellow, I dare not confess   500
  To him what evil I forebode—Who's knocking?
  Each time the door creaks I expect disaster.
  Mistrust and treason lurk in every corner.
  The messengers of force are finding ways

Into the innermost part of the house;
Soon we shall need to bolt and bar the doors.

(*He opens the door and steps back
in astonishment as Werner Stauffacher
comes in.*)

What do I see? Lord Werner! Well, by Heaven,
A worthy, cherished guest—No better man
Has ever stepped across this threshold yet.
You are most welcome, Sir! What brings you here?   510
What are you looking for down here in Uri?
STAUFFACHER: The olden times and olden Switzerland.
WALTER FÜRST: You bring them with you. See, I feel so
    happy,
My heart grows warm just at the sight of you.
—Sit down, Lord Werner—And how did you leave
The Lady Gertrud, your most gracious wife,
Wise Iberg's learned and sagacious daughter?
Your house is praised for hospitality
By all the travelers from German lands
That cross by Meinrad's Cell for Italy.   520
But tell me, you just came from Flüelen
And did not look around you anywhere
Before you set your foot upon this threshold?
STAUFFACHER   (*sits down*):
I did see an amazing new construction
In progress and it did not please me much.
WALTER FÜRST: Friend, there's the situation at a glance.
STAUFFACHER: The like of that has never been in Uri—
The memory of man recalls no fortress,
No dwelling fortified, except the grave.
WALTER FÜRST: It's Freedom's grave. You call it by its name.
                                                        [530]
STAUFFACHER: Lord Walter Fürst, I won't keep secrets
    from you:
No idle curiosity has brought

Me here. I am weighed down with cares. Oppression
I left at home, I find oppression here.
It is insufferable what we endure,
And no end is in sight for this oppression.
Since time's beginning the Swiss have been free,
We are accustomed to be treated well.
This country has not known the like of this
As long as herdsmen have moved on these mountains.   540

WALTER FÜRST: It is unparalleled, the way they're acting!
Even our noble Lord of Attinghausen,
Who has lived through the olden times as well,
Himself believes it is not to be borne.

STAUFFACHER: Below the forest too there are bad doings,
With outcomes no less bloody. Wolfenschiessen,
The Emperor's Burggrave who held Castle Rossberg,
Developed yearnings for forbidden fruit;
Baumgarten's wife, that keeps house in Alzellen,
He tried to misuse her in vile assault;   550
The husband took his ax and murdered him.

WALTER FÜRST: The judgments of Almighty God are just!
Baumgarten, did you say? An upright man!
I trust they rescued him and hid him well?

STAUFFACHER: Your son-in-law got him across the lake,
He is in hiding at my house in Steinen.
The same man has reported worse things still
Of what is going on in Sarnen now.
The heart of every honest man is bleeding.

WALTER FÜRST   (attentively):
What is it, tell me?

STAUFFACHER: Where you enter Melchtal,   560
Right there by Kerns, there lives an upright man,
They call him Heinrich von der Halden, and
His voice is of some weight in the assembly.

WALTER FÜRST: Who does not know him! What has happened
to him?

STAUFFACHER: Well, Landenberg had penalized the son

For some slight fault and ordered his best team
Of oxen to be taken from the plow.
The lad then struck the rascal and took flight.

WALTER FÜRST (*in extreme suspense*):
But what about the father—how is he?

STAUFFACHER: The Landenberger had the father summoned,
He must produce the son immediately,   [570]
And when the father vowed in all good faith
That he knew nothing of the fugitive,
The Bailiff has his torturers come in—

WALTER FÜRST (*jumps up and tries to lead him to the other
                    side of the room*):
No more, be still!

STAUFFACHER (*with voice rising*): "Your son may have escaped,
But I have *you!*", has him thrown on the ground
And has them pierce his eyes with their sharp steel—

WALTER FÜRST: God of Mercy!

MELCHTAL (*rushes out*):   Pierce his eyes, you say?

STAUFFACHER (*in astonishment to Walter Furst*):
Who is this youngster?

MELCHTAL (*seizes him with convulsive vehemence*):
                    Pierce his eyes? Tell me!

WALTER FÜRST: O pitiable old man!

                              But who is this?   580

          (*as Walter Fürst gives him a sign*)

This is the son? Almighty God!

MELCHTAL: And I
Have to be gone!—They put out both his eyes?

WALTER FÜRST: Control yourself! Endure it like a man!

MELCHTAL: All on account of *my* fault, *my* offense!
—He's blind, then? Really blind, completely blind?

STAUFFACHER: That's what I said. The springs of sight gone
    dry,
The sunlight he will never see again.

WALTER FÜRST: Have mercy on his sorrow!

MELCHTAL: Never! Never!

> (*He presses his hand over his eyes and is silent
> for several minutes; then he turns from one to the
> other and speaks in a gentle voice choked with
> tears.*)

O, eyesight is a noble gift of Heaven—
From light all living things derive their being   590
And every happy creature of the earth—
The very plants turn joyously toward light.
And *he* must sit there, groping, in the darkness,
In everlasting gloom—Warm green of meadows
Will gladden him no more, nor flowers' luster;
He cannot even see the sun-red glaciers—
To die is nothing—but to *live* and not
To *see*, there is misfortune.—Why do you
Look at me with such grief? I have two eyes
And cannot give my blinded father one,   600
Nor any shimmer from the sea of light
That breaks in dazzling splendor on my eyes.

STAUFFACHER: Alas, I must increase your sorrow further,
Instead of healing it. He lacks still more,
The Bailiff confiscated all he owned
And left him nothing but his staff wherewith
To wander blind and bare from door to door.

MELCHTAL: The sightless, aged man, with nothing but
His staff! Deprived him even of the sunlight
That poorest men possess in common—Talk   610
No more to me of staying and of hiding!
O what a wretched coward I have been
To take precautions for my safety and
Take none for yours!—To think of your dear head
Left as a hostage in that tyrant's hands!
Faint-hearted caution, leave me! I shall think
Of nothing but of bloody restitution.
I will go over there—No one can stop me—

I'll have my father's eyes from that same Bailiff—
I'll find him even in the midst of all   620
His mounted men—Life is of no importance
If I can cool my hot, enormous sorrow
In his life-blood.

(*He starts to leave.*)

WALTER FÜRST: Stay where you are! What can
  You do against him? He is safe in Sarnen
  In his high lordly castle and can laugh
  At unavailing anger in his fortress.
MELCHTAL: If he lived yonder in the Schreckhorn's palace
  Of ice, or even higher where the Jungfrau
  Sits veiled since all eternity—I still
  Would find a way to him; with twenty youths   630
  That think as I do, I will smash his fortress.
  If no one follows me, if all of you,
  So fearful for your huts and for your herds,
  Will bend beneath the tyrant's yoke—I'll gather
  The herdsmen all together in the mountains,
  Out there beneath the open roof of heaven
  Where minds are clear yet and where hearts are sound,
  And tell the story of this monstrous horror.
STAUFFACHER (*to Walter Fürst*):
  It's reached its peak now—Are we going to wait
  Until the last extreme—
MELCHTAL: What last extreme is there   640
  Yet to be feared, now that the star of eyesight
  Is safe no longer in its socket-pit?
  Are we defenseless? Why have we learned how
  To draw the crossbow, swing the heavy weight
  Of battle-axes? Every creature has
  Been granted its defense in desperation.
  Exhausted stags will make a stand and show
  Their dreaded antlers to the pack of hounds,
  The chamois drags the huntsman down the chasm,—

The very ox, that gently shares the dwellings   650
Of man and bends the mighty sinews of
His neck beneath the yoke to pull the plow,
Will leap up when provoked and whet his horns
And pitch his enemy up to the clouds.

WALTER FÜRST: If all three cantons thought as we three men,
We might perhaps accomplish something now.

STAUFFACHER: If Uri calls, if Unterwalden helps,
Schwyz will stand by its old alliances.

MELCHTAL: My friends in Unterwalden number many,
Not one but will risk life and limb with joy   660
If he has neighbors who will back him up
And shield him.—Reverend elders of this country,
I stand, a youngster merely, here between you,
The much-experienced—My voice has to be
Discreetly silent in the Canton Council.
But do not scorn my words and my advice
Because I am still young and have seen little;
Not wanton youthful blood impels me, but
The painful violence of extreme grief
That would move stones to pity in the field.   670
You both are fathers, heads of families,
And hope to have sons who are virtuous,
Who will revere the sacred hair upon
Your heads and watch out for your star of eyesight.
O just because you have not suffered yet
In property or person, and your eyes
Still move in clarity within their orbits,
Be not unmindful therefore of our pain.
The tyrant's sword hangs over your heads too.
You kept this country free of Austria;   680
My father's crime was nothing more than that,
And you are just as guilty and foredoomed.

STAUFFACHER   (to Walter Fürst):
Well, you decide, and I will follow you.

WALTER FÜRST: Let us first hear what the most worthy lords

Of Sillinen and Attinghausen will
Advise; their names, I think, will gain us friends.

MELCHTAL: Where is a name in all this mountain district
More worthy than *your* name, or *your* name either?
The people have faith in the sterling worth
Of names like these, they ring true in this country.   690
You have a precious heritage of virtue
And you have richly added to it.—Why,
Then, call the nobles? Let us do it by
Ourselves! If we were by ourselves here in
This country, we could manage our defenses!

STAUFFACHER: The nobles do not face an equal peril.
The storm now raging through the lowland regions
Where we are, has not reached yet to the heights.
And yet they will not fail to help us once
They see the country up in arms around them.   700

WALTER FÜRST: If some judge acted between Austria
And us, then law and justice could prevail.
But our oppressor is our Emperor
And highest judge—Hence God must give us help
Through our own arms. Sound out the men of Schwyz,
And I will meanwhile look for friends in Uri.
But whom can we despatch to Unterwalden?—

MELCHTAL: Send me there—Who could be involved more
    closely—

WALTER FÜRST: I won't permit it. You are my guest here
And I must guarantee your safety.

MELCHTAL: Let   710
Me go! I know the by-paths and the trails,
And I'll find friends enough to hide me from
The enemy and furnish me with shelter.

STAUFFACHER: Then let him go with God. There are no
    traitors
Down there. This tyranny is so detested
That it can never find an instrument.
Below the forest that Alzeller man

Can win confederates and rouse the country.
MELCHTAL: How will we manage safe communication
So we deceive suspicions of the tyrants?   720
STAUFFACHER: We could arrange a meeting place at Treib
Or Brunnen, where the merchant ships put in.
WALTER FÜRST: We could not do the job that publicly.
Hear my idea. On the lake's left bank
As you go up toward Brunnen, opposite
The Mythenstein, there is a meadow hidden
By woods; it's called the Rütli by the herdsmen
Because the timber has been cleared from there.
Just at that point our canton borderline

(to Melchtal)

Meets yours, and just a little trip in your   730

(to Stauffacher)

Light boat will carry you across from Schwyz.
Along deserted paths we can get there
By night and hold a quiet consultation.
Let each of you bring ten reliable
Men with him who are one in heart with us,
That way we can discuss the common cause
In common, and with God reach a decision.
STAUFFACHER: So be it. Now give me your good right hands,
And take each other's hands as well, and thus,
As we *three men* now interlock our hands   740
In upright purpose and without deception,
So too shall our *three cantons* stand together,
Defying and defending unto death.
WALTER FÜRST AND MELCHTAL: Unto death!

*(They hold their hands interclasped
for an interval in silence.)*

MELCHTAL: My blind and aged father!
You cannot *see* the day of freedom come,

But you shall *hear* it. When from Alp to Alp
The fiery signals rise aloft in flame
And mighty fortresses of tyrants fall,
Then to your hut Swiss men will pay their call
To bring the joyous tidings to your ear,   750
Then dawn amid your darkness will appear!

(They separate.)

ACT II

SCENE 1

Baron von Attinghausen's manor.

[Morning of November 7 or of November 8, 1307.]

A Gothic hall adorned with blazoned shields and helmets. The Baron, an aged man of eighty-five, of tall and dignified stature, is leaning on a staff on which there is a chamois horn; he is wearing a doublet of fur. Around him are standing Kuoni and six other farmhands with rakes and scythes.

Enter Ulrich von Rudenz in knightly attire.

RUDENZ: Well, Uncle, here I am. What is your will?
ATTINGHAUSEN: Allow me first to share the morning cup,
By ancient family custom, with my workmen.

(*He drinks from a goblet which is
then passed around.*)

I used to be with them in field and forest
Directing all their efforts with my eye,
Just as my banner guided them in battle.
But now I can be no more than their steward,
And if warm sunlight will not come to me,
I cannot seek it on the mountains either.   760
And so, in close and ever closer circles,
I gradually am moving toward the last
And closest of them all, where life stands still.
I am my shadow merely; soon I shall
Be just my name.

KUONI   (*approaching Rudenz with the cup*):
          To your health, Squire.

          (*Rudenz hesitates in accepting the cup.*)

                                                  Drink up!
    It's from one cup and from one heart as well.
ATTINGHAUSEN: Be off, now, boys, and when the evening
    comes
    We'll have a talk about the nation's business.

                  (*The workmen leave.*)

    I see that you are girded and equipped.
    You're bound for Altorf and the Bailiff's castle?   770
RUDENZ: Yes, Uncle, and I must not tarry now—
ATTINGHAUSEN   (*sits down*):
    Are you in such a hurry? Has time been
    So scantily apportioned to your youth
    That you must dole it out to your old uncle?
RUDENZ: I see that you have no real need of me,
    I am a stranger merely in this house.
ATTINGHAUSEN   (*has been scanning him for some time*):
    Yes, that you are. And in your homeland also,
    Unfortunately.—O Uli, Uli, I
    Don't know you any more. You strut in silks,
    And make a great display of peacock feathers,   780
    And hang a purple mantle on your shoulders;
    You gaze upon the peasant with contempt
    And are ashamed of his warm-hearted welcome.
RUDENZ: The honor due him I will gladly pay,
    The privileges he takes I will refuse him.
ATTINGHAUSEN: The entire country lies beneath the heavy
    Anger of the King, and every honest
    Man's heart is troubled by the tyrant force
    That we endure.—The common misery
    Leaves you alone untouched.—As an apostate   790
    From your own people you are seen to stand

On the side of your country's enemies,
And, mocking our distress, you frivolously
Pursue your pleasures, court the Princes' favor,
While underneath the scourge your country bleeds.

RUDENZ: The country is in grave distress—Why, Uncle?
Who is it that brought these afflictions on?
It would cost nothing but a simple word
To be rid of oppression instantly
And win the Emperor's benevolence.   800
But woe to them that keep the people's eyes shut
So they resist what is for their true welfare.
For personal advantage they prevent
The cantons' taking oath to Austria
As all the provinces around have done.
It flatters them to share the Nobles' Bench
With noblemen,—they want the *Emperor* for
Their overlord so they may have *no* master
At all.

ATTINGHAUSEN: Must I hear *this* and from your lips!

RUDENZ: You asked for my opinion, let me finish.   810
—What role is this for you to play here, Uncle?
Have you no more ambition than to be
Chief canton magistrate or standard bearer
And rule alongside of these cattle-drovers?
What? Is it not more laudable a choice
To pay your homage to a royal lord,
Participate in his resplendent court,
Than live here as the peer of your own servants
And sit in the assembly with the peasants?

ATTINGHAUSEN: O Uli! Uli! I can recognize   820
The voices of temptation! They have seized
Your willing ear and filled your heart with poison.

RUDENZ: Yes, I will not conceal it—In my soul
I wince before the mockery of strangers
Who call us peasant aristocracy.
While noble youths around me win high honors

Under Hapsburg's banners, I can't bear
To sit here idly on ancestral land
And waste the springtime of my life away
In menial labors of the day. Elsewhere   830
Great things are happening, a world of fame
Is splendidly a-stir beyond these mountains—
My helmet and *my* shield rust in the hall;
The ringing call of martial trumpets and
The cry of heralds summoning to tourneys,
These do not penetrate into these valleys;
Here I hear nothing but monotonous
Cowherders' songs and jingling cattle-bells.

ATTINGHAUSEN: Deluded man, misled by idle splendor!
Despise your native land! And be ashamed   840
Of ancient pious customs of your forefathers!
With burning tears you will some day be sick
With yearning for your own ancestral mountains,
And that nostalgic melody of cowherds
Which in your haughtiness you now disdain,
Will seize you with an anguished homesickness
When it strikes on your ear in alien lands.
The impulse to the fatherland is mighty!
The false and foreign world is not for you;
Up at the proud Imperial court you will   850
Remain an alien with your true heart!
The world abroad requires quite different virtues
From those you have acquired amid these valleys.
Go up there, sell your independent soul,
Take land in fief, become a Prince's lackey,
When you can well be your own master and
A prince on your free and ancestral lands.
O Uli! Uli! Stay among your people
And do not go to Altorf. O do not
Forsake your native country's sacred cause!   860
I am the last one of my race. My name
Will end with me. There hang my shield and helmet;

These they will put into my grave with me.
And must I think as I draw my last breath
That you are waiting only for my death
To go before this new fief-giving court
To get from Austria my noble lands
That I had once received from God in freedom?

RUDENZ: It is in vain that we resist the King,
The world belongs to him. Are we alone   870
To hold out stubbornly and to persist
In breaking up the chain of territories
Which he has mightily set up around us?
His are the markets and the courts, *his* are
The merchant roads; the very beasts of burden
That travel through the Gotthard pay his levies;
We are encompassed round about and closed
In by his territories like a net.
And will the Empire save us? Can it save
Itself against the growing might of Austria?   880
If God does not help us, no emperor can.
What is the good of emperors' promises,
When they, in time of war or money-troubles,
Can pawn the cities that have taken refuge
Behind their Eagles, and sell them off to
The Empire? Uncle, No! It is a blessing
And wise precaution in these times of faction
To make alliance with a mighty chief.
The Emperor's crown can pass from clan to clan
And has no memory for faithful service,   890
But an hereditary lord well served
Means sowing seed for times to come.

ATTINGHAUSEN: Are you so clever?
You think you see more clearly than your ancestors
Who fought heroically with blood and treasure
For the sake of the precious jewel, Freedom?
Go take a boat down to Lucerne and ask
How Austria's dominion sits with *them*.

They'll come up here and count our sheep and cattle,
Measure off our Alps, put our wild fowl
And large game animals into preserves   900
In our free forests, set up toll-gates at
Our gates and bridges, pay their purchases
Of lands out of our poverty, and pay
For all the wars they wage out of our blood.
No, if we are to risk our blood for something,
Let it be *for ourselves!* We will not pay
Less for our freedom than for slavery!
RUDENZ: How can we,
Mere herder folk, stand up to Albrecht's armies!
ATTINGHAUSEN: O learn to know these herder people, Boy!
I know them, I have led them into battle,   910
And I saw how they fought before Faënza.
Just let them come to force a yoke upon us
That we have made our minds up *not* to bear!
O learn to feel of what stock you are born!
And do not cast away the true pearl of
Your worth for idle show and tinsel glitter—
To be known as the head of a *free* people
Devoted to you out of love alone
And loyal to you both in war and death—
Such pride be yours, boast *such* nobility—   920
And grip your native bonds more tightly to you,
Ally yourself with your dear fatherland,
And with your heart entire hold fast to it!
The sturdy roots of your best strength are here;
Out in the alien world you stand alone,
A weak reed snapped in two by any storm.
Come, you have not seen us for a long time,
Try it with us for just one day—Just for
Today do not go up to Altorf, not
Today! Grant your own people this one day!   930

(*He takes his hand.*)

RUDENZ: I gave my word. Excuse me. I am bound.

ATTINGHAUSEN   *(releases his hand, with gravity)*:
  Yes, you are bound—Oh yes, unhappy man,
  You are, but not by word and vow,
  It's with the bonds of love that you are bound!

(Rudenz turns away.)

  Hide as you will. It is the noble lady
  Berta von Bruneck who lures you up to
  The palace, binds you to the Emperor's service.
  It is the noble lady that you hope
  To win by your defection—Do not be deceived!
  They show the girl to lead you on, but they   940
  Will not bestow her on your innocence.

RUDENZ: I have heard quite enough. Good day to you.

(Exit.)

ATTINGHAUSEN: You crazy youngster, wait!—Ah, he is gone.
  And I cannot restrain him, cannot save him.
  This is the way young Wolfenschiessen turned
  Against his country—and still more will follow.
  The alien magic carries youth away,
  Aspiring mightily beyond our mountains.
  Accursed hour when this alien thing
  Arrived amid these tranquil blessed valleys   950
  Destroying innocence of our old ways!
  The new makes its way in by force, the old,
  The venerable, departs, new times come on,
  A different-thinking generation lives.
  What am I doing here? All those with whom
  I lived and worked are in their graves. *My* time
  Lies buried under earth already. Happy
  Are they who do not have to live amid the new one.

(Exit.)

SCENE 2

A meadow surrounded by cliffs and woods.

[Night of November 7-8, 1307]

On the cliffs are paths with railings, also ladders, from which the countrymen are subsequently seen climbing down. In the background the lake is visible, above which at first a lunar rainbow is seen. High mountains close the prospect, with still higher ice-capped peaks towering over them. It is completely dark on stage; only the lake and white glaciers gleam in the moonlight.

Enter Melchtal, Baumgarten, Winkelried, Meier von Sarnen, Burkhard am Bühel, Arnold von Sewa, Klaus von der Flüe, and four more countrymen, all with weapons.

MELCHTAL   (*still offstage*):
  The path is widening out, just follow *me!*
  I recognize the cliff with the cross on it.   960
  This is our goal, here is the Rütli.

               (*They come in with torches.*)

WINKELRIED: Hark!
SEWA: Deserted.
MEIR: Not a countryman in sight yet.
  We are the first ones here, we Unterwaldners.
MELCHTAL: How late at night is it?
BAUMGARTEN: The fire watchman
  In Selisberg has just called two o'clock.

         (*A bell is heard in the distance.*)

MEIER: Be still!
AM BÜHEL: The matin bell down in the forest chapel
  Rings clear across to us from Schwyzerland.

VON DER FLÜE: The air is pure and carries the sound far.
MELCHTAL: Some of you go and make a fire of brushwood
So that it will burn bright when the men come.

(*Two countrymen go out.*)

SEWA: It is a fine and moonlight night. The lake
Lies there as quiet as a level mirror.
AM BÜHEL: They have an easy crossing.
WINKELRIED (*points toward the lake*): Hey, look there!
Look there! Do you see something?
MEIER: What?—Of course!
A rainbow in the middle of the night.
MELCHTAL: It is the moonlight that is causing it.
VON DER FLÜE: That is a strange and wondrous sign! There's many
A living person that has never seen it.
SEWA: It's double; there's a fainter one above it.
BAUMGARTEN: There is a boat just passing underneath.   980
MELCHTAL: That will be Stauffacher in his small boat.
The good man does not keep us waiting long.

(*He goes with Baumgarten toward the shore.*)

MEIER: The men from Uri are the slowest coming.
AM BÜHEL: They have to come the long way round here through
The mountains to avoid the Bailiff's spies.

(*Meanwhile the two countrymen have
built a fire in the middle of the area.*)

MELCHTAL   (*at the shore*):
Who is it? Give the password!
STAUFFACHER   (*from below*):   Friends of the country.

(*They all go toward the rear to meet the new ar-
rivals. Out of the boat step Stauffacher, Itel Reding,
Hans auf der Mauer, Jörg im Hofe, Konrad Hunn,*

Ulrich the smith, Jost von Weiler, and three other
countrymen, all with weapons also.)

ALL   (*shouting*):
          Welcome!

          (*While the others remain at the rear exchanging*
          greetings, Melchtal comes forward with Stauff-
          acher.)

MELCHTAL: O Lord Stauffacher, I have
  Seen him who never can see *me* again!
  I laid my hands upon his eyes and drew
  A burning feeling of revenge out of   990
  The dead and vanquished sunlight of his glance.
STAUFFACHER: Do not talk of revenge. Our purpose is
  Not venegeance for things done but warding off
  A threatened evil. Tell me what you have
  Accomplished for the cause in Unterwalden,
  And what the people think, and how you managed
  Yourself to slip out of the snares of treason.
MELCHTAL: Along the dread peaks of Surennen pass,
  Across the waste and spreading fields of ice
  Where no sound comes but croaking of the vultures,   1000
  I made my way up to the mountain pasture
  Where herdsmen from the Engelberg and Uri
  Shout greetings and merge herds for common grazing,
  Quenching my thirst with milky glacier waters
  That foam their way in runlets down the slopes.
  I stayed in isolated herdsmen's huts
  Where I was host and guest, until I came
  To dwellings where men live gregariously.
  Report already had spread through those valleys
  Of the new monstrous horror that had happened,   1010
  And my misfortune won me deep respect
  At every door to which I came and knocked.
  I found those upright souls profoundly outraged

At the new tyranny of government.
For just as their Alps on and on forever
Breed the same plants, and streams flow uniformly,
And clouds themselves and winds unvaryingly
Pursue their same familiar courses, so
Our ancient customs from our grandsires to
Our grandsons have kept on without a change.   1020
They will not stand for sudden innovations
In their accustomed, even way of life.
They all extended their hard hands to me,
From their walls they reached me down their rusty swords,
And in their eyes there flashed the joyous feeling
Of courage when I named to them the names
Which to those mountain countryfolk are sacred,
Your name and Walter Fürst's—Whatever you
Consider right they vowed that they would do,
They swore to follow you to death itself.   1030
And thus protected by the sacred law
Of hospitality, I passed from farm
To farm until I reached my native valley,
Around which many of my kinsmen dwell,
And then I found my father, blind and plundered,
On strangers' straw, existing on the gifts
From strangers' charity—

STAUFFACHER: O Lord in Heaven!

MELCHTAL: I did not weep! I did not spend the force
Of my hot grief in floods of helpless tears;
Deep in my bosom like a precious treasure   1040
I buried it and thought of action only.
I crawled through every turning of the mountains,
No valley was so hidden but I found it;
Up as far as the glacier's ice-shod foot
I searched and found all huts where men inhabit,
And everywhere I set my foot I found
An equal hatred for this tyranny;
For right up to that final boundary

Of living Nature where the frozen ground
No longer yields, the Bailiff's greed has plundered.   1050
I stirred the hearts of all those honest people
And goaded them to anger with my words,
And all of them are ours with heart and tongue.

STAUFFACHER: You have accomplished much in this short time.

MELCHTAL: I did still more. It's those two fortresses,
Rossberg and Sarnen, that the people fear.
Behind those walls of stone the enemy
Finds easy shelter and works us his harm.
I thought I would explore with my own eyes:
I was in Sarnen and went through the castle.   1060

STAUFFACHER: You dared to venture in that tiger's lair?

MELCHTAL: I was disguised there in a pilgrim's habit,
I saw the Bailiff reveling at table—
Judge now if I can keep my heart's control:
I saw my enemy and did not kill him.

STAUFFACHER: Indeed your boldness had good fortune's
blessing.

*(The other countrymen have meanwhile
come forward and draw around these two.)*

But tell me now, who are the friends and men
Of upright character who came with you?
Make me acquainted with them so that we
Can join in trust and open up our hearts.   1070

MEIER: Who would not know *you* Sir, in these three cantons?
My name is Meier von Sarnen; this here is
My sister's son, named Struth von Winkelried.

STAUFFACHER: You do not name me any unknown names.
It was a Winkelried that slew the dragon
In Weiler Swamp and in that conflict lost
His life.

WINKELRIED: That was my ancestor, Lord Werner.

MELCHTAL *(points out two countrymen)*:
Those live beyond the forest, cloister people

Down from the Engelberg. You surely will not
Scorn them for all that they are serfs and do not   1080
Live free like us on their ancestral lands.
They love this country and are well reputed.
STAUFFACHER   (to these two):
Give me your hands. Let any man rejoice
Who is not bound in service in this world;
But uprightness will thrive in any class.
KONRAD HUNN: This is Lord Reding, our ex-chief-magistrate.
MEIER: I know him well. He is my adversary
At law with me about a piece of land.
—Lord Reding, we are enemies in court,
Here we are friends.

(He shakes his hand.)

STAUFFACHER: Ah, this is nobly spoken.   1090
WINKELREID: You hear? They're coming. Hear the horn of Uri!

(To right and left armed men are seen
climbing down the cliffs with torches.)

AUF DER MAUER: Look! Isn't that the servant of the Lord,
Our worthy pastor, climbing down? He does
Not shun the terrors of the road and night,
A faithful shepherd caring for his people.
BAUMGARTEN: The sexton's with him, and Lord Walter
Fürst.
But I do not see Tell among their numbers.

(Enter Walter Fürst, Rösselmann the pastor,
Petermann the sexton, Kuoni the herdsman, Werni
the huntsman, Ruodi the fisherman, and five other
countrymen.
All of them together, thirty-three in number,
advance and take up positions around the fire.)

WALTER FÜRST: This is the way we have to sneak around
Like murderers to meet together on

Our native soil and our paternal lands,
By night, that lends its cloak of blackness only
To crimes and to conspiracies that shun
The sunlight, just to get our proper rights,
Which, after all, are evident and clear
As splendor of the open noonday sun.

MELCHTAL: That doesn't matter. What dark night has spun
Shall freely forth to the light of the sun.

RÖSSELMANN: Hear what God bids me say, Confederates!
We represent a cantonal assembly
And we may well pass for an entire people.   1110
So let us meet according to the ancient
Rules of the country, as in times of peace;
Whatever is unlawful in this session
Must be excused by hardship of the times.
But God is everywhere where right is practiced,
And we are standing underneath His heaven.

STAUFFACHER: Yes, let us follow ancient usage here,
And though it may be night, our right shines clear.

MELCHTAL: We lack in numbers, but the entire people's
Hearts are here, *the best men* are here present.   1120

KONRAD HUNN: And if the ancient books are not at hand,
Still they are all inscribed upon our hearts.

RÖSSELMANN: Then let the ring be formed immediately
And let the swords of office be set up.

AUF DER MAUER: Now let the magistrate assume his place
And let the bailiffs stand on either side.

THE SEXTON: There are three nations. Which one will be
honored
To furnish the assembly with a leader?

MEIER: Schwyz may contest with Uri for the honor,
We Unterwaldners willingly withdraw.   1130

MELCHTAL: We will withdraw; we are the suppliants here
Who seek assistance from their powerful friends.

STAUFFACHER: In that case Uri will assume the sword;
Its banner has led in the trips to Rome.

WALTER FÜRST: Then let the honor of the sword be Schwyz's:
   From its race we are all of us descended.

RÖSELMANN: Let me adjust this quarrel amicably.
   Schwyz leads in council, Uri in the field.

WALTER FÜRST   (*hands Stauffacher the swords*):
   Take them.

STAUFFACHER: Not I; the eldest has the honor.

IM HOFE: The eldest man here is Ulrich the smith.   1140

AUF DER MAUER: A worthy man but not of free estate;
   No serf can have the post of judge in Schwyz.

STAUFFACHER: Lord Reding's here, the ex-chief-magistrate,
   Why should we look for anyone more worthy?

WALTER FÜRST: Let him preside as head of the assembly!
   All who agree to that, hold up their hands.

         (*All raise their right hands.*)

REDING   (*steps into the middle*):
   I cannot place my hand upon the books,
   So I shall swear by those eternal stars
   That I shall never stray from what is right.

       (*The two swords are set up before him, the ring
       forms around him, with Schwyz holding the center,
       Uri on the right, and on the left Unterwalden. He
       stands leaning on his battlesword.*)

   What is it that has brought together these   1150
   Three mountain peoples at this ghostly hour
   Here on this lake's inhospitable shore?
   What shall the purport be of this new league
   That we shall found here under Heaven's stars?

STAUFFACHER   (*steps into the ring*):
   We are not founding a new league; it is
   An old alliance from our fathers' times
   Which we renew. Know, then, Confederates,
   Though lake or mountain may divide us and
   Though every nation may rule of itself,

We are however of one race and blood,   1160
We all proceeded from a single homeland.
WINKELRIED: Then it is true, the way the old songs say,
   That we came from far off into this country?
   O tell us what you know about it so
   The new league will be strengthened by the old.
STAUFFACHER: This is the story that old herdsmen tell:
   Away back in the midnight lands up north
   There lived a numerous nation plagued with famine.
   In that distress the council made a rule
   That every tenth man as the lots should fall   1170
   Should leave his fathers' lands. And that was done.
   With lamentation men and women left
   In a vast host down toward the noonday sun
   And fought their way with swords through Germany
   Down to the uplands of these mountain forests.
   Nor did that marching host of people weary
   Until they had arrived in that wild valley
   Where now the Muotta flows between the meadows.
   No sign of human life was to be seen there
   Except one hut that stood beside the shore,   1180
   And there a man sat tending ferry-crossings.
   The lake was raging wildly at that moment
   And was not passable, so they examined
   The land more closely and perceived fine stands
   Of timber, and they found good running streams,
   And then they felt as though they were back home
   Again. So they made up their minds to stay,
   And built the ancient hamlet known as Schwyz,
   And many was the bitter day they had
   Before they cleared the forest's tangled roots.   1190
   Then later, when the ground no more sufficed
   The people's numbers, they moved on again
   To the black mountain, yes, on to the Whiteland,
   Where hidden by eternal walls of ice
   A different people speaks with different tongues.

The hamlet Stanz they built beside the Kernwald,
The hamlet Altorf by the river Reuss.
Yet they were always mindful of their source
Of origin. From all the alien races
That since have settled in their country's midst   1200
The men of Schwyz can always be distinguished;
There's heart and blood to make them know each other.

(*He clasps hands to right and left.*)

AUF DER MAUER: Yes, we are of one heart and of one blood!
ALL   (*clasping each other's hands*):
We are one nation and shall act as one.
STAUFFACHER: The other peoples bear a foreign yoke,
They have submitted to their conquerors.
Within our country's borders live great numbers
Of tenants who endure the rule of others,
Whose servitude is passed on to their children.
But *we*, the ancient Swiss of purest stock,   1210
We have invariably preserved our freedom.
We have not bowed the knee before the Princes,
We freely chose the Emperor's protection.
RÖSSELMANN: We freely chose the Empire's shield and shelter:
That's how it reads in Emperor Friedrich's charter.
STAUFFACHER: The freest man is not without a master.
There has to be a head, a supreme judge,
Where justice may be sought in any quarrel.
Thus for the territory which our fathers
Had wrested from the ancient wilderness   1220
They gave that honor to the Emperor who
Is called the lord of German and French lands,
And like the other free men of his Empire
Pledged him the noble service of their arms.
This is the only duty of free men,
To shield the Empire that gives them protection.
MELCHTAL: Beyond that, anything is slavery.
STAUFFACHER: Whenever came the call to arms, they followed

The Empire's banners and they fought its battles.
And under arms they went to Italy   1230
To place the Roman crown upon his head.
At home they ruled themselves quite cheerfully
By ancient usages and their own laws.
Death sentences alone the Emperor passed.
And for those some high Count was authorized
Who had no residence within the country.
When blood guilt did occur, they summoned him
And underneath the open sky he clearly
Pronounced his judgment with no fear of persons.
What traces are there here that we are slaves?   1240
If anyone knows otherwise, speak out!

IM HOFE: No, everything is just as you have stated,
We never tolerated despotism.

STAUFFACHER: And we defied the Emperor himself
When he once twisted law to suit the priests.
For when the people from the monastery
Einsiedeln claimed our mountain pasture land
That we had grazed on since ancestral times,
And when the Abbot showed an ancient charter
That granted him the unclaimed wilderness—   1250
They had suppressed the fact of our existence—
Then we cried out: "The charter is a fraud!
No Emperor can make gifts of what is ours,
And if the Empire fails to render justice,
We can, amid these mountains, do without
The Empire." So our fathers said. Shall *we*
Endure the infamy of this new yoke
And from a foreign lackey stand for what
No Emperor in his might dared do to us?
We made this soil of ours, created it   1260
From nothing by our diligence of hands,
Transformed the ancient forest that housed bears
Into a dwelling seat for human beings;
We slew the dragon's brood that used to rise

All poison-swollen from the swamps; we tore
The veil of mist away that used to shroud
This wilderness in everlasting grey;
We sprung hard cliffs apart and spanned safe paths
Across the chasms for the traveler;
Ours is this soil through thousand-year possession—   1270
And now the lackey of an alien master
Should come and forge his chains upon us here
And heap disgrace on us on our own soil?
Is there no help against such tyranny?

(Great commotion among the
countrymen.)

No, there's a limit to a tyrant's power.
When men oppressed can not find justice, when
The burden gets to be unbearable,—
Then they with confidence and courage reach
To Heaven and fetch their eternal rights
From where they hang as indestructible   1280
And as inalienable as stars themselves.
Then Nature's old primaeval state recurs
Where man to man stands up in opposition,
And as a last resort when nothing else
Is of avail, the sword is given them.
Supreme possessions we may well defend
Against tyrannic power.—We guard our country,
And we protect our wives, protect our children!

ALL   *(clashing their swords)*:
    And we protect our wives, protect our children!

RÖSSELMANN   *(steps into the ring)*:
    Before you seize your swords, consider well!   1290
    Things can be peaceably adjusted with
    The Emperor. It will cost you just one word
    And your oppressors will turn flatterers.
    Accept the offer they have often made,
    Renounce the Empire, recognize the rule

Of Austria—

AUF DER MAUER: What's this the priest is saying?
We swear to Austria!

AM BÜHEL: Don't listen to him!

WINKELRIED: It's traitor's counsel!

REDING: Peace, Confederates!

SEWA: Do Austria homage after such disgrace!

VON DER FLÜE: What! Let ourselves be bullied into
something   1300
We had refused when we were kindly asked!

MEIER: We would be slaves and would deserve to be so.

AUF DER MAUER: Abolish any man's Swiss citizenship
Who talks surrender now to Austria!
Chief Magistrate, I urge that this be made
The first law of the land that we enact.

MELCHTAL: So be it! Anyone who talks surrender
To Austria shall be stripped of his rights,
No countryman shall seat him at his hearth.

ALL   (raise their right hands):
Yes, we want that to be the law!

REDING   (after a pause):   It is.   1310

RÖSSELMANN: Now we are free, this law has made you free.
Now Austria will not extort by force
What it could not obtain by friendly asking—

JOST VON WEILER: Continue with the order of the day!

REDING: Confederates! Have you tried all mild measures?
Perhaps the King is not aware; it is
Not by his will that we are suffering.
We ought to try this final measure first
And lay our grievances before his ear
Before we take up weapons. Force is always   1320
Monstrous, even when the cause is just.
God only helps when man will help no longer.

STAUFFACHER   (to Konrad Hunn):
Now your report would be in order. Speak.

KONRAD HUNN: I was at Rheinfeld at the Emperor's court

To plead against the Bailiff's harsh oppression
And claim the charter of our ancient freedom
Which every other new King has confirmed.
I found there messengers from many cities,
From Swabia and from along the Rhine,
And all of them received their charters and   1330
Returned with satisfaction to their countries.
But *me,* your delegate, they just referred
To councillors who dismissed me with cold comfort:
"The Emperor had no time just then; but doubtless
He would consider us some other time."
As I was walking sadly through the halls
Of the King's palace I saw Duke John weeping
Where he stood in a window bay, the noble
Lords of Wart and Tegerfeld beside him.
They called to me and said; "God help yourselves!   1340
And do not look for justice from the King.
Has he not robbed his very brother's son
And kept him from his rightful heritage?
The Duke has begged him for his mother's lands,
He said he was of age and it was time
For him to rule his land and people now.
What answer did he get? The Emperor gave him
A wreath to wear,—'the ornament of youth.'"
AUF DER MAUER: You heard what they said. Do not look for
    right
Or justice from the Emperor. Help yourselves.   1350
REDING: We have no further course. Take counsel now
    How we shall guide things to a happy outcome.
WALTER FÜRST   (*steps into the ring*):
    We want to rid ourselves of hated force;
    Our ancient rights as we inherited
    Them from our fathers, we want to preserve,
    Not grab for new ones by illegal means.
    What is the Emperor's, the Emperor keeps,
    And he who has a master, let him serve him.

MEIER: Well, I hold lands in fief from Austria.

WALTER FÜRST: Then you continue serving Austria.   1360

JOST VON WEILER: I pay tax to the lords of Rappersweil.

WALTER FÜRST: Then you continue with your tax and tribute.

RÖSSELMANN: I took oath to Our Lady's Convent in Zürich.

WALTER FÜRST: What is the convent's render to the convent.

STAUFFACHER: I hold no fiefs except those of the Empire.

WALTER FÜRST: What has to be, let it be done, no more.
   We want to drive these Bailiffs out, and all
      Their henchmen too, and smash the fortress castles,
      If possible, with no blood spilled. And let
   The Emperor see that we have cast aside   1370
   Respectful habits only from compulsion.
   If he sees us remaining within bounds,
   He may in wisdom overcome his anger.
   A nation will inspire a just fear if
   With sword in hand it shows its self-control.

REDING: But let us hear *how* this can be accomplished.
   The enemy holds weapons in his hands
   And he will not give way to peaceful means.

STAUFFACHER: He will when he sees we are under arms.
   We'll take him by surprise before he's ready.   1380

MEIER: An easy thing to say, but hard to do.
   Two fortress castles tower in this country.
   They give the enemy a place of safety
   And will prove fearful if the King attacks.
   Rossberg and Sarnen must be overcome
   Before the sword is raised in these three cantons.

STAUFFACHER: If we delay that long, the enemy
   Will be forewarned. Too many share the secret.

MEIER: There are no traitors in the Forest Cantons.

RÖSSELMANN: Zeal too, though well intended, can betray. 1390

WALTER FÜRST: Postpone it, and the fortress will be finished
   In Altorf, and the Bailiff will gain strength.

MEIER: You're thinking of yourselves.

THE SEXTON: And you are quite

Unjust.

MEIER   *(flaring up)*:
    Unjust! Must we hear that from Uri!

REDING: Peace! By your oaths!

MEIER: If Schwyz and Uri have
    An understanding, *we* are forced to silence.

REDING: In face of this assembly I must warn you
    Your show of temper here disturbs the peace!
    Do we not all stand here in the same cause?

WINKELRIED: If we postpone the matter until Christmas,   1400
    There is a custom by which all the tenants
    Bring gifts up to the castle for the Bailiff.
    In that way ten or twelve men can assemble
    Inside the palace unsuspected and
    Take sharp-edged weapons with them secretly
    Which can be quickly fixed in staffs for handles,
    For no one comes with weapons to the castle.
    The main force will be waiting close by in
    The woods, and when the others seize the gate,
    Some one will blow a horn and they will rush   1410
    Out of their hiding place. In such a way
    The castle will be ours with little effort.

MELCHTAL: The Rossberg I will undertake to scale.
    Inside the castle there's a girl that likes me
    And I can easily get her to let
    Rope ladders down to me for a night visit.
    Once there, I'll pull my friends up after me.

REDING: Does everyone agree to the postponement?

(The majority raise their hands.)

STAUFFACHER *(counts the votes)*:
    It is a twenty to twelve majority.

WALTER FÜRST: If on the given day the castles fall,   1420
    We'll send smoke signals up from mountain top
    To mountain top; the People's Levy will
    Be swiftly summoned to the capital.

Then when the Bailiffs see the threat of arms.
Believe me, they will soon give up the struggle
And will be glad to take safe-conduct offers
To get beyond the borders of the country.

STAUFFACHER: From Gessler, though, I fear some stiff
   resistance;
He is surrounded fearfully with troopers;
He won't give in without blood shed; and even   1430
In exile he will be a terror to us.
It's hard and almost dangerous to spare him.

BAUMGARTEN: Where there is mortal danger, let *me* go!
I owe the saving of my life to Tell
And I will gladly risk it for the country.
I've made my honor safe and satisfied
My heart.

REDING: Things will be solved with time. Be patient.
Some things must be entrusted to the moment.
—But see, while we have gone on talking here
By night, the morning on the highest peaks   1440
Has posted glowing sentinels.—Come, let
Us go before day's brightness overtakes us.

WALTER FÜRST: Have no fears, night yields slowly from these
   valleys.

(Involuntarily they have all removed
their hats and are gazing at the dawn in
silent contemplation.)

RÖSSELMANN: By this light which gives us its greeting first
Of all the peoples who dwell down below us
With heavy breathing in the fume of cities,
Let us pronounce the oath of this new league.
We mean to be a single folk of brothers
Inseparable in peril or distress.

(They all repeat the words after him
with three fingers raised.)

We mean to be free as our fathers were
And sooner go to death than live in bondage.

(*As before.*)

We mean to have faith in Almighty God
And not to be afraid of human might.

(*As before. The countrymen embrace
one another.*)

STAUFFACHER: Let every man now go his way in silence
Back to his friends and fellow citizens.
All who are herdsmen, winter herds in peace
And quietly enlist friends for the cause.
Whatever must yet be endured till then,
Endure it. Let the tyrants' reckoning
Increase until a single day will settle   1460
Both general and private debts at once.
Let every man restrain his righteous rage
And spare his venegeance for the common weal,
For it is theft from all and pilferage
When one man helps himself in private zeal.   [1465]

(*As they leave in perfect calm in three different
directions, the orchestra strikes up an imposing
strain. For a time the stage remains open to the
view and displays the spectacle of the sunrise over
the ice-capped mountain peaks.*)

ACT III

SCENE 1

The yard in front of Tell's house.

[Ten days later: November 18, 1307.]

Tell is busy with a carpenter's ax, Hedwig with some household task. Walter and Wilhelm are playing at the rear with a small crossbow.

WALTER   (*sings*):

> Crossbow-armed and steady,
> Down his mountain way
> Comes the archer, ready
> At the dawn's first ray.
>
> As in airy spaces   1470
> Hawk and kite are kings,
> Over mountain places
> Archers rule all things.
>
> All out-doors is his,
> As his arrow leaps;
> There his quarry is
> All that flies and creeps.

(*He comes skipping up.*)

My bowstring snapped in two. Please fix it, Father.
TELL: Not I. A proper huntsman helps himself.

(*The boys go away.*)

HEDWIG: The boys are learning early how to shoot.   1480
TELL: It's early practicing that makes the master.

57

HEDWIG: Ah, would to God they never learned!

TELL: They must learn everything. Whoever means
  To make his way through life must be prepared
  For thrust and parry.

HEDWIG: No one ever will
  Find peace at home.

TELL: Well, Mother, I can't either.
  Nature did not intend me for a herdsman,
  And restless, I pursue a fleeting goal.
  I do not honestly enjoy my life
  Unless I conquer it anew each day.   1490

HEDWIG: And you give no thought to the woman's anguish
  Who meanwhile waits for you and grieves and worries.
  A shuddering comes over me at what
  The servants tell about your feats of daring.
  At each farewell my heart is seized with trembling
  For fear you never will come back again.
  I see you lost up on the savage glacier,
  Or making a false leap from one cliff to
  The other; I see the chamois jumping back
  And dragging you into the chasms with them,   1500
  Or avalanches burying you deep,
  As underneath your foot the treacherous snow
  Gives way and you go down into a living
  Grave deep in the horrible crevasse.
  Death has a hundred changing forms in which
  He catches rash and daring Alpine huntsmen!
  It is a sorry trade that makes men risk
  Their lives along the brink of the abyss.

TELL: A man that has sharp eyes and healthy senses
  And trusts in God and his own nimble strength   1510
  Will easily get out of any danger.
  The mountains do not scare men born among them.

*(He has finished his work and lays
his tools aside.)*

I think this gate will hold for years to come.
An ax at home saves you the carpenter.

(He takes his hat.)

HEDWIG: Where are you going?
TELL: To Altorf, to your father's.
HEDWIG: You're planning nothing dangerous? Confess.
TELL: What makes you think that, Wife?
HEDWIG: There's something brewing
    Against the Bailiffs. There was some assembly
    Held at the Rütli. You are in it too.
TELL: I wasn't present at it—but I will   1520
    Not fail my country when it calls.
HEDWIG: They'll give
    You an assignment where the danger is.
    Your share as usual will be the hardest.
TELL: Each man will be assessed as he is able.
HEDWIG: You also took that man across the lake
    During the storm. It was a miracle
    That you escaped. You didn't think at all
    Of child and wife.
TELL: Dear wife, I thought of you;
    That's why I saved the father for his children.
HEDWIG: To think of sailing on that raging lake!   1530
    Why, that's not trusting God! That's tempting God!
TELL: Those who reflect too much accomplish little.
HEDWIG: Yes, you are good and you help everyone,
    And when you are in need yourself no one
    Will help you.
TELL: God keep me from needing help!

(He picks up his crossbow and arrows.)

HEDWIG: Why need you take your crossbow? Leave it here.
TELL: Without a weapon I'm without an arm.

(The boys come back.)

WALTER: Where are you going, Father?
TELL: To Altorf, Boy,
   To Grandpa's. Want to come along?
WALTER: Oh yes!
HEDWIG: The Bailiff is there now. Stay out of Altorf.   1540
TELL: He *leaves* today.
HEDWIG: Then wait till he is gone.
   He has a grudge against us: don't remind him.
TELL: His ill will isn't going to harm me any.
   I do right and fear no enemy.
HEDWIG: Those who do right are those he hates the most.
TELL: Because he can't get at them. I suspect
   The knight will probably leave me alone.
HEDWIG: Do you know that for sure?
TELL: Some time ago
   I was out hunting in the wild ravines
   Of the deserted Schächen River valley,   1550
   And just as I was climbing up a trail
   Among the rocks where two men could not pass,
   For over me the wall of cliff hung sheer
   And down below the Schächen fiercely roared,

            (*The boys press close on either
            side of him and look at him with
                  intense curiosity.*)

   There was the Bailiff coming toward me all
   Alone, and I was also there alone,
   Just man to man, and with the gorge beneath us,
   And when the gentleman caught sight of me
   And saw it was the man he recently
   Had harshly punished for some slight infraction,   1560
   And saw me coming forward carrying
   This splendid weapon with me, he turned pale,
   His knees began to shake, and I could see
   That he was going to fall against the cliffside.
   —Then I felt sorry for him, I went up

Respectfully and said: It's I, Lord Bailiff.
But not one feeble sound could he bring forth
Out of his mouth. He only motioned with
His hand for me to go along my way.
I did, and sent him up his retinue.   1570
HEDWIG: He has once trembled at you, he will never
   Forgive you for the fact you saw his weakness.
TELL: So I avoid him; nor will he be looking
   For *me.*
HEDWIG: Stay out of there today. Go hunting.
TELL: What are you thinking of?
HEDWIG: I am afraid.
   Don't go.
TELL: How can you worry for no reason?
HEDWIG: *Because* there is no reason—Tell, stay here.
TELL: But, my dear Wife, I promised I would come.
HEDWIG: Go if you must— but leave the boy with me.
WALTER: No Mother, I will go along with Father.   1580
HEDWIG: Walty, do you want to leave your mother?
WALTER: I'll bring you something nice with me from
   Grandpa's.

(*He leaves with his father.*)

WILHELM: Mother, I will stay with you!
HEDWIG   (*embraces him*):   Yes, you
   Are my dear boy and all that I have left!

(*She goes to the gate and gazes after the depart-
ing ones for a long time.*)

SCENE 2

[A short time later.]

A wild and secluded spot in the forest. Misting

waterfalls plunge from the cliffs. Enter Berta in
hunting attire, and directly afterwards, Rudenz.

BERTA: He's following me. At last I can explain.

RUDENZ   *(enters swiftly)*:
My Lady, I find you alone at last.
We are surrounded here by precipices,
I fear no witness in this wilderness;
I must get this long silence off my heart—

BERTA: Are you quite sure the hunting party has   1590
Not followed us?

RUDENZ: They're way out there. It's now
Or never! I must seize this precious moment.
My destiny must be decided, even
If it forever separates me from you.
—O do not arm your kindly glances with
That grim severity! For who am I
To lift up my audacious wish to you?
Fame has not yet pronounced my name; I cannot
Array myself alongside all those knights
That woo you in their glitter and their glory.   1600
A heart of love and loyalty is all
I have—

BERTA   *(solemnly and severely)*:
You talk of love and loyalty
And are disloyal to your closest duties?

                    (Rudenz falls back.)

The slave of Austria who sells out to
The foreigner, oppressor of his people?

RUDENZ: Do I hear this reproach from you, my Lady?
Whom am I seeking on that side but you?

BERTA: You fancy you will find me on the side
Of treason? I would sooner give my hand
To Gessler, to the tyrant's very self,   1610
Than the unnatural son of Switzerland

Who turns himself into his instrument!
RUDENZ: Good Lord, what do I hear!
BERTA: What can be closer
  To a good man than his own people? Are
  There finer duties for a noble heart
  Than to defend the innocent and to
  Protect the rights of those who are oppressed?
  My soul is bleeding for your people's sake,
  I suffer *with* them, for I love them dearly:
  They are so modest, yet so full of strength.   1620
  My heart is wholly drawn to them and I
  Come to respect them more with every day.
  But you, by Nature and chivalric duty
  Born to be their defender, and who now
  Desert them, faithlessly go over to
  The enemy, and forge chains for your country,
  You are the one who hurts me and offends me.
  I force my heart to keep from hating you.
RUDENZ: Do I not seek what is best for my people?
  To give them peace beneath the mighty scepter   1630
  Of Austria—
BERTA: You give them servitude!
  You are expelling Freedom from the last
  Stronghold that still remains to her on earth.
  The people judge their happiness more wisely.
  No false appearances mislead their feelings.
  O they have cast a net about your head—
RUDENZ: Berta! You hate me, you despise me!
BERTA: If
  I did, it would be better for me. But
  To *see* the man despised and despicable
  Whom I would like to love—
RUDENZ: O Berta! Berta!   1640
  You show me the supreme delight of heaven
  And cast me down at one and the same moment.

BERTA: No, what is noble in you is not stifled
   Entirely! It is only sleeping; I
   Shall wake it. You must practice violence
   Against yourself to kill your innate virtue;
   But it is stronger, fortunately, than you,
   Despite yourself you are still good and noble.
RUDENZ: Then you believe in me? O Berta, your
   Love can make me be anything at all!   1650
BERTA: Then be what glorious Nature made you! Fill
   The place where she has stationed you on earth,
   Stand with your people and your country, and
   Fight for your sacred right.
RUDENZ: Alas for me!
   How can I ever win you or possess you
   If I rebel against the Emperor's power?
   Does not your relatives' despotic will
   Control the disposition of your hand?
BERTA: But my estates are in the Forest Cantons,
   And if the Swiss are free, I too am free.   1660
RUDENZ: Berta, what a prospect you have opened!
BERTA: Through Austria's favor do not hope to win me.
   Their hands are stretched toward my inheritance
   To merge it with their own inheritance.
   That greed for land which is now seeking to
   Devour your freedom threatens mine as well.
   O Friend, I have been destined as a victim,
   Perhaps to be some favorite's reward.
   They want to drag me to the Emperor's court,
   Where treachery lives side by side with plots.   1670
   Detested marriage chains await me there,
   And only love—your love can rescue me!
RUDENZ: You could resolve your mind to living here
   And being mine in my own fatherland?
   O Berta, all my yearning for the world,
   What was it but a striving after you?

I sought you only on the path of fame,
All my ambition was nothing but love.
If you can shut yourself in this still valley
And there renounce the glory of the world—   1680
Then I have found the goal of all my striving.
Then let the stream of the tempestuous world
Beat on the steadfast shore of these great mountains,
I have no further fugitive desire
To cast abroad into life's distances.
Then let these precipices here around us
Spread out a firm, impenetrable wall
And let this closed and blessed valley only
Be open to the heavens and have light.

BERTA: Now you are wholly as my dreaming heart   1690
   Imagined you, my faith has not deceived me.

RUDENZ: Farewell, you vain illusion that deceived me!
   I shall find happiness in my own fatherland.
   Here where the boy grew up in happiness,
   By memories of a thousand joys surrounded,
   Where for me stream and tree in life abounded,
   You will be mine in my own homeland sweet.
   Oh, I have always loved it! And without it
   All happiness on earth was incomplete.

BERTA: Where would the Islands of the Blessed be   1700
   If not here in this land of innocence?
   Here where the old fidelity still dwells,
   Where guile has not yet found an entrance way,
   No envy will roil happiness's fountain
   And hours forever bright will fly away.
   There I will see *you* in true manhood's worth,
   Revered with honest homage unconstrained
   As first among free men of equal birth
   And great as any king that ever reigned.

RUDENZ: There I will see you crown of womanhood,   1710
   By charming feminine activity

Creating in my house the realms of good,
And like the springtime's blossoms, bountifully
Adorning my whole life with lovely grace
And making all things live in every place.
BERTA: Beloved Friend, you see why I was sad
At seeing you destroy this happiness
Of life yourself.—Alas, where would I be
If I were forced to follow that proud knight,
The country's despot, to his dismal castle!   1720
There is no castle here. No walls divide
Me from a people whom I can make happy.
RUDENZ: But how can I escape, how slip the snare
That I have placed upon my head in folly?
BERTA: Tear it to pieces with a manly will!
Let come of it what may: stand by your people!
It is your rightful place.

(*Hunting horns in the distance.*)

                    The hunting party
Is coming closer. We must part. Fight for
Your fatherland, and you fight for your love!
There is one enemy whom we all dread,   1730
One freedom gives us all our liberty!

(*Exeunt.*)

SCENE 3

A meadow near Altorf.

[Early afternoon of the same day.]

*In the foreground there are trees, at the rear
is the hat on a pole. The prospect is closed by the
Bannberg, over which a snowcapped mountain
towers.*

Hardheart and Folklove are standing guard.

HARDHEART: Our guard is all for nothing. No one will
  Come near to do the hat obeisance.
  It used to be just like a country fair,
  And now the meadow is almost deserted
  Since that scarecrow has been on that pole.
FOLKLOVE: Nothing but riff-raff turns up any more,
  They swing their tattered caps just to annoy us.
  The decent people all prefer to make
  A detour half way round the village rather   1740
  Than have to bend their backs before the hat.
HARDHEART: But they will have to come this way when they
  Come from the City Hall around the noon-hour.
  I thought I'd made a catch the other day.
  No one remembered to salute the hat.
  Just then the priest, that Rösselmann, came by
  On his way from a sick call—and he went
  And held the Host right there beside the pole.
  The sexton had to ring the little bell,
  And they all genuflected—I did too—   1750
  Saluting thus the monstrance, not the hat.
FOLKLOVE: I get the feeling, Friend, that we are standing
  Here in the pillory before this hat.
  It's after all an insult for a trooper
  To mount guard here before an empty hat
  And any honest fellow must despise us.
  To do obeisance to just a hat,
  That is, you must admit, a silly order.
HARDHEART: Why not before an empty, hollow hat?
  You bend as much to lots of hollow skulls.   1760

  (*Enter Hildegard, Mechtild, and Elsbeth with
  children and stand around the pole.*)

FOLKLOVE: You're just the kind of fawning rascal, too,
  To get the honest people into trouble.

Let anyone that wants to, pass this hat,
I shut my eyes and don't see anything.
MECHTILD: There hangs the Bailiff—Show respect, you boys!
ELSBETH: I wish to God he'd go and leave his hat
Behind; the country would be no worse off!
HARDHEART   (chases them away):
Will you clear out! Accursed womenfolk!
Who sent for you now? Send your husbands over
If they feel like defying the command.   1770

(The women leave.)

(Enter Tell with his crossbow, leading the boy
by the hand. They pass downstage in front of the
hat without paying any attention to it.)

WALTER   (points to the Bannberg):
Father, is it true that on that mountain
The trees will bleed if anybody hits
Them with an ax?
TELL: Who says they do that, Boy?
WALTER: The master herdsman says they do. He says
The trees are banned by magic and a person
That does them harm, his hand will grow out of
His grave.
TELL: The trees are banned, that much is so.
You see those glaciers there, those icy peaks
That disappear into the sky?
WALTER: Those glaciers?
They are the ones that thunder so at night   1780
And send the heavy avalanches down.
TELL: That's right. Those avalanches would have buried
The town of Altorf long ago beneath
Their weight without that forest over there
To stand up as a kind of bulwark for us.
WALTER   (after some thought):
Father, are there countries with no mountains?

TELL: If you go down out of these mountains here
  And keep on going, following the streams,
  You will come to a large and level land
  Where forest rivers no more toss their foam   1790
  And where the streams run leisurely and quiet;
  There you can see all over heaven's dome,
  The grain grows there in fair fields manifold,
  The country is a garden to behold.
WALTER: Well, Father, why don't we go down there quickly,
  Down where that country is so beautiful
  Instead of living here in toil and trouble?
TELL: The country is as beautiful as heaven,
  But those that till it, *they* do not enjoy
  The fruits of what they sow.
WALTER: But don't they live   1800
  As free as you do on their patrimony?
TELL: The fields belong to bishops and to Kings.
WALTER: But they can surely hunt free in the forests?
TELL: The game and fowl belong to overlords.
WALTER: But they can surely fish free in the streams?
TELL: The streams, the sea, the salt, are all the King's.
WALTER: Who is the King that everybody fears?
TELL: He is the one who feeds them and protects them.
WALTER: Then they aren't able to protect themselves?
TELL: Down there no neighbor dares to trust his
    neighbors.   1810
WALTER: Father, I feel too close in that wide land.
  I'd rather live among the avalanches.
TELL: Yes, it is better, Child, with avalanches
  Behind your back than with such wicked people.

(They start to pass on.)

WALTER: Oh, Father, see that hat there on the pole.
TELL: What is the hat to us? Come, let us go.

(As he starts to go, Hardheart
steps toward him with pike lowered.)

HARDHEART: In the Emperor's name! Stop and stand where
   you are!

TELL   (*grabs the pike*):
   What do you want? Why are you stopping me?

HARDHEART: You violate the mandate. Come with us.

FOLKLOVE: You did not do obeisance to the hat.   1820

TELL: Friend, let me go.

HARDHEART: Come, off with you to prison!

WALTER: No, you can't put my father into prison!
   Help! Help!

(calling offstage)

Come here, you men! Good people, help!
Help! Help! They're going to put him into prison.

*(Enter Rösselmann the priest and
Petermann the sexton with three other men.)*

SEXTON: What is it?

RÖSSELMANN: Why should you arrest this man?

HARDHEART: He is the Emperor's enemy, a traitor!

TELL   (*seizes him violently*):
   A traitor, I!

RÖSSELMANN: You are mistaken, Friend.
   Why, this is Tell, an upright citizen.

WALTER   (*catches sight of Walter Fürst and hurries toward
   him*):
   Grandfather, help! They're going to take my father.

HARDHEART: To prison, off with you!

WALTER FÜRST   (*hurrying up*):   Stop! I will be   1830
   Security for him!—In God's name, Tell,
   What happened?

(Enter Melchtal and Stauffacher.)

HARDHEART: He disdains the Bailiff's sovereign
   Authority and will not recognize it.

STAUFFACHER: Could Tell do such a thing?
MELCHTAL: You lie, you rascal!
FOLKLOVE: He did not do the hat obeisance.
WALTER FÜRST: And he should go to prison just for that?
  Friend, take my guarantee and let him go.
HARDHEART: You guarantee yourself and your own person!
  We're doing as we're told. Take him away!
MELCHTAL   (to the countrymen):
  This is an outrage! Are we going to stand for it   1840
  And let them take him off before our eyes?
THE SEXTON: We are the stronger. Friends, don't stand for it!
  We have one back against another here.
HARDHEART: Who is resisting orders from the Bailiff?
THREE MORE COUNTRYMEN   (hurrying up):
  We'll help you. What's going on? Let's knock them down.

(Reenter Hildegard, Mechtild, and
Elsbeth.)

TELL: I'll help myself. Just go along, good people.
  Do you think, if I wanted to use force,
  That I would be afraid before their pikes?
MELCHTAL   (to Hardheart):
  Just try to take this man out of our midst!
WALTER FÜRST AND
    STAUFFACHER: Be quiet! Still!
HARDHEART   (shouting):   Rebellion and revolt!   1850
THE WOMEN: Here comes the Bailiff!
HARDHEART   (raises his voice): Mutiny! Revolt!
STAUFFACHER: Shout so you burst, you rascal!
RÖSSELMANN AND MELCHTAL: Shut your mouth!
HARDHEART   (shouts louder still):
  Help! Help! Help for the servants of the law!
WALTER FÜRST: Here is the Bailiff! What will happen to us!

(Enter Gessler on horseback with his falcon on
his wrist, Rudolf the Equerry, Berta and Rudenz,

and a large retinue of armed servants who form
a ring of pikes around the entire stage.)

RUDOLF THE EQUERRY: Make way there for the Bailiff!
GESSLER: Scatter them!
Why all this crowd of people? Who cries help?

(General silence.)

Who was it? I want to know.

(to Hardheart)

                         You there, step forward!
Who are you, and why have you seized this man?

(He hands the falcon to a servant.)

HARDHEART: Most gracious Lord, I am your man-at-arms
And your appointed guard here by the hat.   1860
I caught this man right in the act of failing
To do obeisance before the hat.
I started to arrest him as you ordered,
And these folks want to stop me now by force.
GESSLER *(after a pause)*:
Do you disdain your Emperor so greatly,
Then, Tell, and me, who rule here in his stead,
That you refuse the honors to the hat
Which I hung up to test obedience?
You have betrayed your evil purposes.
TELL: Forgive me, Sir. It was from thoughtlessness   1870
I did so, not from disrespect for you.
My name would not be Tell if I were cautious.
I beg your pardon. It won't occur again.
GESSLER *(after a silence)*:
You are a master at the crossbow, Tell.
They say you will compete with any archer?
WALTER TELL: And that's the truth, Sir. He can shoot an
    apple

Out of a tree a hundred paces off.

GESSLER: Is that your boy there, Tell?

TELL: Yes, gracious Lord.

GESSLER: Do you have other children?

TELL: Two boys, Sir.

GESSLER: And which one is it that you love the most?   1880

TELL: Sir, I love both my children equally.

GESSLER: Well, Tell, since you can shoot an apple from
   The tree a hundred paces off, you shall
   Put your skill to the test.—So take your crossbow—
   You have it right there with you—and prepare
   To shoot an apple off from your boy's head.
   But I advise you to aim well so that
   You hit the apple with a single shot,
   For if you miss it your own head is lost.

(Everyone shows signs of horror.)

TELL: Sir—what atrocious thing are you requiring   1890
   Of me?—An apple from my own child's head—
   Oh no, no, gracious Lord, that can't be what
   You mean—Merciful God forbid!—You cannot
   Ask that of any father seriously.

GESSLER: Yes, you will shoot the apple off from that
   Boy's head. That is my order and my will.

TELL: I am supposed to aim my crossbow at
   My own child's much-loved head? I'd rather die!

GESSLER: You will die *with* the boy unless you shoot.

TELL: I am to be my own child's murderer!   1900
   You have no children, Sir, you do not know
   What things go on inside a father's heart.

GESSLER: Why, Tell, you are so cautious suddenly!
   They told me that you were a dreamer and
   Aloof from other people's ways of action.
   You love odd things—That's why I have selected
   Such a unique objective for your daring.

Another man might well be cautious—*you*
Will shut your eyes and do it like a man.

BERTA: Sir, do not push this jest with these poor people. 1910
You see them standing here all pale and trembling—
They are so little used to jests from you.

GESSLER: Who told you I was jesting?

*(He reaches for a branch of the tree
that hangs above him.)*

Here is the apple.
Make room there—let him take his distance as
The custom is—I give him eighty paces,
No less, no more. He boasted that he could
Hit his man from a hundred paces off.
Now, Archer, hit your mark and do not miss.

RUDOLF THE EQUERRY: My God, he means it. Get down on
your knees
There, Boy, and beg the Bailiff for your life. 1920

WALTER FÜRST *(aside to Melchtal, who can hardly control
his impatience)*:
Control yourself, I beg you. Keep your head.

BERTA *(to the Bailiff)*:
Sir, call a halt to this! It is inhuman
To play this way with any father's anguish.
If this poor man should have deserved to die
Because of his slight guilt, by God in heaven,
He has already perished ten times over.
Release him to his hut unharmed. He has
Learned who you are by now. This hour will be
Remembered by him and his children's children.

GESSLER: Open a lane there—Quick, what are you waiting 1930
There for? Your life is forfeit, I can kill you.
You see how in my mercy I have placed
Your fate into your own well-practiced hand.
A man cannot complain of a harsh sentence

When he is made the master of his fate.
You boast of your keen eye. All right! Here is
Your chance now, *Archer*, to display your skill.
The aim is worthy and the prize is large.
A bull's-eye hit is something any man
Can manage; I call Master only one   1940
Who is sure of his skill in any place,
Whose heart is neither in his hand nor eye.

WALTER FÜRST (*throws himself down before him*):
Lord Bailiff, we acknowledge your high power.
But now let mercy pass for justice! Take
The half of my possessions, take them all,
But spare a father from this ghastly thing!

WALTER TELL: Grandfather, do not kneel to that false man!
Just tell me where to stand. I'm not afraid.
Why, Father hits a bird in flight, so he
Won't miss when he aims at his own child's heart.   1950

STAUFFACHER: Lord Bailiff, does this innocence not move you?

RÖSSELMANN: Remember that there is a God in heaven
Whom you must answer to for all your doings.

GESSLER (*points to the boy*):
Tie him to that linden tree.

WALTER TELL: Tie me!
No, I will not be tied. I will hold still
Just like a lamb and I won't even breathe.
But if you tie me, no, then I can't do it,
Then I will surely fight against my bonds.

RUDOLF THE EQUERRY: Just let them put a blindfold on your
eyes, Boy.

WALTER TELL: Why on my eyes? Do you think I'm afraid
of   [1960]
The arrow from my father's hand? I'll face
It firmly and won't even blink my eyes.
Come, Father, show them that you are an archer!
He can't believe it, he thinks he'll destroy us.

To spite the tyrant shoot and hit the mark!

*(He goes over to the linden tree,
where the apple is placed on his head.)*

MELCHTAL   *(to the countrymen)*:
What? Is this outrage to be carried through
Before our eyes? What did we take the oath for?
STAUFFACHER: It is no use. We have no weapons with us.
You see the forest of their pikes around us.
MELCHTAL: O if we only had gone straight to action!   1970
May God forgive those who advised postponement!
GESSLER   *(to Tell)*:
To work now! Weapons are not borne for nothing.
It's dangerous to carry murder-weapons,
The arrow may rebound upon the archer.
This proud right which the peasants have assumed
Offends the sovereign ruler of this country.
None but those in command should carry arms.
If you like wielding arrows and the bow,
Well, I will designate a target for you.
TELL   *(stretches the crossbow and inserts the arrow)*:
Open a lane! Make room!   1980
STAUFFACHER: What, Tell? You mean to—Never! You're
   unsteady,
Your hand is shaking and your knees are trembling—
TELL   *(lets the crossbow sink down)*:
My eyes are dazzling!
WOMEN: O Lord God in heaven!
TELL   *(to the Bailiff)*:
Excuse me from this shot. Here is my heart!

(He tears open his shirt.)

Call to your mounted men and mow me down!
GESSLER: I do not want your life, I want this shot.
There's nothing you can't do, Tell, nothing daunts you;
You steer a boat as well as bend the bow,

No storm dismays you when there's need of rescue.
Now, Savior, help yourself—you have saved others!   1990

> (*Tell stands in ghastly struggle, his hands twitch-*
> *ing and his rolling eyes directed now on the Bailiff,*
> *now toward heaven. Suddenly he reaches into his*
> *quiver, takes out a second arrow, and sticks it into*
> *his doublet. The Bailiff notes all these actions.*)

WALTER TELL   (*under the linden tree*):
Shoot, Father! I'm not afraid.
TELL: It must be done!
RUDENZ   (*who all this time has stood in the greatest suspense*
and kept control of himself by sheer force, now comes for-
ward):
Lord Bailiff, you're not going to press this further,
You surely will *not*—It was just a test—
You have achieved your end—Severity
When pressed too far will miss its own wise goal,
And overtightly stretched, a bow will snap.
GESSLER: You will be silent till you're called.
RUDENZ: I *shall* speak,
I have a right to! I hold the King's honor
Sacred, but such rule as this breeds hatred.
This is not the King's will—that I maintain—   2000
Such cruelty as this my people do not
Deserve. You do not have authority
For this.
GESSLER: Ha! You turn bold!
RUDENZ: I have kept silent
At all these grievous actions I have seen,
I shut my eyes when they saw all too clearly,
My overflowing and indignant heart
I forcibly repressed within my bosom.
But any further silence would be treason.
Both to my fatherland and to the Emperor.
BERTA   (*throws herself between him and Gessler*):

You will provoke this raging madman further.   2010
RUDENZ: My people I abandoned, I forsook
The kindred of my blood, I tore asunder
All bonds of Nature to join you. I thought
That I was furthering the good of all
By strengthening the Emperor's power—but
The blind has fallen from my eyes. With horror
I see I have been led up to the brink
Of an abyss.—You have misled my judgment,
Deceived my upright heart— With all the best
Intentions I was ready to destroy   2020
My people.
GESSLER: Rash man, such talk to your Lord!
RUDENZ: The Emperor is my Lord, not you—I was
Born free as you, and I will pit myself
Against you any day in knightly virtue.
And if you did not stand here for the Emperor,
Whom I revere, though you disgrace him now,
I would throw down my glove before you and
You would by knightly custom answer to me.
Yes, call your mounted men. I do not stand
Defenseless here like *them*—

    (pointing toward the people)

          I have a sword,   2030
If they come near me—
STAUFFACHER *(shouts)*: He has hit the apple!

    While everyone has been looking this way and
    while Berta has thrown herself between Rudenz
    and the Bailiff, Tell has shot his arrow.)

RÖSSELMANN: The boy's alive!
MANY VOICES: And he has hit the apple!

    (Walter Fürst staggers and is about
    to fall. Berta supports him.)

GESSLER   (*amazed*):
  He shot that arrow? What? The man is crazy!
BERTA: The boy's alive! Compose yourself, good Father!
WALTER TELL   (*comes running with the apple*):
  Father, here is the apple. I knew all
  The time that you would not hit your own son.

> (*Tell has stood with his body bent forward as
> if he were trying to follow the arrow; the crossbow
> drops from his hand. As he sees the boy coming he
> runs to meet him with outstretched arms and with
> ardent emotion lifts him to his heart. In this posture
> he collapses unconscious. Everyone stands moved.*)

BERTA: O gracious Heaven!
WALTER FÜRST   (*to father and son*): Children! O my children!
STAUFFACHER: Praise be to God!
FOLKLOVE: That was a shot! It will
  Be talked about until the end of time!
RUDOLF THE EQUERRY: They'll talk of Tell the Archer as
    long as   2040
  These mountains still remain on their foundations.

> (*He hands the Bailiff the apple.*)

GESSLER: By God, the apple is shot through the center!
  It was a master shot, and I must praise it.
RÖSSELMANN: The shot was good. But woe to him that forced
  Him to it, making him tempt God thereby.
STAUFFACHER: Come to your senses, Tell, stand up. You have
  Redeemed yourself and are free to go home.
RÖSSELMANN: Come on, and bring the son back to his mother!

> (*They start to lead him away.*)

GESSLER: Tell, listen!
TELL   (*comes back*): What is your command, my Lord?
GESSLER: You hid a second arrow on your person—Yes,   2050
  I noticed it—What did you mean by that?

TELL   (*embarrassed*):
  That is a sort of custom, Sir, with archers,
GESSLER: No, Tell, I will not let that answer pass.
  There must have been some other meaning to it.
  Now speak the truth quite frankly, Tell. Whatever
  It is, I guarantee your life. What was
  That second arrow for?
TELL: All right, then, Sir,
  Since you have guaranteed my life, I will
  Tell you the truth in its entirety.

> (*He draws the arrow out of his doublet
> and gazes at the Bailiff with a dreadful
> glance.*)

  I would have used this second arrow to—   2060
  Shoot *you*, if I had hit my own dear child,
  And *you*—there would have been no missing there.
GESSLER: Well, Tell, I guaranteed your life for you,
  I gave my knightly word, and I will keep it.
  But since I have perceived your evil thought,
  I'll have you taken and put under guard
  Where neither moon nor sun will shine on you
  So I may be in safety from your arrows.
  Arrest him there, you men, and tie him up!

> (*Tell   is   bound.*)

STAUFFACHER: What, Sir? How can you treat a man this way
  In whom God's hand is clearly manifest?   [2070]
GESSLER: Let's see if it saves him a second time.
  Put him aboard my ship. I'll come at once
  Myself to pilot him across to Küssnacht.
RÖSSELMANN: You seize him and take him out of the
     country?
COUNTRYMEN: You can't do that! The Emperor can't do that!
  That goes against the charters of our freedom!

GESSLER: Where are they? Has the Emperor confirmed them?
No, he has not confirmed them; such a favor
Has to be earned first by obedience.   2080
You all are rebels to the Emperor's courts
And fostering an impudent rebellion.
I know the lot of you, I see right through you.
I'm taking this one from your midst right now,
But all of you are sharers in his guilt.
The wise will learn obedience and silence.

> (*He withdraws. Berta, Rudenz, the Equerry, and
> servants follow him. Hardheart and Folklove re-
> main behind.*)

WALTER FÜRST: It's over now. He has made up his mind
To ruin me and all my family.
STAUFFACHER   (*to Tell*):
Why did you have to rouse the tyrant's fury?
TELL: Let them control themselves who felt my anguish.   2090
STAUFFACHER: Now everything is lost, yes, everything!
And we are all in chains and fetters with you!
COUNTRYMEN   (*gather around Tell*):
With you our last support has given way.
FOLKLOVE   (*comes up*):
Tell, I am sorry—but I must obey.
TELL: Farewell.
WALTER TELL   (*clinging to him with intense sorrow*):

> O Father! Father! Dearest Father!

TELL   (*raises his arms to heaven*):
Up yonder is your Father. Call on Him!
STAUFFACHER: Tell, shall I take your wife some word from you?
TELL   (*lifts the boy with fervor to his bosom*):
The boy is safe. God will look after me.   [2098]

> (*He tears himself away quickly
> and follows the men-at-arms.*)

ACT IV

SCENE 1

The eastern shore of Lake Lucerne. [*The same afternoon.*]

The oddly shaped, steep cliffs in the west close the prospect. The lake is rough; violent rushing and roaring; intermittent flashes of lightning and claps of thunder.

Kunz von Gersau. A Fisherman [Ruodi] and his son.

KUNZ: I saw it with my very eyes, you can
    Believe me. It all happened as I told you.   2100

FISHERMAN: Tell taken as a prisoner to Küssnacht,
    The best man in the land, the bravest arm,
    If we should ever make a stand for freedom!

KUNZ: The Bailiff's taking him across the lake
    Himself. They were just getting on board ship
    When I left Flüelen; but the storm that is
    Now on its way and which compelled me also
    To make a sudden landing on this shore
    May well have forced them to postpone departure.

FISHERMAN: Tell in fetters, in the Bailiff's power!   2110
    O he will bury him far down enough
    So he will never see the light of day!
    For he must fear the righteous vengeance of
    The free man he has grievously offended.

KUNZ: The ex-chief-magistrate, the noble Lord
    Of Attinghausen too, they say, is at
    The point of death.

FISHERMAN: There breaks our hope's last anchor!
   He was the only one who still could raise
   His voice in favor of the people's rights.
KUNZ: The storm is getting worse. Farewell. I'll find   2120
   Some quarters in the town. Departure is
   Impossible today in any case.

                    (*Exit.*)

FISHERMAN: Tell in captivity, the Baron dead!
   Now, Tyranny, lift up your haughty brow,
   Cast all your shame away! The mouth of truth
   Is mute, the seeing eye is blinded, and
   The arm that was to save us is in chains.
THE BOY: It's hailing hard. Come to the cottage, Father.
   It isn't pleasant out here in the open.
FISHERMAN: Rage on, you winds! Descend in flames, you
      lightnings!   [2130]
   You clouds, burst open! Rivers of the sky,
   Pour down and drown the land! Annihilate
   The unborn generations in their seed!
   You raging elements, become our master!
   Come back, you bears, come back you wolves of old
   In this great wilderness! Yours is the land.
   Who wants to live here now without our freedom!
THE BOY: Hark, how the chasm roars and whirlpools bellow.
   The gorge has never raged like this before.
FISHERMAN: To aim at his own child's beloved head,   2140
   Never was father asked to do the like!
   And in wild fury Nature should not rise
   Up in revolt? I would not be surprised
   If these cliffs bent and stooped into the lake,
   Or if those jagged peaks, those icy towers
   Which since Creation Day have never thawed,
   Should melt away and fall from their high ridges,
   If the mountains burst apart, if ancient gorges

Collapsed, and if a second deluge came
That would engulf the dwellings of the living!   2150

(*A bell is heard.*)

THE BOY: You hear? A bell is ringing on the mountain.
Some ship is surely sighted in distress
And they have rung the bell to call to prayer.

(*He climbs up a rise of ground.*)

FISHERMAN: Woe to the vessel that, now underway,
Is rocked and cradled in that fearsome cradle!
Here neither helm nor helmsman can avail,
The storm is master, wind and waves play ball
With human beings. Neither near nor far
Is there a port to give him friendly shelter.
Precipitous and out of reach the crags,   2160
Unpitying and hostile, stare at him,
Displaying to him only hard and stony bosoms.

THE BOY   (*points toward the left*):
Father, a ship! It's coming up from Flüelen.

FISHERMAN: God help those wretched people! If the storm
Once gets engaged within this narrow gorge
It will thrash like a beast of prey that flings
Itself against its cage's iron bars;
Howling, it seeks in vain to find a door,
For precipices close it all around
To wall the narrow passage to the sky.   2170

(*He climbs up the mound.*)

THE BOY: It is the Bailiff's boat from Uri, Father,
I know it by its red deck and its flag.

FISHERMAN: The judgment of the Lord! Yes, that is he,
The Bailiff, travelling there. He sails along
And carries his crew with him on his boat:
The arm of vengeance has been swift to find him,

And now he knows the stronger Lord above him.
These waves will not pay heed to words of his,
Nor will these precipices bow their heads
Before his hat. Give up your praying, Boy,   2180
And do not stay the arm of the Almighty!
THE BOY: I am not praying for the Bailiff but
For Tell, who is also on that boat with him.
FISHERMAN: O blind unreason of the element!
To catch a single guilty man must you
Destroy the boat together with the helmsman!
THE BOY: Look, look, they just had gotten safely past
The Buggisgrat, but the force of the storm
Rebounding now off of the Teufelsmünster
Is hurling them back toward the Axenberg.   2190
I can't see them now.
FISHERMAN: There stands the Hackmesser
Where more than one ship has already foundered.
If they're not pretty cautious steering past it
Their boat will smash to pieces on the spur
That juts out steeply there into the depths.
They have an able helmsman on board with them;
If anyone can save them it is Tell,
But they have put his arms and hands in fetters.

> (Enter William Tell with his crossbow. He
> comes with rapid steps, glances around in amaze-
> ment, and displays the most vehement agitation.
> As he reaches the middle of the stage, he throws
> himself down, touching the earth with his hands
> and then spreading them aloft toward heaven.)

THE BOY   (notices him):
Look, Father! Who is that man kneeling there?
FISHERMAN: He clutches at the earth with both his hands 2200
And seems to be beside himself.
THE BOY   (comes forward):

What do I see! Come, Father, come and look!

FISHERMAN   (*approaches*):

Who is it?—God in heaven! Why, it's Tell!
How did you get here? Tell me!

THE BOY: Were you not
A captive on that boat and bound in chains?

FISHERMAN: Were they not taking you away to Küssnacht?

TELL   (*rises*):

I was set free.

FISHERMAN AND THE BOY: Set free? A miracle!

THE BOY: Where do you come from?

TELL: From that boat there.

FISHERMAN: What!

THE BOY   (*simultaneously*):

Where is the Bailiff?

TELL: Drifting on the waves.

FISHERMAN: Can it be possible? But how did *you* get here? 2210
Did you escape your fetters *and* the storm?

TELL: By God's own blessed providence. Now hear me.

FISHERMAN AND THE BOY: O speak, speak!

TELL: You already know what happened
In Altorf?

FISHERMAN: I know all about that. Speak!

TELL: Of how the Bailiff had me seized and bound
And tried to take me to his Küssnacht fortress?

FISHERMAN: And boarded ship with you at Flüelen.
We know all that. But how did you escape?

TELL: I lay there in the boat bound fast in chains,
Defenseless, a lost man, without a hope   2220
Of seeing the sun's cheerful light again,
Or the dear faces of my wife and children,
And sadly gazed across the waste of waters—

FISHERMAN: Poor man!

TELL: And we were sailing on, the Bailiff,
Rudolf the Equerry, and the attendants.

But both my quiver and my crossbow lay
Down by the stern next to the pilot's rudder.
Then, just as we came opposite the point
Of Little Axen, God ordained it so
That such a viciously destructive storm   2230
Burst forth abruptly from the Gotthard chasms
That all the oarsmen thought with sinking hearts
That drowning was to be their wretched fate.
And then I heard one of the men turn toward
The Bailiff and address these words to him:
"Sir, you can see your plight and ours as well,
And how we hover on the brink of death.
The pilots are at their wits' end, however,
From the excess of terror and they are
Not skilled at sailing. But a strong man is   2240
This Tell, and he knows how to steer a boat.
How would it do to use him in our need?"
And then the Bailiff said to me: "Tell, if
You ventured to help us escape this storm,
I might consent to free you from your fetters."
And I replied: "Sir, with God's help, I will
Assume the task of getting us away."
I was relieved then of my chains and went
Up to the helm and stoutly steered the course.
I cast a sideward glance at where my weapons   2250
Were lying and kept sharp eyes on the coast
Where there might be a chance for my escape.
And when I spied a shelf of rock that came
Down level where it thrust into the lake—
FISHERMAN: I know it,—at the foot of the Great Axen,
   But I can't think it's possible—It rises
   Too steep—to reach it from a boat by jumping.
TELL: I shouted to the men to strain their oars
   Till we got opposite that shelf of rock;
   By then, I cried, the worst part would be over.   2260

And then as, briskly rowing, we got there,
I prayed for God's high mercy and I pressed
With all my might and main against the tiller
And swung the stern around and toward the cliffside.
Then quickly seizing up my weapons, I
Jumped out and flung myself upon the ledge
While with a mighty kick I shoved the boat
Back out into the chasm of the waters—
There let it pitch, as God wills, on the waves!
And here I am, delivered from the storm's   2270
Abuse and from the worse abuse of men.

FISHERMAN: Tell! Tell! The Lord has wrought a miracle
Upon you. I can hardly trust my senses.
But tell me, where do you intend to go
Now? For there is no safety for you if
The Bailiff comes out of this storm alive.

TELL: While I was still in fetters on his boat
I heard him say he meant to land at Brunnen
And take me to his fortress by the way
Of Schwyz.

FISHERMAN: Then he will travel overland?   2280

TELL: He plans to.

FISHERMAN: Hide yourself without delay!
God will not rescue you from his hands twice.

TELL: Tell me the nearest way to Arth and Küssnacht.

FISHERMAN: The open highway runs by way of Steinen,
But there's a shorter road and more concealed
My boy can take you by the way of Lowerz.

TELL (gives him his hand):
May God repay your kindly deed. Farewell.

(He leaves and comes back again.)

Weren't you one of the Rütli oath-men too?
It seems to me they named you.

FISHERMAN: I was there

And did pledge my allegiance to the League.   2290
TELL: Then be so kind and hurry down to Bürglen,—
My wife despairs of me,—and tell her that
I have escaped and that I am well hidden.
FISHERMAN: But where shall I tell her that you have fled?
TELL: You'll find my father-in-law there with her too,
And others who swore their oaths at the Rütli.
Bid them have courage and be of good cheer:
Tell is now free and master of his weapon;
They presently will hear more word of me.
FISHERMAN: What do you have in mind? Tell me quite
frankly.   [2300]
TELL: Once it is *done* it will be talked about.

(Exit.)

FISHERMAN: Show him the way, Jenni. May God be with him!
He'll carry out whatever he sets out to do.

(Exit.)

SCENE 2

The baronial hall at Attinghausen.

*The Baron is in an armchair, dying. Walter
Fürst, Stauffacher, Melchtal, and Baumgarten are
busy around him. Walter Tell is kneeling in front
of the dying man.*

WALTER FÜRST: It is all over with him, he is gone.
STAUFFACHER: He does not lie there like a dead man. See,
Upon his lips the feather stirs! His sleep
Is quiet and his features gently smile.

*(Baumgarten goes to the door and
speaks with someone.)*

WALTER FÜRST   (to Baumgarten):
   Who is it?
BAUMGARTEN   (comes back): It's your daughter, Lady Hedwig.
   She wants to speak to you and see the boy.

   ·   (Walter Tell gets up.)

WALTER FÜRST: How can I comfort her? Do I have comfort 2310
   Myself? Is all grief heaped upon my head?
HEDWIG   (forcing her way in):
   Where is my child? Let me, I must see him—
STAUFFACHER: Control yourself! This is a house of death—
HEDWIG   (rushes to the boy):
   My Walty! O, he is alive!
WALTER TELL   (clings to her): Poor Mother!
HEDWIG: Can it be really true? You are unharmed?

   (She examines him with anxious care.)

   Can it be possible he aimed at you?
   How could he? O, he has no heart—he could
   Despatch the arrow at his very child!
WALTER FÜRST: He did so with grief-stricken soul, with anguish.
   He had to do it. His life was at stake.   2320
HEDWIG: If he had had a father's heart before
   He did it, he would have preferred to die
   A thousand times!
STAUFFACHER: You should give praise to God
   Whose mercy so disposed—
HEDWIG: Can I forget
   How it might have turned out? Good Lord in heaven!
   If I live eighty years I still will see the boy
   Standing there tied, his father aiming at him,
   And still that arrow flying toward my heart.
MELCHTAL: If you knew how the Bailiff goaded him!
HEDWIG: O, the hard hearts of men! When once their pride 2330
   Is hurt, they care for nothing any more.

In the blind rage of sport they risk their own
Child's head and the heart of the mother too!

BAUMGARTEN: O, is your husband's lot not hard enough
Without your hurting him with harsh reproach?
Have you no feeling for *his* sufferings?

HEDWIG (*turns toward him and faces him squarely*):
Are tears the most that you can offer for
A friend's misfortune?—Where were you when they
Put that good man in chains? Where was your help?
You just looked on and let the infamy be done.   2340
And you permitted them to take your friend
Out of your midst. When did Tell ever act
In such a way toward you? Did he just stand
Commiserating when the Bailiff's horsemen
Were after you and when the raging lake
Roared there before you? Not with idle tears
Did he bemoan your state; he leaped into
The boat, forgot his wife and child, and saved you—

WALTER FÜRST: What could we have done to rescue him
When we were few in numbers and unarmed!   2350

HEDWIG (*throws herself upon his bosom*):
O Father! You have lost him too! The country,
And all of us have lost him! We all feel
The lack of him, and he the lack of us.
May God preserve his soul from sheer despair.
No consolation of his friends can reach
His dismal dungeon. What if he fell ill?
Down in that prison's musty darkness he
Will surely sicken. Like the Alpine rose
That fades and withers in the air of swamps,
There is no life for him except in sunlight   2360
And in the aromatic stream of air.
In prison! He! His very breath is freedom,
The dungeon's reek is more than he can bear.

STAUFFACHER: Compose yourself. We all intend to work

To open up his prison doors.

HEDWIG: What can *you* do without him? Just as long
As Tell was free, yes, then there was still hope.
Then Innocence still had a friend and there
Was still a helper for the persecuted.
Tell rescued all of you—yet all of you   2370
Together could not strike *his* fetters off!

(The Baron wakes.)

BAUMGARTEN: He stirs. Be still.

ATTINGHAUSEN *(sitting upright)*: Where is he?

STAUFFACHER: Who?

ATTINGHAUSEN: I need him,
And he deserts me in this final moment.

STAUFFACHER: He means the squire. Have they sent out for
him?

WALTER FÜRST: He has been sent for. And you may take
comfort,
For he has found his heart, he stands with us.

ATTINGHAUSEN: Has he declared then for his fatherland?

STAUFFACHER: With heroism.

ATTINGHAUSEN: Why does he not come
So that he may receive my final blessing?
I feel my end approaching swiftly now.   2380

STAUFFACHER: O noble Sir, that is not so! This brief
Sleep has refreshed you and your eye is clear.

ATTINGHAUSEN: Pain is a sign of life, and it has left me.
My sufferings are over, like my hope.

(He notices the boy.)

Who is the boy?

WALTER FÜRST: Give him your blessing, Sir.
He is my grandson and he has no father.

*(Hedwig kneels down with the boy in
front of the dying man.)*

ATTINGHAUSEN: And I must leave you all, all fatherless
  Behind. Alas for me that my last gaze
  Has seen the ruin of the fatherland.
  Have I attained life's fullest measure only   2390
  To perish utterly with all my hopes?
STAUFFACHER   (to Walter Fürst):
  Is he to die amid this gloomy sorrow?
  Shall we not brighten up this final hour
  With some fair ray of hope?—O noble Baron,
  Lift up your spirits! We are not entirely
  Abandoned, we are not lost utterly.
ATTINGHAUSEN: Who is to save you?
WALTER FÜRST: We will save ourselves.
  Listen to what I tell you: the three cantons
  Have pledged their word to drive the tyrants out.
  The compact has been sealed; a sacred oath   2400
  Binds us together. Action will be taken
  Before the year begins another cycle.
  Your dust will have its rest in a free country.
ATTINGHAUSEN: What do you say! The compact has been sealed?
MELCHTAL: On the appointed day the forest cantons
  Will all three rise. To that end everything
  Is ready, and the secret is well kept
  Till now, though hundreds share in it.
  Hollow is the ground beneath these tyrants.
  The days of their dominion have been counted   2410
  And soon no more trace of them will be found.
ATTINGHAUSEN: What of the fortresses among the cantons?
MELCHTAL: They all will fall on the appointed day.
ATTINGHAUSEN: And do the nobles share in this alliance?
STAUFFACHER: We look for their assistance when the time comes,
  But only peasants have sworn up to now.
ATTINGHAUSEN: (rises slowly to his feet in great astonishment):
  If peasants have dared such a thing as that,
  With their own means, with no help from the nobles,

If they put so much faith in their own strength,—
Why, then there is no further need of ours.   2420
We can descend in comfort to our graves.
The splendor of mankind lives after us
And is sustained by other strength than ours.

*(He lays his hand on the head of the boy who is
kneeling in front of him.)*

Upon this head where once the apple lay
Will bloom for you a new and better freedom.
The old goes down, the times are changed about,
And new life comes to flower in the ruins.

STAUFFACHER   *(to Walter Fürst)*:
See what a radiance shines in his eyes!
That is not the extinction of mere Nature,
That is the ray of light from a new life.   2430

ATTINGHAUSEN: The nobles come down from their ancient castles
And swear their civic oaths unto the cities.
It has begun in Üchtland and in Thurgau,
And noble Bern lifts up its ruling head,
The free have a safe citadel in Freiburg,
And lively Zürich arms its guilds to form
A warrior host; and there the might of kings
Will break against her everlasting walls—

*(He speaks the following in the tone of a seer; his
speech rises to inspiration.)*

I see the Princes and the noble lords
Approaching in their armor to make war   2440
Against an inoffensive folk of herdsmen.
The struggle will be unto death, and many
A pass will be made glorious by bloody
Decision. With bare breast the peasant will
Fall a free martyr in the host of lances,
But he will break them, and the flower of nobles

Will fall, and freedom lift victorious banners.

(seizing Walter Fürst's and Stauffacher's hands)

Therefore stand firm together—inseparable—
Let no free place be alien to another—
Set beacon fires a-top your mountains so   2450
That league with league may swiftly be assembled—
Be one—Be one—Be one—

(He falls back upon the pillow—His hands even in
death still hold the others clasped. Fürst and Stauffacher go on gazing at him for a time in silence,
then they step away, each one given over to his own
sorrow. Meanwhile servants have entered quietly
and approach with signs of a more silent or of a
more agitated grief; some kneel beside him and
weep over his hand. During this mute scene the
castle bell is tolled.)

(Enter Rudenz swiftly.)

RUDENZ: Is he alive yet? Can he hear me still?
WALTER FÜRST: (motions and averts his face):
   You are our liege-lord now and our protector,
   And now this castle has a different name.
RUDENZ   (notices the corpse and stands seized with intense
      sorrow):
   O gracious God! Is my remorse too late?
   Could he not live just a few pulse-beats longer
   So that he might behold my altered heart?
   His loyal voice I scorned to heed while yet
   He walked beneath the light. Now he is gone,   2460
   Is gone for all eternity and leaves
   Me with this heavy debt I cannot pay.
   O tell me! Did he die displeased with me?
STAUFFACHER: Before he died he heard what you had done
   And blessed the courage with which you had spoken.
RUDENZ: (kneels down beside the dead man):

Yes, consecrate remains of a dear man,
Yes, lifeless corpse, here I will take my oath
Upon your hand now cold in death: I have
Forever broken all my alien bonds;
I am once more restored to my own people;   2470
I am a Swiss and I intend to be so
With my whole soul.

                    (rising)

                    Mourn for your friend, the father
Of all of us, but do not be dismayed!
It is not just his lands that I inherit,
His heart and spirit have descended to me
And my fresh youth shall do for you whatever
His grey old age was still indebted for.
—O reverend Father, let me have your hand.
And give me yours. And Melchtal, yours as well.
Do not hold back! O do not turn away!   2480
Receive my solemn oath and promise now.
WALTER FÜRST: Give him your hands. His heart which has re-
    turned
Deserves our trust.
MELCHTAL: You used to scorn the countrymen.
    So tell us what we can expect of you.
RUDENZ: Do not think of the error of my youth!
STAUFFACHER   *(to Melchtal)*:
    "Be one"—That was our father's final word.
    Be mindful of him now.
MELCHTAL: Here is my hand.
    The peasant's handclasp, noble Lord, is also
    A man's good word. What are the knights without us?
    And our estate is older far than yours.   2490
RUDENZ: I honor it and my sword shall defend it.
MELCHTAL: *That* arm, Lord Baron, that subjects the hard
    Earth to itself and fructifies her womb

Can also be protection for men's bosoms.
RUDENZ: You shall protect *my* breast, I will protect
Your breast. That way we make each other strong.
—Why talk, however, when our fatherland
Is still a prey to alien tyranny?
Not till the soil is cleansed of enemies
Can we adjust our differences in peace.   2500

(after he has paused for a moment)

Still silent? Do you have no word for me?
I still do not deserve to have you trust me?
Then I must force my way against your will
Into the secret of your war alliance.
You met and swore an oath up at the Rütli.
I know—know everything that went on there,
And what was not disclosed to me by you
I have kept secret as a sacred pledge.
I never was my country's foe, believe me,
I never would have acted there against you.   2510
But you did quite unwisely to postpone.
The hour is urgent, action must come fast.
Tell was the victim of your hesitation—
STAUFFACHER: We took an oath to wait till after Christmas.
RUDENZ: I was not there. I did not take the oath.
Go on and wait, but I will act.
MELCHTAL: What? You would—
RUDENZ: I count myself one of the country's leaders,
And my first duty now is to protect you.
WALTER FÜRST: To lay this precious dust within the earth
Is your first duty now and holiest.   2520
RUDENZ: When we have freed the country we will lay
The fresh-cut victory wreath upon his bier.
O Friends! I do not have your cause alone,
I have my own cause also to fight out
Now with these tyrants. Hear and know: my Berta

Has disappeared, abducted secretly
With daring impudence out of our midst.

STAUFFACHER: The tyrant has committed such an outrage
Against an independent noblewoman?

RUDENZ: O my good friends! I promised you assistance,   2530
But first I must myself beg some from you.
My dear one has been seized and carried off
And who knows where the madman has concealed her
Or to what violence they yet may go
To force her heart to a detested union!
Do not abandon me, O help me save her—
She loves me, she deserves it of the country
To have all arms take weapons to defend her—

WALTER FÜRST: What do you plan to do?

RUDENZ: How should I know?
O, in this darkness that beshrouds her fate,   2540
In the great anguish of uncertainty
With nothing definite to fasten on
Just this one thing is clear within my soul:
Beneath the ruins of these tyrants' power
Alone is she to be dug up and found.
The fortresses must one by one be taken
To find the dungeon where she is forsaken.

MELCHTAL: Come, lead us! We will follow you. Why leave for
Tomorrow what can yet be done today?
Tell was still free when we swore at the Rütli.   2550
The monstrous thing had not yet taken place.
The times have brought about a different law.
Who is so cowardly as to wait longer!

RUDENZ   (to Stauffacher and Walter Fürst):
With weapons meanwhile and prepared for action
You will await the mountains' signal fires.
For swifter than the sails of messengers
The tidings of our victory will reach you.
And once you see the flames blaze up around,

Then strike the enemy like lightning bolts
And tear the tyrant structure to the ground.   2560

(Exeunt.)

SCENE 3

The Sunken Road near Küssnacht.
Descent is from above between cliffs and the way-
farers are seen on the higher ground before they
appear on the stage. Cliffs surround the entire
scene; on one of those furthest forward there is a
projection overgrown with bushes.

Enter Tell with his crossbow.

TELL: He has to come along this sunken road,
    There is no other way to Küssnacht. Here
    I'll do the thing. The land lies favorably.
    That clump of elders there will hide me from him
    And down from there my arrow can well reach him.
    The narrow passage will hold up pursuers.
    So settle your account with Heaven, Bailiff,
    Your time has run its course and you must go.
       I lived in tranquil innocence. My missile
    Was only aimed at creatures of the forest,   2570
    My thought had not the slightest taint of murder.
    You startled me from my tranquillity,
    And into seething dragon-poison you
    Transformed the milk of my good sentiments.
    You have accustomed me to monstrous things.
    A man who took his own child's head for target
    Can also shoot into a foeman's heart.
       My tender children in their innocence,
    My loyal wife I must protect against
    Your fury, Bailiff—When I stretched that bowstring tight, 2580

And when my hand was trembling as it did so,
And when with devilish cruelty of pleasure
You forced me to take aim at my child's head,
And when I pleaded helplessly before you,
Then I within my breast was vowing with
A fearful oath that only God could hear
That my *next* arrow's *first and foremost* target
Would be your heart. The oath that I pronounced
Amid the hellish torments of that moment
Is a sacred debt, and I will pay it.   2590

You are my lord, the Bailiff of my Emperor,
But never would the Emperor have permitted
Himself what *you* did. To this land he sent you
To render justice—harsh, for he is wroth—
But not to practice every cruel deed
With murderous joy and with impunity.
There lives a God to punish and avenge.

Now come you forth, you bringer of sharp pain,
My precious jewel now, my highest treasure—
I will set you a target which till now   2600
Has been impenetrable to worthy pleas—
But it shall find *you* irresistible.
And you, my trusty bowstring that so often
Have served me loyally in joyous sport,
Do not desert me in dread earnestness!
Hold fast just this one time, you faithful cord
That have so often winged my bitter arrow—
If this one speeds too feebly from my hand,
I have no second one at my command.

(Wayfarers pass across the stage.)

Upon this bench of stone I will sit down,   2610
Placed to afford wayfarers some brief respite,
For here there is no homeland. Each man presses
Onward in haste to pass the others by

And does not ask about their sorrows. Here
The careworn merchant passes, and the lightly
Girded pilgrim and the pious monk,
The somber highwayman, the merry minstrel,
The driver with the heavy laden horse
Who comes from far off in the lands of men,
For every road leads to world's end at last.   2620
All these are passing on their way, each one
Concerned with his affairs—and mine is murder!

(He sits down.)

Before, when Father went away, dear children,
There was great joy when he came back again.
He never came unless he brought you something,
Perhaps a pretty Alpine flower, perhaps
An unfamiliar bird or fossil shell
Such as a traveler finds upon the mountains.
But he pursues a different quarry now.
By the wild way he sits with thoughts of murder;   2630
It is a foeman's heart that he is stalking.
And yet he thinks of you, dear children, now,
And to protect you in your lovely innocence
Against the tyrant's vengeance he intends
To do a murder with the bow he bends.

(He gets up.)

It is a noble prey I stalk. Why, hunters
Are not discouraged when they have to wander
For days on end amid the winter's rigor,
And risk their lives in leaps from cliff to cliff,
And climb smooth walls of precipices where   2640
They use their blood to keep their feet from slipping,
Just so that they can catch a wretched chamois.
A far more precious prize is here in question,
A foeman's heart who seeks my own destruction.

*(From a distance is heard lively music
which comes closer.)*

All my life long I have been wielder of
The bow, observing always archer's rules.
And I have often hit the bull's eye and
Brought home fine prizes more than once with me
From shooting matches. But today I mean
To shoot my mastershot and win the best   2650
Thing that exists in all this mountain region.

*(A wedding party passes across the stage and up the
sunken road. Tell, leaning on his bow, observes it.
Stüssi the game warden joins him.)*

STÜSSI: There goes the Mörlischachen cloister steward,
    That's whose this wedding party is—a rich man
    Who owns at least ten dairies on the Alps.
    He's taking his bride down to Imisee.
    Tonight will see some revelling in Küssnacht.
    Come! Every honest fellow is invited.
TELL: A solemn guest is not fit for a wedding.
STÜSSI: If some care troubles you, throw it aside
    And take whatever comes. The times are hard,   2660
    A man must catch his pleasure as he can.
    It's marry here and bury somewhere else.
TELL: And often one leads right into the other.
STÜSSI: So goes the world. There's trouble everywhere
    A-plenty. Up in Canton Glarus they
    Have had a landslide; one whole side of Glärnisch
    Caved in.
TELL: What? Do the very mountains totter?
    There's nothing left to stand firm on the earth.
STÜSSI: And elsewhere too we hear of wondrous things.
    I talked to one man who had come from Baden.   2670
    A knight was travelling to see the King
    And on the way a swarm of hornets met him;

They fell upon his horse and stung it so
That it dropped dead upon the ground from pain,
And he came on by foot to where the King was.
TELL: Unto frail creatures sting is also given.

*(Enter Armgard with several children and stations
herself at the entrance to the sunken road.)*

STÜSSI: They say it bodes some great disaster to
The country, some grave deeds opposed to Nature.
TELL: No day goes by but brings that kind of deeds,
It takes no portents to proclaim their coming.   2680
STÜSSI: Yes, they are fortunate who tend their field
In peace and sit at home untroubled with
Their own.
TELL: The best man cannot be at peace
If some malicious neighbor does not like it.

*(Tell keeps looking up toward the high
part of the road in uneasy expectation.)*

STÜSSI: Farewell, then. Are you waiting here for someone?
TELL: I am.
STÜSSI: A prosperous homeward journey to you.
Have you come up from Uri? They expect
Our lord the Bailiff back from there today.

(A wayfarer comes along.)

THE WAYFARER: The Bailiff won't be coming any more
Today. The streams have overflowed from these   2690
Big rains and swept the bridges all away.

(Tell gets up.)

ARMGARD: *(comes forward):*
The Bailiff won't be coming?
STÜSSI: Do you have
Some business with him?

ARMGARD: Yes.

STÜSSI: Why do you stand
Then in this sunken road right in his way?

ARMGARD: He can't evade me here, he has to hear me.

HARDHEART (*comes hurrying down the sunken road and
shouting offstage*):
Make way! Make way! My gracious lord the Bailiff
Is riding close behind me here.

               (*Tell goes out.*)

ARMGARD (*eagerly*):   The Bailiff
Is coming!

         (*She comes downstage with her children. Gessler
         and Rudolf the Equerry appear on horseback on
         the high part of the road.*)

STÜSSI: How did you get through the water
Now that the stream has swept away the bridges?

HARDHEART: We had our tussle with the lake, my Friend, 2700
And have no fear of any Alpine stream.

STÜSSI: You were on shipboard in that mighty storm?

HARDHEART: Yes, that we were. I never will forget it.

STÜSSI: Tell me about it!

HARDHEART: Let me go, I have to
Announce the Bailiff's coming at the castle.

                 (*Exit.*)

STÜSSI: If there had been good people in that boat
It would have sunk with all hands to the bottom.
These people, they are proof to fire and water.

            (*He looks around.*)

Where did that huntsman go that was just here?

                 (*Exit.*)

         (*Enter Gessler and Rudolf the Equerry
            on horseback.*)

GESSLER: Say what you will, I am the Emperor's servant   2710
And have to think about how I can please him.
He did not send me to this country here
To pet these people and be sweet to them.
He wants obedience. The issue is:
Are peasants or the Emperor to be master?
ARMGARD: Now is the moment. I will bring it to him.

(She approaches timidly.)

GESSLER: I did not set the hat up as a joke
In Altorf, or to test the people's hearts.
Those I knew long ago. I set it up
To teach them how to bend their neck for once.   2720
Those necks that they have held so stiffly upright.
I had that *inconvenient* thing set up
Right in their path where they had to pass by
So it would hit them in the eye and they
Would think about the master they forget.
RUDOLF: The people have, however, certain rights—
GESSLER: Which there is no time now to weigh and ponder!
Things of far-reaching import are in progress.
The Imperial House intends to grow, and what
The father gloriously began, the son   2730
Intends to finish. This small people is
A stone upon our path—This way or that—
It must give in.

*(They start to pass on. The woman
throws herself down before the Bailiff.)*

ARMGARD: My husband is
In prison; his poor orphans cry for bread.
Have mercy, Lord, on our great misery.
RUDOLF: Who is your husband?
ARMGARD: A poor cutter of

Wild hay, Sir, from up on the Rigiberg.
He mows the unclaimed grass that overhangs   2740
The gorges and grows on steep sides of cliffs
Where cattle do not venture to go down—

RUDOLF   (to the Bailiff):
A wretched living and a pitiable!
I beg you to let this poor man go free.
However gravely he may have offended,
His grisly work is punishment enough.

(to the woman)

You shall have justice—Go present your plea
Inside the castle. This is not the place.

ARMGARD: No! I will not budge from this spot until
The Bailiff has restored my husband to me!   2750
This is the sixth month he has been in prison
And waited vainly for the court's decision.

GESSLER: Woman, would you try to force me? Stand back!

ARMGARD: Justice, Lord Bailiff! You are judge here in
This country in the stead of God and Emperor.
Do your duty! As you hope for justice
Yourself from Heaven, show us justice now!

GESSLER: Out of my sight with these high-handed people!

ARMGARD   (seizes the bridle of his horse):
No, no, no! I have nothing more to lose.
You shall not leave this spot, Lord Bailiff, till   2760
You render justice to me! Knit your brows
And roll your eyeballs as you will. We are
In such unbounded misery that we
No longer care about your anger—

GESSLER: Woman,
Stand back or else my horse will ride you down.

ARMGARD: Then let it ride me down—Here—

(She pulls her children to the ground and together with them throws herself into his path.)

Here I lie

With all my children—Now let these poor orphans
Be trampled by your horse's hooves to death.
It will not be the worst thing you have done.

RUDOLF: Are you insane?

ARMGARD (*continuing more frantically*):

You long have trampled down   2770

The Emperor's country underneath your feet!
O, I am just a woman! If I were
A man, I would do something more than lying
Here in the dust.

> (*The previous music is heard again on the high
> part of the road, but muffled now.*)

GESSLER: Where are my servants? Have
Them carry her away from there or I will
Forget myself and do what I'll regret.

RUDOLF: The servants, Sir, cannot get through. This narrow
Defile is blocked up by a wedding party.

GESSLER: I still am much too mild a ruler for
These people. Tongues are still too free. They have   2780
Not yet been tamed the way they need to be.
But this shall all be changed, I promise you.
I will yet break this arrogance of temper
And this bold will to freedom I will bend.
I will proclaim a new law in these cantons.
I will—

> (*An arrow pierces him. He puts his hand to his
> heart and starts to fall. In a dull voice*)

Have mercy on me, God!

RUDOLF:

Lord Bailiff—

My God! What is it? Where did that come from?

ARMGARD (*starting up*):
He's falling! Murder! Murder! He is hit!

He has an arrow squarely in his heart!

RUDOLF (*jumps down from his horse*):
O what a ghastly thing to happen—God— 2790
Lord Knight—Implore the mercy of your God!
You are a dead man now.

GESSLER: This is Tell's arrow.

> (*He has slipped off the horse into the arms of
> Rudolf the Equerry and is now laid on the bench.*

TELL (*appears above on the top of the cliffs*):
You know the archer, seek no other one!
Our homes are free, the innocent are safe
From you. You will not further harm this land.

> (*He disappears from the cliff.
> People rush in.*)

STÜSSI (*in front*):
What is the matter? What has happened here?

ARMGARD: The Bailiff has been stricken by an arrow.

PEOPLE (*rushing in*):
Who has been shot?

> (*As the leaders of the wedding procession come
> on stage, the rear ones are still up the hill and the
> music continues.*)

RUDOLF: He's bleeding here to death.
Hurry, get help! Pursue the murderer!
Lost man, this is the way you have to end, 2800
But you would not pay heed to my fair warning.

STÜSSI: By God, he lies there pale and lifeless!

MANY VOICES: Who
Has done this thing?

RUDOLF: What! Are these people mad,
Providing music for a murder? Have
Them stop!

(*The music breaks off suddenly. Still more
people come in.*)

Lord Bailiff, speak, if you are able—
Do you have nothing to confide to me?

(*Gessler makes a sign with his hand and repeats
it vehemently when it is not immediately understood.*)

Where shall I go? To Küssnacht? No, I do
Not understand you. Do not be impatient.
Leave earthly things now, make your peace with Heaven.

(*The whole wedding party is standing around
the dying man with a horror devoid of emotion.*)

STÜSSI: How pale he's turning. Death is in possession   2810
Of his heart now. His eyes are glazed and set.
ARMGARD   (*raises one child up*):
See, children, how a tyrant perishes.
RUDOLF: You crazy womenfolk, have you no feeling,
To gape and feast your eyes upon this horror?
Help, lend a hand! Will no one help me draw
The agonizing arrow from his heart?
WOMEN   (*step back*):
We should touch him whom God has stricken down?
RUDOLF: Curse and damnation on you!

(*He draws his sword.*)

STÜSSI: Try it, Sir!
Your rule is at an end. The tyrant of
This land has fallen. We will stand for no   2820
Compulsion any more. We are free people.
ALL   (*tumultuously*):
The land is free!
RUDOLF: So it has come to that!
Fear and obedience are so soon ended?

(to the men-at-arms who come
throngingin)

You see the ghastly deed of murder that
Has happened here. All help is futile now.
And it is useless to pursue the killer.
We now face other worries. On to Küssnacht
So we can save the Emperor's fortresses!
For at this instant all the bonds of order
And all the bonds of duty are dissolved   2830
And no man's loyalty is to be trusted.

(As he is leaving with the men-at-arms
six Brothers of Mercy come in.)

ARMGARD: Make way! Make way! Here come the Brothers of
                    Mercy.
STÜSSI: The victim falls and now the ravens come.
THE BROTHERS OF MERCY   (form a semicircle around the dead
                    man and sing in a deep tone):
            Death swiftly summons man to go,
                It grants no respite or delay;
            In mid-career it strikes him low,
                Sweeps him in prime of life away.
            Prepared or not, with joy or fear,
                He must before his Judge appear.   [2839]

(As the last lines are being repeated
the curtain falls.)

ACT V

SCENE 1

A public square near Altorf.

[A couple of days later. November 20 or 21.]

At right rear the Fortress Keep of Uri with its construction scaffolding still standing as in Act 1, Scene 3; to the left a prospect out into many mountains, on all of which signal fires are burning. It is just at daybreak; bells are heard ringing from various distances.

Ruodi, Kuoni, Werni, the Master Stonemason, and many other countrymen; also women and children.

RUODI: You see the fire signals on the mountains? 2840
STONEMASON: You hear the bells beyond the forest there?
RUODI: The foe is driven out.
STONEMASON: The fortresses are taken.
RUODI: And we in Canton Uri still endure
  The tyrant's fortress on our native soil?
  Are we the last ones to declare our freedom?
STONEMASON: Is this *yoke* yet to stand that was intended
  To force us? Tear it down!
ALL: Down, down with it!
RUODI: Where is the Bull of Uri?
THE BULL OF URI: Here. What's wanted?
RUODI: Climb up the beacon tower, blow your horn

III

Till it resounds throughout the mountains and   2850
Wakes all the echoes in the rocky gorges
To summon all the dwellers in the mountains
Together quickly.

(*Exit the Bull of Uri.*
Enter Walter Fürst.)

WALTER FÜRST: Wait, Friends! Wait! We still
Lack information as to what has happened
In Schwyz and Unterwalden. Let us first
Wait for the messengers.

RUODI: Why wait? The tyrant
Is dead, the day of freedom has appeared.

STONEMASON: Aren't these flaming messengers enough
That blaze on all the mountain tops around us?

RUODI: Come everyone, take hold, women and men!   2860
Tear down the scaffolding! Stave in those arches!
Break through those walls! Leave no stone on another!

STONEMASON: Come on, you workmen there! We built it up
And we can tear it down.

ALL: Come, tear it down!

(*They fall upon the structure from all sides.*)

WALTER FÜRST: It's started. I can't stop them any more.

(*Enter Melchtal and Baumgarten.*)

MELCHTAL: What? Is this fortress standing yet, when Sarnen
Is ashes and the Rossberg is torn down?

WALTER FÜRST: Is that you, Melchtal? Do you bring us
freedom?
Are all the cantons free of enemies?

MELCHTAL   (*embraces him*):
Pure is the soil. Rejoice, old Father! At   2870
This very moment we are talking here
There are no tyrants left in Switzerland.

WALTER FÜRST: Tell me, how did you seize the fortress?

MELCHTAL: Rudenz it was who captured Fortress Sarnen
  With manly and audacious act of daring.
  The Rossberg I had scaled the night before.
  But hear what happened. When we had set fire
  To that one, with the enemy removed,
  And crackling flames were shooting to the sky,
  Out rushed young Diethelm, Gessler's boy, and shouted 2880
  The Bruneck woman was on fire inside.
WALTER FÜRST: Great God!

(*The scaffold beams are heard crashing.*)

MELCHTAL: And she it was. She had been locked
  Up secretly upon the Bailiff's orders.
  In frenzy Rudenz rose, for we already
  Had heard the beams and stout supports go crashing
  And out from somewhere in the smoke the shriek
  Of the unhappy woman.
WALTER FÜRST: She was saved?
MELCHTAL: Then was the time for swiftness and decision!
  Had he been *nothing but* our nobleman,
  We surely would have prized our lives too dear,   2890
  But he was our confederate, and Berta
  The people honored. So, with confidence
  We risked our lives and plunged into the fire.
WALTER FÜRST: But she was saved?
MELCHTAL: She was. Rudenz and I,
  We carried her together from the flames
  As rafters fell behind us with a crash.
  Then when she realized she had been saved
  And opened up her eyes to heaven's light,
  The Baron threw himself upon my heart
  And silently a compact then was sworn   2900
  Which firmly tempered in the fire's heat,
  Will last through all the trials Fate may send.
WALTER FÜRST: And where is Landenberg?

MELCHTAL: Across the Brünig.
    It was no fault of mine if he who blinded
    My father got away with his own eyesight.
    I followed him and caught him in mid-flight,
    From where I dragged him to my father's feet.
    My sword was brandished over him already
    When from the pity of that blind old man
    He won the gift of life that he implored.   2910
    He swore his solemn oath not to come back,
    And he will keep it: he has felt our arm.
WALTER FÜRST: You did well not to put the stain of blood
    On your untainted triumph.
CHILDREN (hurry across the stage with fragments of the scaf-
    folding):
                        Freedom! Freedom!

    (The horn of Uri is sounded with might.)

WALTER FÜRST: Look, what a festival! *This* day will be
    Remembered by these children to old age.

            (Girls bring in the hat on a pole.
            The stage is filled with people.)

RUODI: Here is the hat to which we had to bow.
BAUMGARTEN: Let's have suggestions what to do with it.
WALTER FÜRST: Good Lord! Beneath that hat my grandson
    stood!
SEVERAL VOICES: Destroy that emblem of the tyrant's power!
    Burn it up!   [2920]
WALTER FÜRST: No, let it be preserved!
    It had to be the tool of tyranny,
    Now let it serve as Freedom's sign forever.

        (The citizens, men, women, and children, are
        standing and sitting on the beams of the shattered
        scaffolding, picturesquely grouped in a great semi-
        circle.)

MELCHTAL: So we stand happy now upon the ruins
 Of tyranny, and what we vowed up at
 The Rütli has been splendidly fulfilled.
WALTER FÜRST: Our work has been begun but not completed.
 We need strong harmony and courage now.
 For, be assured the King will lose no time
 In taking vengeance for one Bailiff's death   2930
 And bringing back by force the one expelled.
MELCHTAL: Let him come on with all his armies' might.
 The enemy within is driven out,
 And we will face the one that comes from outside.
RUODI: Just a few passes lead into the country,
 And those we'll cover with our very bodies.
BAUMGARTEN: We are united by eternal bonds,
 And never will his armies frighten us!

   (*Enter Rösselmann and Stauffacher.*)

RÖSSELMANN (*as he is coming in*):
 These are the dreadful judgments of the Lord!
PEOPLE: What is it?
RÖSSELMANN: What times we are living in! 2940
WALTER FÜRST: What is it, tell us!—Ah, it's you, Lord Werner?
 What do you bring?
PEOPLE: What is it?
RÖSSELMANN: Hear and marvel!
STAUFFACHER: We are delivered from a dreadful fear—
RÖSSELMANN: The Emperor has been murdered.
WALTER FÜRST: God in heaven!

   (*The people are in commotion and throng
    around Stauffacher.*)

ALL: What? Murdered! What? The Emperor! Hear! The
 Emperor!
MELCHTAL: Impossible! Where did you get this news?
STAUFFACHER: It's definite. At Bruck King Albrecht fell
 By an assassin's hand. A trustworthy man,

Johannes Müller,* heard it in Schaffhausen.

WALTER FÜRST: Who would have dared so terrible a deed? 2950

STAUFFACHER: The doer makes it still more terrible.
It was his nephew, his own brother's child.
Duke John of Swabia who did the deed.

MELCHTAL: What drove him to this deed of parricide?

STAUFFACHER: The Emperor had withheld his patrimony
From the impatient claimant. Rumor had it
He planned to cut him out of it entirely
And compensate him with a Bishop's hat.
But be that as it may, the young man lent
Ear to the evil counsels of his friends,   2960
And with the noble Lords of Eschenbach,
Of Tegerfelden, von der Wart, and Palm,
He plotted, when he could not get his rights,
To take revenge on him with his own hand.

WALTER FÜRST: O tell us how this dreadful thing was done.

STAUFFACHER: The King had ridden down from Stein zu
    Baden
To Rheinfeld, where the court was, and he had
The Princes Hans and Leopold with him
And a large retinue of noble lords.
And when they came up to the River Reuss   2970
Where crossing by a ferry is required,
The murderers got on the boat and parted
The Emperor from his retinue. Then when
That Prince was riding down across a field
Of grain—a great and ancient city of
The heathen time is said to lie beneath it—
With ancient Fortress Hapsburg now in sight
From whence the power of his race proceeded—

---

*Schiller here whimsically and gracefully compliments his contemporary, the distinguished Swiss historian Johannes Müller (1752-1809), whose *History of Switzerland* was one of the poet's principal source works for this play.

Duke Hans then plunged a dagger in his throat,
Rudolf of Palm transfixed him with a spear,   2980
And Eschenbach stove in his skull, so that
He fell in his own blood, slain by his kin
On his own territory. People on
The other shore were witness to the deed
But cut off by the stream they could do nothing
But raise a futile cry of lamentation.
There by the roadside a poor woman sat,
And in her lap the Emperor bled to death.

MELCHTAL: And so he only dug an early grave,
  Who wanted all and never ceased to crave.   2990

STAUFFACHER: A monstrous horror is abroad now in the land.
  All passes of the mountains are blockaded,
  And each estate has fortified its borders.
  Old Zürich has itself closed up its gates
  That have stood open thirty years, for fear of
  The murderers and still more—the avengers.
  Armed with the ban of outlawry, stern Agnes,
  The Queen of the Hungarians, is coming,
  Who does not know the gentleness of her
  Mild sex, to avenge her father's royal blood   3000
  On the assassins' entire families,
  Their servants, children, and their children's children,
  Yes, on the very stones of their great castles.
  Whole generations she has sworn to send
  Down to her father's grave, and bathe herself
  In blood as if it were the dew of May.

MELCHTAL: Is it known where the murderers have fled?

STAUFFACHER: They fled immediately the deed was done
  In five opposed and different directions
  And separated, not to meet again.   3010
  Duke John, they say, is wandering in the mountains.

WALTER FÜRST: Then they will reap no fruit from their
  misdeed.

Revenge does not bear fruit. It is itself
Its ghastly food, assassination is
Its joy, and horror its satiety.

STAUFFACHER: Their misdeed will not profit the assassins.
But at the same time we with hands untainted
May pick the blessed fruit of this foul outrage.
For we have been relieved of a great fear.
The greatest foe of freedom has been slain.   3020
And it is said the scepter will pass from
The House of Hapsburg to another race;
The Empire will assert its free election.

WALTER FÜRST AND OTHERS: What have you heard?

STAUFFACHER: The Count of Luxemburg
Already has been chosen by most votes.

WALTER FÜRST: We have done well in holding loyal to
The Empire. Now there is some hope for justice.

STAUFFACHER: The new lord will be needing sturdy friends.
He will protect us from the wrath of Austria.

(*The countrymen embrace one another.*)

(*Enter the Sexton with an Imperial
messenger.*)

SEXTON: Here are the country's noble leaders.

RÖSSELMANN AND OTHERS: Sexton,   3030
What is it?

SEXTON: An Imperial messenger
Brings you this letter.

ALL   (*to Walter Fürst*) Break the seal and read it.

WALTER FÜRST   (*reads*):
"To men of Uri, Schywz, and Unterwalden
Queen Elsbeth sends her grace and all things good."

MANY VOICES: What does the Queen demand? Her reign is over.

WALTER FÜRST   (*reads*):
"In her great suffering and widow's grief
In which the bloody passing of her lord

Has plunged the Queen, she still is mindful of
The old good faith and love of the Swiss cantons."
MELCHTAL: She never did when she was in her heyday.   3040
RÖSSELMANN: Be quiet! Listen!
WALTER FÜRST   (reads):
"And she relies upon this loyal people
To bear a strong and just abhorrence toward
The cursed perpetrators of this deed.
Hence she will now expect of the three cantons
That they will no wise aid the murderers
But rather that they loyally will help
In their surrender to avengers' hands,
In memory of the love and former favor
That they have had from Rudolf's princely house."   3050

(Signs of indignation among the
countrymen.)

MANY VOICES: The love and favor!
STAUFFACHER: We did receive the favor of the father,
But what such can we boast of from the son?
Did he confirm the charter of our freedom
As all preceding Emperors had done?
Did he judge in accordance with just laws
And lend afflicted innocence protection?
Did he so much as hear the messengers
That we had sent to him in our distress?
Not one of all these things did the King do   3060
For us, and if we had not gotten our
Rights for ourselves with our own doughty hands
Our woes would not have moved him. Gratitude?
He sowed no gratitude amid these valleys.
He stood in his high place; he could have been
A father to his peoples; but it pleased him
To be concerned for no one but his own.
By those that he enriched let grief be shown.

WALTER FÜRST: We will not find rejoicing in his fall
   Nor now remember evil done. Far be   3070
   That from us. But that we should take revenge
   For this King's death, who never did us good,
   Pursuing those who never troubled us,
   Is not our duty, nor can ever be so.
   For love must be a voluntary service.
   Death sweeps forced obligations all away,
   To him we have no further debts to pay.
MELCHTAL: And if the Queen is weeping in her chamber
   And carrying her frantic grief to Heaven,
   She may look here upon a people freed   3080
   From anguish thanking that same God above—
   Whoever would reap tears must first sow love.

(Exit the Imperial messenger.)

STAUFFACHER   *(to the people)*:
   But where is Tell? Must he alone be missing
   Who is the founder of our freedom? He
   Accomplished most and he endured the worst.
   To his house let us go together, all
   Of us, and hail the savior of us all.

(They all leave.)

SCENE 2

The main room of Tell's house.

*A fire is burning on the hearth. The open door affords
a view outside.*

Hedwig. Walter and Wilhelm.

HEDWIG: Your father comes today. Dear boys, dear boys,
   He is alive, and free, and we are free,
   And everybody! And it was your father   3090

That saved the country.

WALTER: I was there too, Mother!
I have to be included. Father's arrow
Just grazed my life, and I did not so much
As tremble.

HEDWIG (*embraces him*):
                Yes, you have been given back
To me! I have borne you a second time.
A second time I suffered birthpangs for you.
But that is past—I have you both now, both!
And your dear father will be home today!

(A monk appears at the door.)

WILHELM: Look, Mother, look—there stands a pious friar.
He surely will be asking you for alms.   3100
HEDWIG: Have him come in so he may have refreshment.
He should feel he is in a house of joy.

*(Shes goes inside and comes back
directly with a goblet.)*

WILHELM (*to the monk*):
Come in, good man. My mother will refresh you.
WALTER: Come in and rest and go away the stronger.
THE MONK (*glancing around fearfully with haggard looks*):
Where am I? Tell me in what canton am I?
WALTER: Why, are you lost that you should not know that?
You are in Bürglen, Sir, in Canton Uri,
Just where the Schächen valley opens out.
THE MONK (*to Hedwig as she comes back in*):
Are you alone? Your husband is not home?
HEDWIG: I expect him soon now—but what is the matter? 3110
You do not look as though you brought good things.
Whoever you may be, you are in want:
Take this.

(She hands him the goblet.)

THE MONK: Thirst as my parched heart may, I will
   Touch nothing here until you promise me—
HEDWIG: Do not come near me, do not touch my garment,
   Stand far off if I am to listen to you.
THE MONK: Now by this fire here blazing hospitably
   And by your children's precious heads which I
   Embrace—

(He seizes the boys.)

HEDWIG: What are you thinking of? Stand back,
   Man, from my children! You are no monk! That   3120
   You are not! Peace should live inside that habit,
   And in your features there abides no peace.
THE MONK: I am the most unhappy of mankind.
HEDWIG: Misfortune mightily speaks to the heart,
   And yet the sight of you chokes up my bosom.
WALTER   *(jumping up)*:
   Mother! Here's Father!

(He hurries out.)

HEDWIG: O my God!

*(She starts to follow, trembles, and
steadies herself.)*

WILHELM   *(hurries after him)*:   It's Father!
WALTER   *(outside)*:
   You're back again!
WILHELM   *(outside)*: O Father, dearest Father!
TELL   *(outside)*:
   Yes, I am back again. Where is your mother?

(They enter.)

WALTER: There she is by the door and can't get further,
   She's trembling so with terror and with joy.   3130
TELL: O Hedwig! Hedwig! Mother of my children!
   God helped. No tyrant can part us again.

HEDWIG   (*on his neck*):
  O Tell! What anguish I have felt for you!

  (*The monk becomes attentive.*)

TELL: Forget that now and live for joy alone!
  I am back home again. This is my cottage.
  I stand again on my own property.
WILHELM: But what have you done with your crossbow,
    Father?
  I don't see it.
TELL: You won't see it again.
  It is preserved now in a holy place,
  And henceforth will not serve in any hunt.   3140
HEDWIG: O Tell! Tell!

  (*She steps back and releases his hand.*)

TELL: What has frightened you, dear Wife?
HEDWIG: How—*how* have you come back to me? This hand
  —Do I dare touch it?—This hand—Lord in Heaven!
TELL   (*heartily and courageously*):
  This hand defended you and saved the country.
  I dare to lift it freely up to Heaven.

  (*The monk makes a sudden movement and
    he notices him.*)

Who is the friar here?
HEDWIG: O, I forgot him!
  You speak with him, I shudder in his presence.
THE MONK   (*comes nearer*):
  Are you the Tell by whom the Bailiff died?
TELL: I am, and I conceal it from no man.
THE MONK: So you are Tell! It is the hand of God   3150
  That has directed me beneath your roof.
TELL   (*sizes him up*):
  You are no monk! Who are you?

THE MONK: You have killed
  The Bailiff who had done you wrong—I too
  Have slain an enemy who had denied me
  My rights—He was your enemy as well—
  And I have rid the country of him.
TELL *(falling back)*:   You
  Are—Horror!—Children! Children! Go inside!
  Go in, dear Wife! Go, go!—Unhappy man,
  You are—
HEDWIG: My God, who is it?
TELL: Do not ask!
  Away! Away! The children must not hear it.   3160
  Go, leave this house—go far away—you can
  Not live beneath a single roof with them.
HEDWIG: Alas, what is it? Come!

           (She leaves with the children.)

TELL *(to the monk)*:   You are the Duke
  Of Austria—That's it! And you have murdered
  The Emperor, your uncle and your lord.
JOHANNES PARRICIDA: He was the thief of my inheritance.
TELL: To kill your uncle and your Emperor!
  And earth still bears you, sun still shines upon you!
PARRICIDA: Tell, hear me first before you—
TELL: Dripping with
  The blood of parricide and Emperor murder,   3170
  You dare to step into my stainless house?
  You dare to show your face to a good man
  And ask the right of hospitality?
PARRICIDA: From you I looked for mercy. You took vengeance
  Upon your enemy.
TELL: Unhappy man!
  Can you confuse the blood guilt of ambition
  With what a father did in self-defense?
  Did you defend beloved heads of children?

Did you protect the hearth's pure sanctity? Did you
Ward off the worst and utmost from your own?   3180
I lift my stainless hands aloft to Heaven
And curse you and your deed. I have avenged
The sacredness of Nature, which you have
Disgraced—We share no common ground—*You* murdered,
While *I* defended what was dearest to me.

PARRICIDA: You cast me out, forlorn and in despair?

TELL: I feel a horror when I speak with you.
Begone! And travel down your fearful road.
This home of innocence, let it stand pure.

PARRICIDA (*turns to go*):
I *can* not, *will* not go on living thus!   3190

TELL: And yet I pity you—O God in Heaven!
So young, of such aristocratic race,
My Lord and Emperor Rudolf's grandson here,
A fugitive from murder, at my threshold,
A poor man's threshold—desperate, imploring—

(*He covers his face.*)

PARRICIDA: If you can weep, allow my destiny
To move you; it is terrible. I am
A Prince—I *was* one—I could have been happy
If I had bridled my desires' impatience.
But envy gnawed upon my heart. I saw   3200
My cousin Leopold in youthful prime
Rewarded with great lands and crowned with honor,
And myself, who was of an age with him,
Held down in slavish status of a minor—

TELL: Unhappy man, your uncle knew you well
When he refused to give you lands and people!
You with your wild and sudden deed of madness
Fearfully justify his wise decision.
Where are the bloodstained helpers in your murder?

PARRICIDA: Wherever the avenging spirits took them.   3210

I have not seen them since the direful deed.

TELL: You know the ban pursues you, that friends may
   Not help you and your enemies may kill you?

PARRICIDA: That is why I avoid all public highways.
   I do not dare to knock at any cottage,
   Out to the wilderness I turn my steps.
   A horror to myself I wander through
   The mountains and shrink at sight of myself
   When brooks reflect my own unhappy image.
   If you feel pity and humanity—   3220

(*He falls on his knees before him.*)

TELL   (*averting his gaze*):
   Stand up! Stand up!

PARRICIDA: No, not until you lend your hand to help me.

TELL: Can I help you? Can any mortal sinner?
   But do stand up. Whatever horror you
   Have done—you are a man—and so am I—
   And no one shall go comfortless away
   From Tell. I will do what I can.

PARRICIDA   (*leaping up and seizing his hand with vehemence*):
                                                    O Tell!

   You rescue my poor soul from desperation!

TELL: Release my hand. You must be gone. Here you
   Can not stay undiscovered, and discovered,   3230
   You cannot count on shelter. Where will you
   Go hoping to find peace?

PARRICIDA: How can I tell?

TELL: Hear what God prompts me. You must go into
   The land of Italy and to Saint Peter's
   City; cast yourself at the Pope's feet,
   Confess your guilt, and win your soul's release.

PARRICIDA: Will he not turn me over to avengers?

TELL: Accept what he may do as sent from God.

PARRICIDA: How will I get down to that unknown land?

I do not know the way and do not dare   3240
  To join my steps to other travelers.
TELL: I will describe the way for you. Mark well!
  You go upstream along the River Reuss
  That plunges from the mountain in wild falls—
PARRICIDA   (terrified):
  I see the Reuss? It flowed beside my deed.
TELL: The roadway skirts the gorge, and many crosses
  Mark it, erected to the memory
  Of travelers killed by the avalanche.
PARRICIDA: I have no fear of Nature's terrors if
  I tame the frantic torments of my heart.   3250
TELL: Before each cross fall on your knees, atoning
  Your guilt with scalding tears of true contrition—
  And if you safely pass that way of terror,
  And if the mountain does not send its snowdrifts
  Down over you from its ice-covered ridge,
  You will come to the bridge that spans the spray.
  If this does not give way beneath your guilt,
  When once you safely have put it behind you
  A black hole in the cliff will open up;
  No light has shone there—but you will pass through;   3260
  It leads into a cheerful vale of joy.
  But you must hasten on with rapid foot.
  Wherever there is peace you must not linger.
PARRICIDA: O Rudolf! Rudolf! Royal ancestor!
  Thus comes your grandson's foot upon your Empire's soil!
TELL: Thus climbing you come to the Gotthard peaks
  Where the eternal lakes are to be found
  Which are filled by the very streams of heaven.
  There you will bid farewell to German earth.
  Another stream with cheerful course will lead you   3270
  Into the land of Italy, your promised land—

       (*The cowherd's song is heard sounded
           on many Alphorns.*)

But I hear voices. Go!

HEDWIG *(hurries in)*: Where are you, Tell?
Here comes my father. And in glad procession
All the confederates are drawing near—

PARRICIDA *(covers his face)*:
Alas! I may not linger with the happy.

TELL: Go in, dear Wife, and give this man refreshment.
Heap gifts in plenty on him, for his way
Lies far and he will not find any shelter.
Quick! They are near.

HEDWIG: Who is it?

TELL: Do not ask.
And when he goes away, avert your eyes   3280
So that they will not see the road he travels.

*(With a sudden movement Parricida advances
toward Tell, but the latter beckons him away and
leaves. When both have gone out on opposite
sides, the stage is transformed and there is seen
in the*

FINAL SCENE

*the entire valley in front of Tell's dwelling, to-
gether with the peaks that enclose it, occupied by
countrymen who are grouped in a picturesque en-
semble. Others are coming across a high footbridge
that spans the Schächen. Walter Fürst with the two
boys, Melchtal, and Stauffacher come forward,
others press after them. As Tell steps out they all
greet him with loud jubilation.)*

ALL: Hurrah for Tell, the archer and the savior!

*(As the foremost ones crowd around Tell and
embrace him, Rudenz and Berta also appear, the*

*former embracing the countrymen, the latter em-
bracing Hedwig. The music from the mountain-
side accompanies this mute scene. When it con-
cludes, Berta steps into the midst of the people.)*

BERTA: My countrymen! Confederates! Take me
  Into your league as the first happy woman
  To find protection in the land of freedom.
  In your courageous hands I place my rights.
  Will you protect me as a citizen?
COUNTRYMEN: That we will do with our life blood!
BERTA: I can
  Then, and I do extend this youth my hand,
  A free Swiss woman to this free Swiss man!   3290
RUDENZ: And I set free all bondsmen on my land.

> (*As the music quickly strikes up
> again, the curtain falls.*)

DEMETRIUS

INTRODUCTION

The fragment of Schiller's play *Demetrius* is pure diamond. It shines in the memory when whole dramas, including some of Schiller's own, have been forgotten. In the form translated here, the text of this remarkable work is essentially the product of two months' work, March and April, 1805, though the notion of writing such a play had been clearly formed in the author's mind very shortly after the completion of *William Tell* in February of 1804. The Russian subject may well have suggested itself to him as early as 1799, the year when his brother-in-law, Wilhelm von Wolzogen, went to Petersburg to assist in the negotiations for the marriage of Marya Pavlovna, sister of Alexander I of Russia, to Karl Friedrich, the heir to the ducal throne of Weimar. Curiosity about the vast empire to the east led to readings in Russian history, and these in turn inevitably revealed the immense dramatic possibilities in the story of that youth who, in 1605, led Polish armies into his homeland to make himself Tsar and who, as Tsar Dmitri I, was assassinated the following year. The mystery attendant upon those events would strike any reader, for, to this day, no one knows for sure precisely who that "Dmitri" was. Quite possibly the young man himself did not know. He may have been, as Russian historians generally claim he was, no more than an impudent adventurer who cynically assumed the identity of the lost Crown Prince Dmitri, who had presumably perished as an eight-year-old boy in 1591; or he may have been the innocent dupe of other cynics, and, if so, he may have been monstrously disillusioned at some point or other of his flamboyant career. By temperament Schiller was attracted to the second interpretation of Dmitri's character, especially as he found it eloquently presented in Levesque's *Histoire de Russie*

iii

(1800), and it was on the basis of that interpretation that he began his play in March of 1804.

Scenario and partial text still survive for an Act I which would have portrayed the events in Sambor during the hero's obscure youth, events which in our version are rapidly summarized in the hero's speech before the Polish Assembly. Writing of this scene, rejection of this scene, composition of new scenes, elaboration of the total scenario, all these things occupied the better part of a year, a year unfortunately interrupted repeatedly by protracted illnesses and by other distractions. A journey consumed the month of May; July found the author temporarily swayed by the attraction of a different theme, *The Princess of Celle;* November brought at last the actual marriage of the Russian Princess so long in preparation. Schiller's consumptive lungs could hardly bear the strain put upon them by the production of his one-act *Homage of the Arts,* the courtly stage-allegory in verse which he had composed in honor of the distinguished bride. Exhaustion from that experience forced him to his sickbed through the next three months. There he whiled away the hours with a translation of Racine's *Phèdre,* and not until the end of February did he summon the vitality for original composition. March and April saw the creation of *Demetrius* to line 1288 or into the second half of Act II. On May 5, 1805 the poet was dead.

The political situation in Russia at the opening of the seventeenth century, as Schiller's readings revealed, invited intrigue. The ancient line of rulers of Kiev and subsequently of Moscow, descendants of the half-legendary Viking chieftain Rurik of "852" A.D., had become extinct in 1598 with the death of Tsar Theodore I (Fyodor Ivanovich), the son of Ivan the Terrible. Through much of the troubled reign of Ivan and through all of the reign of the incompetent Theodore power had actually been wielded by Boris Godunov, a nobleman of Tatar origin, whose sister was Theodore's wife. When no legitimate ruler was left to succeed Theodore in 1598, Boris rigged an assembly vote to have himself elected Tsar and thereafter sustained his unsafe position by means of an oppressive secret police.

His accession may well have been long planned in advance, for, as far back as 1584 when Theodore came to the throne, Boris had banished Theodore's infant half-brother Dmitri, the only remaining heir of Ivan, together with the infant's ex-Empress mother, to the village of Uglich on the Volga. Six years later, in May of 1591, the little boy, then aged eight, was murdered in that village. Or, at least, some child was murdered. Godunov's official investigating committee reported that the child was epileptic and had fatally wounded himself by falling upon a knife while playing. Conflicting rumors prevailed at the time as to precisely what had taken place and why, including the rumor that the wrong child had been slain and that the little prince had been spirited away to safety. All members of the boy's mother's family, the Nagois, were hurried off to banishment in remote places, as were the innocent inhabitants of the town of Uglich. Even the bell that sounded the alarm that day was deported to Siberia.

Again some years later and shortly before Theodore's death a youth named Yuri (George) Otrepev, known as the son of a small landholder north of Moscow, came to the capital and served as a domestic in various noble households, particularly with the Romanovs, the family of Theodore's mother, whom Godunov rightly suspected as his determined enemies. After an interval in domestic service young Otrepev became a monk, taking Grigori as his name in religion. His skill in letters was noticed by the Patriarch Job, head of the Russian church, who made him a clerk. From his monastery the new monk was reported as having made statements to the effect that he would some day be Tsar, and for these shocking statements he had to flee the country. It was remarkable with what ease he escaped through the frontier guards into Lithuania. The common Russian belief has it that Grigori—contemptuously designated as Grishka Otrepev—was a sly scoundrel whose clerkship gave him access to secret archives and that his own impudent mind gathered from those archives certain information which he could use in a grand imposture of passing himself off as the lost Dmitri. Non-Slavic scholars have suspected that he may have been an illegitimate son of Ivan's who meant to have his "rights."

It has never been proven that the person appearing in Poland shortly after Otrepev's famous escape into Lithuania was precisely this same Otrepev, though presumably it was. At any rate, in 1603 a twenty-year-old youth with red hair, unprepossessing features, and uncommonly quick wits entered the service of Prince Wiśniowiecki in Poland, and according to Polish accounts this youth disclosed to his patron the fact that he was the lost Prince Dmitri, escaped from the murderous henchmen of Boris Godunov at Uglich in 1591. That this youth was the runaway monk Otrepev is highly probable; that he was Dmitri is possible but dubious. Whatever his identity, it seems well nigh certain that he had been primed for his "mission" by Godunov-hating parties in Moscow and that his escape into Lithuania had been prearranged by those parties. In short, he was the instrument of a long-range plot by Muscovite nobles to overthrow the usurper Godunov, and his backers were willing to undertake the dire and treasonable risk of inviting Poland, then a far more powerful state than Russia, to use this figurehead of a prince as a pretext for invasion of their native land from abroad. What the Poles actually thought of the pretender is not recorded, but it is not difficult to imagine how they envisaged "Dmitri" as their own puppet-ruler of Russia once their armies had installed him as Tsar in Moscow. The already complex situation was further complicated by a love affair. "Dmitri" fell quite in love with Maryna, the beautiful daughter of Mniszek, the powerful Wojewoda (Palatine) of Sandomierz (Sendomir), while Maryna, for her part, entertained relentless ambitions of becoming Empress of Russia.

Plans were made and carried out. In 1604 "Dmitri" at the head of Polish and Cossack armies prepared to enter Russia. Dissidents from Godunov flocked everywhere to his banners, and in spite of fulminations of the usurper and of the Patriarch Job, resistance crumbled before the triumphant forces moving against Moscow. Suddenly Boris Godunov died, apparently of anxiety, before they took his capital. Popular acclaim hailed Tsar Dmitri Ivanovich and angry mobs slaughtered all of Godunov's family.

The mother of the actual Prince Dmitri acknowledged the new-comer as her lost son—a statement which she was to retract a year later. Patriarch Job was sent into exile.

Once Tsar, "Dmitri" bore himself with utter self-assurance without the remotest resemblance to a man beholden to helpers to win his throne. In fact, it was his self-assurance that undid him. Compared with Poland, he felt his native Russia was backward in the extreme. He began at once and with vigor to liberalize the country, displaying the will and the vision of the future Peter the Great in the process. Unquestionably he moved too fast. His economic measures angered the nobles, his European-mindedness offended the mass of the people, and his Roman Catholic wife, Maryna, made him religiously suspect in the eyes of the clergy. In 1606 he was murdered at the instigation of Prince Vasili Shuiski—whom a hand-picked group of nobles then proclaimed Tsar before any representative assembly could be convoked to deal with the situation.

Nor was this by any means the end of the business. Within a short time Polish and Cossack armies were again moving against Moscow with a "Prince Dmitri" at their head. "Pseudo-Dmitri II" was clearly an impostor, it matters little where he came from or who he actually was. Yet the willful and the credulous accepted his claim to be identical with the man "escaped" from Shuiski's henchmen just as the boy-prince had "escaped" from Godunov's henchmen. Maryna's father paid his daughter a large sum to recognize this new impostor as her husband, whereupon the proud and beautiful young woman found herself "Empress" of a rude military camp and in time mother of a child borne to a nameless ruffian who was certainly not her consort. In 1609 Swedish armies, called into Russia by Shuiski to stave off the forces of the new pretender, advanced into the country to gain what territory they might. Poland, in a countermove, invaded anew, and "Pseudo-Dmitri II," seeing himself bypassed, fled in panic before the outcome was decided, leaving his Russian supporters in the lurch. He returned after the defeat of the Swedes and after the deposition of Shuiski himself in July of 1610, only to meet, before the end of the year, with assassination instead of supreme office. At the beginning of 1611 utter confusion prevailed: Cossack troops were "protecting" Maryna and her infant son; Polish forces held the Moscow Kremlin; popular and hastily improvised armies of Russians were in possession of large areas of the country, including Moscow, where they were holding the Poles at bay inside the city's fortress; and the nobles were making an agreement to accept Ladislas, Prince of Poland, as Tsar. The native improvised armies finally won the day after three years of chaotic civil war, and in 1613 a national assembly elected as Tsar the sixteen-year-old boy, Michael Romanov, the uneven fortunes of whose descendants determined Russian history until 1917.

Not even Schiller's dramatic plan, immense as his prose scenario reveals it to have been, could accommodate so many characters, such diverse action. In the course of 1804 he had already rejected his sketch of an Act I dealing with the emergence of the pretender from obscurity, probably because it exceeded the limits his play would tolerate. In its place he composed the superb scene in the Polish Assembly with which the work now begins. Hardly twenty lines of prose from a German history book sufficed for his inspiration here, and those lines dealt largely with the bare facts of Russian and Polish politics as of 1603. The role of Odowalsky is also entirely Schiller's creation, resting on no historical basis; patently it is a dark role compounded of both cynicism and passion in stark contrast to the deceived innocence of the hero. Maryna, on the other hand, is close to her historical counterpart, even if her wild will is now infused with demonic force. The brief and splendid scene between her and her father at the end of Act I likewise shows, not what history records, but what the author rightly felt "must have been," and the same description applies to the more elaborate convent scene of Act II with its confrontation of the ex-Empress-mother and the Patriarch Job. Not even the unfinished sentences of this unfinished draft of the play can obscure the fact that everywhere, up to this point, a brilliant dramatic imagination is at work, nor the fact that the poet's language attains a splendor and an intensity *as poetry* never before realized by Schiller.

The second scene of Act II is good as far as it goes but it is over-brief; perhaps the author would have enlarged its scope if he had been granted sufficient time. Scene 3 is the roughest of rough sketches for the *beginning* of a scene, and from the point where it breaks off we are dependent upon Schiller's prose scenario to determine the course and outcome of the drama. This scenario, a purely private journal about a work in progress and never intended for other eyes, is clear enough in general outlines, though the writer often debates with himself alternate means of portraying this or that theme or event. Its full text occupies twenty-eight pages in the Sekulär edition of Schiller's works, but the present translation selects only essentials from it. The plans for Act III are impressive indeed. The death-scene of Boris Godunov portrays an able ruler overtaken by the Nemesis of his own early crime and constitutes a somber Baroque tragedy incapsulated within the larger play. With the usurper's death triumph is assured for Demetrius, but there, at the peak of his fortunes, comes the revelation that he is not the lost Tsarevich, that he is, in fact, the mere dupe of a small man's small revenge. In the fine ensuing scene, which is based partly on historical fact, Marfa wavers between acknowledgment of Demetrius and rejection of him, yet for a moment the two are visible to the public gaze in what *seems* to be the desired reunion of mother and son. The proposed Act IV sounds less promising, especially in respect to the wistful—and nonhistorical—love which Demetrius feels for Godunov's daughter Axinia. Act V provides for melodrama on the grand scale when the hero is slain at his putative mother's feet because she will not publicly sustain the lie by which he has lived and briefly ruled. Characteristically Schillerian is the effective final curtain provided by the last straggler from the murderous mob who picks up some item of lost insignia from the fallen Tsar and is seized with the idea of becoming "Pseudo-Dmitri II".

Both text and scenario of *Demetrius* were withheld from the public for a decade following Schiller's death, and only selections, rather irresponsibly edited, were made available in print for another fifty years, the first complete version bearing the date of 1876.

Schiller's failure to complete his drama about the false Dmitri is one of German literature's major losses. Oddly enough the failure was to be repeated half a century later. The gifted writer Friedrich Hebbel saw the possibilities of the theme as early as 1838, when he was twenty-five years old, but postponed the ambitious task for another twenty years; when he did at last begin composition of his grandiosely conceived five-act verse-play with prologue, his task was interrupted again and again and finally broken off altogether by his final illness. His manuscript, painfully written with rheumatism-twisted fingers trails off in the middle of a sentence at line 3305 of his text, approximately half way through the final act. An early twentieth century treatment of the theme by Paul Ernst has only slight value. Prosper Merimée created a French Dmitri-play of moderate success, while Pushkin's blank verse drama of 1827, landmark that it is in Russian literature, is neither Pushkin's greatest work nor the fullest treatment of the subject. Mussorgski's opera, *Boris Godunov,* which had its première in 1874, follows Pushkin's play in part, and, like it, is really concerned, not with Dmitri, but with his opponent. The same qualification applies to the imposing trilogy of verse-plays by A. K. Tolstoi: *The Death of Ivan the Terrible* (1866), *Tsar Fyodor Ivanovich* (1868), and *Tsar Boris* (1870). In all Russian versions Dmitri is a secondary figure into whose character the worst possible of variant interpretations is read. His story, in the nobly tragic terms proposed by Schiller, still awaits the hand of a great dramatist.

A NOTE ON THIS TRANSLATION

The present translation follows the textual arrangement and line-numbering system given in Volume VIII of *Schillers Sämtliche Werke,* edited by Gustav Kettner (1904). Place names are given in the form most likely to be familiar to English readers. Personal names, in disregard of Schiller's German usage, have been given their Polish spelling in so far as they are Polish and a standard transliteration in so far as they are Russian; the same process was applied to occasional Polish and Russian words in the text. Schiller's variant spellings, often dictated by exigencies of meter, have been retained, e.g., Demetrius (Latin), Dmitri (Russian), Dimitri (pseudo-Greek).

CHARACTERS

Act I:

King Sigismund III of Poland
The Crown Chancellor
The Grand Marshal
The Archbishop of Gnesen
The Archbishop of Lemberg
The Bishop of Cracow
The Bishop of Wermeland
The Castellan of Cracow
Prince Leo Sapieha
Mniszek, Wojewoda of Sendomir
Odowalsky
Korela, Hetman of the Ukrainian Cossacks
Rokol
Opalinsky
Ossolinsky } "Noblemen"
Zamosky
Demetrius, who claims to be the lost Prince Dmitri Ivanovich, heir to the throne of Russia
Maryna, daughter of Mniszek
Bishops, Palatines, Senators, Provincial Deputies of the Polish Assembly
"Noblemen"

MARFA, the name in religion of Empress Marya Nagaya, last wife of Tsar Ivan the Terrible and mother of Prince Dmitri Ivanovich

OLGA ⎫
XENIA ⎬ nuns at Marfa's convent
ALEXIA ⎭

A FISHER LAD

JOB, PATRIARCH OF MOSCOW

NUNS

DEMETRIUS

ODOWALSKY

RAZIN, AN ARMY OFFICER

ARMY OFFICERS

GLEB ⎫
ILYA ⎬ peasants in a rural village
TIMOSHKA ⎭

OLEG ⎫
IGOR ⎬ peasants from a second village

IVANSKA ⎫
PETRUSHKA ⎬ peasants from a third village

THE POSADNIK (village mayor)

Peasants with their wives and children

Place: Act I in Cracow, Poland
       Act II in Russia and at the Russian border
Time: 1603-1605

Note: Asterisks in the text indicate illegible lines or words, or lines never composed by Schiller.

ACT I

SCENE I

The Imperial Diet in Cracow

As the curtain rises, the Polish Imperial Assembly is seen in session in the great Senate Chamber. The rear of the stage is a dais elevated by three steps and covered with red carpet, on which is the royal throne overhung by a canopy. On either side hang the coats-of-arms of Poland and Lithuania.[1]

The King is seated on the throne. To his right and left on the dais stand the ten Officials of the Crown. Below the dais, on either side of the stage, sit the Bishops, Palatines, and Castellans, with heads covered. Behind them stand the Provincial Deputies in two rows with heads uncovered and all of them armed. The Archbishop of Gnesen, as Primate of the Realm, sits nearest the proscenium. Behind him his chaplain holds up a golden cross.

THE ARCHBISHOP OF GNESEN:[2]   This stormy session of the Diet,
   then,
   Has been brought to a fortunate conclusion.
   The King and the estates part amicably,
   The nobles are agreed to lay down arms,
   And the unruly Rokosz[3] to disband.
   The King, however, gives his sacred word
   To grant redress to justified complaints,
   Nothing   *   *   *   *   *

[1]The marriage of Princess Jadwiga of Poland to Grand Prince Jagiello of Lithuania in 1386 had brought the two countries under a single ruler.
[2]Gnesen — (Polish) Gniezno.
[3]Rokosz — the organized resistance of the nobles against increase of the King's centralized power at their expense.

3

As the *pacta conventa* stipulate.[4]
And now that there is peace within, we can   10
Direct our eyes to lands abroad.
*   *   *   *   *   *

Is it the will of the illustrious
Estates that Prince Demetrius, who claims
The Russian crown as true son of Ivan,
Shall come before the bar to demonstrate
To this Seym Walny[5] the justice of his claim?

THE CASTELLAN OF CRACOW: Honor requires it and propriety.
It ill befits us to deny his plea.

THE BISHOP OF WERMELAND:[6] The documents pertaining to his claim
Have been investigated and found valid.   20
He *can* be heard.

SEVERAL DEPUTIES: He *must* be given hearing.

LEO SAPIEHA: To hear him means to recognize him.

ODOWALSKY: Not
To hear him means rejecting him unheard.

THE ARCHBISHOP OF GNESEN: Is it your pleasure to give him a hearing?
I ask you for the second time and third time.

THE CROWN CHANCELLOR: Let him appear before our throne.

SENATORS: Hear him!

PROVINCIAL DEPUTIES: We want to hear him!

> (*The Grand Marshal of the Crown gives the
> usher a sign with his staff, and the latter goes out
> to open the door.*)

LEO SAPIEHA: Chancellor, write this down:
I raise objection to this whole proceeding,
And all that may come of it, contrary to
The peace of Poland with the crown of Moscow.   30

---

[4]*pacta conventa* — constitutional limitations on royal authority; they were formally read aloud at the openings of Diet meetings.
[5]Seym Walny — (Polish) Imperial Diet or "grand assembly."
[6]Wermeland — Värmland in Sweden.

(Enter Demetrius.

*He advances several steps toward the throne and
with covered head makes three bows, one to the
King, then to the Senators, finally to the Provincial
Deputies. From each section in question he is
answered with a bow of the head.*

*Immediately he takes a position such that, without
turning his back on the royal throne, he can survey
a large part of the assembly and of the audience,
of which it is assumed that they are also present at
the Diet.)*

THE ARCHBISHOP OF GNESEN: Prince Dmitri and son of Ivan,
  if splendor
Of this royal Diet overawes you,
If sight of majesty holds you tongue-tied,
You may—the Senate grants you such permission—
Select an advocate of your own choice
And of another's lips avail yourself.

DEMETRIUS: My Lord Archbishop, I stand here to claim
An empire and a royal scepter. It
Would ill beseem me to be frightened at
A noble people and its King and Senate.   40
I never have beheld a circle so
Exalted. But the sight makes my heart swell
And does not frighten me. The more distinguished
The hearers, the more welcome. I can not
Address a more resplendent gathering.

THE ARCHBISHOP OF GNESEN: * The illustrious Republic[7]
Inclines to give you audience. *   *   *   *

DEMETRIUS: High and mighty King! You worthy, mighty
Bishops and Palatines, and Deputies
And Lords of the illustrious Republic!   50
Astounded and with thoughtful wonderment
I see myself, the son of Tsar Ivan,

[7]The elected monarch and the Diet of regional rulers.

At this assembly of the Polish nation.
Hate bloodily divided our two realms
And peace was not established while he lived.
But Heaven has now so brought things about
That I, his blood, who with my nurse's milk
Sucked in that ancient hatred, have to come before you
As suppliant and in the midst of Poland
Must seek my rights. Therefore, before I speak,   60
Forget magnanimously all that has happened
And that the Tsar whose son I say I am
Had overrun your boundaries in war.
I stand before you as a prince despoiled.
I seek protection. Men oppressed may claim
A sacred right to every noble breast.
But who upon this earth can well be just
If not a great, courageous nation which,
Free in supreme totality of power,
Is bound to no accounting but its own,   70
And unrestricted by   *   *   *   *
Can give obedience to fine humaneness?
The Archbishop of Gnesen: You claim to be the son of
      Tsar Ivan;
And your demeanor does not contradict,
Nor does indeed your speech, that splendid claim.
Convince us all the same that you are he,
   *   *   *   *   *   *   *

Then hope the utmost from the nobleminded
Republic. — It has never feared the Russians
In battle, and it loves in equal measure
To be a noble foe and courteous friend.   80
Demetrius: Ivan Vasilevich, the mighty Tsar[8]
Of Moscow, in the long duration of
His reign had wed a series of five consorts.
The first one, from the many-heroed race

[8]Ivan Vasilevich ("John son-of-Basil") — Ivan IV, "the Terrible,"
1533-1584.

Of the Romanovs, bore him Feodor,
Who ruled next in succession. One son only,
Dmitri, the late blossom of his strength,
Was borne by Marfa, of the race Nagoi,
A tender child yet when his father died.
Tsar Feodor, a youth of feeble strength   90
And feeble wits, allowed his Equerry-
in-chief to rule, one Boris Godunov,
Who with sly courtier-cunning governed *him*.
Fyodor was childless, and the sterile womb
Of the Tsaritsa gave no hope of heirs.
Now when the sly Boyar[9] by flattery
Had gained the people's favor for himself,
He raised his wishes to the very throne.
A young prince yet was all that stood between him
And his proud aspiration, Prince Dimitri   100
Ivanovich, who then was growing up
In Uglich, the seat of his widowed mother.
Now with his black design ripe for fulfillment,
He sent assassins to the town of Uglich
To murder the Tsarevich and to blame
The deed   *   *   *   *   *   *
Amid the darkest of the midnight hours
Fire caught the castle wing where the young prince
Was living separately with his attendants.
The house fell prey to overwhelming flames,   110
The prince quite vanished from the eyes of men
And so remained. All mourned for him as dead.
I tell familiar things that all of Moscow knows.
THE ARCHBISHOP OF GNESEN: What you report is well known to
    us all.
The news resounded all about the world
That Prince Dimitri met his death amid
That conflagration in the town of Uglich.
And since his death proved advantageous to

[9]Boyar — "nobleman."

The Tsar now reigning, no one felt a scruple
About accusing him of that grave murder.   120
The theme now is, however, not his death.
That prince is still alive. He lives in you,
Is your assertion. Give us proof of that.
Whereby do you attest that you are he?
And by what signs can you be recognized?
How did [that prince] remain   *   *
And now comes, after sixteen years of silence,
Quite unexpectedly back to the light?

DEMETRIUS: Less than a year ago I found myself.
Till then I had lived hidden from myself,   130
Without suspicion of my princely birth.
I found myself a monk with monks when I
Began to waken into self-awareness,
And with monastic rigor on all sides.
Against the narrow clerical existence
My eager mind rebelled and darkly in my veins
My knightly blood revolted violently.
I cast the monk's garb from me with a will
And fled to Poland, where the noble Prince
Of Sendomir,[10] the gracious friend to man,   140
Received me kindly in his princely house
And trained me in the noble use of weapons.

THE ARCHBISHOP OF GNESEN: * * * What? You did not
    know yourself,
And yet report had filled the world already
That Prince Demetrius was still alive?
Tsar Boris trembled on his throne already
And stationed his zastavs[11] along the borders
To scrutinize all travelers with care.
What? That report did not proceed from you?
You had not at that time made claim to be   150

---

[10]Sendomir — (Polish) Sandomierz.
[11]zastavs — (Russian) "border guards." (Properly: *zastava* "a toll-
gate, check-point.")

Demetrius?

DEMETRIUS: I tell you what I know.
 If any rumor spread of my existence,
 Some god officiously had made it current.
 I did not know myself. In the house of
 The Palatine and lost among his servants
 I lived out youth's obscure and cheerful time.
 Still unknown to myself, I worshiped his
 Attractive daughter with a silent homage
 Yet was still far from the audacity
 Of venturing such happy aspirations.   160
 The Castellan of Lemberg,[12] then her suitor,
 Took umbrage at my passion. Haughtily
 He challenged me and in his blinded fury
 Forgot himself so far as to strike at me.
 *   *   *   *   *   *

 Provoked so grievously, I seized my weapon.
 He, wildly raging, ran against my sword
 And died by my involuntary hand.

MNISZEK: Yes, that is how   *   *   *   *

DEMETRIUS: My mischance was extreme. Without a name,
 A Russian and an alien, I had killed   170
 A grandee of the realm, committed murder
 In the house of my patron and protector,
 And slain his future son-in-law and friend.
 My innocence could be of no avail;
 Neither the sympathy of the whole court
 Nor favor of the Palatine could save me,
 Because the law, which favors Poles alone
 But is strict with all foreigners, condemned me.
 My sentence was decreed. I was to die.
 I was already kneeling at the block   180
 With bare neck ready for the sword.

              (*He stops short and*   *   *   *)

12Lemberg — (Polish) Lwow.

At just that moment there was seen a cross
Of gold inset with precious gems which had
Been hung about my neck at baptism.
As is the custom with my people, I
Had always worn concealed around my neck
From childhood years the sacred pledge of Christ's
Redemption, and now at the very moment
When I was on the verge of leaving life,
I clasped it as my final consolation   190
And pressed it to my lips with reverence.
The object was observed, its worth and splendor
Roused wonderment and curiosity.
I was freed from my bonds, interrogated,
But I could not remember any time
When I had been without that precious token.
Now as it chanced, three scions of Boyars,
In flight from persecution by their Tsar,
Came on a visit to my lord at Sambor.
They saw the precious thing and recognized it   200
By the nine emeralds there interlaced
With amethysts as being the same one
That Knyaz Mstislavskoi had hung about[13]
The last son of the Tsar at baptism.
They scrutinized me closer and perceived
An odd caprice of Nature, that I was
Born with my right arm shorter than the other.
Then as they were harassing me with questions,
I chanced to think about a little Psalter
That I had taken with me in my flight.   210
Greek words had been inscribed inside that Psalter
By the Igumen with his very hand,[14]
But I had never read the words myself
Because the language is unknown to me.
The Psalter was then fetched, the words were read;

[13]Knyaz — (Russian) "Prince."
[14]Igumen — (Russian) "Abbot."

The purport was that Brother Philaret[15]
(That was my cloister name), who owned the book,
Was Prince Dimitri, youngest son of Tsar
Ivan, whom Andrei, an upright d'yak,[16]
Had spirited away that night of murder;   220
Attesting records were preserved in two
Precisely designated monasteries.
Therewith all three Boyars fell at my feet,
Convinced by the force of these attestations,
And hailed me as the son of Tsar Ivan.
Thus swiftly destiny swept me up from
Misfortune's depths to fortune's pinnacle.

THE ARCHBISHOP OF GNESEN: [How odd! Extraordinary and
    most odd!
Yet Providence's ways are wondrous strange.][17]

DEMETRIUS: Then, as it were, the scales fell from my eyes!   230
All of a sudden memories revived
In the remotest depths of my past life,
And as the furthest towers of the distance
Will gleam amid the gold of sunlight, so
Within my soul two images shone forth,
The sunlit pinnacles of consciousness.
I saw myself in *flight* in dark of night
And I beheld a flashing flame blaze up
As I looked backward through the black night's horror.
It must have been a distant, early image,   240
For what preceded it and what came after
Was blotted out in distances of time;
Disjointed only, solitary gleaming,
That picture had stuck in my memory.
And yet I well recalled from later years
How one of my companions once in anger
Called me son of the Tsar. I thought it was

[15]"Philaret" was the name in religion of Michael Romanov's father.
[16]D'yak — (Russian) "scribe, clerk."
[17]Lines in brackets supplied from an earlier draft of Schiller's.

To twit me and avenged it with a blow.
All this now flashed like lightning through my mind;
It stood in dazzling certainty before me   250
That I was the Tsar's son who was thought dead.
Then all enigmas of my dark existence
Were with that single word resolved. Not merely
By tokens which can be deceiving, but
Within my inmost breast, by my own heartbeats
I felt   *   *   *   *   *
And I will sooner shed it drop by drop
Than   *   *   *   *   *

THE ARCHBISHOP OF GNESEN: And are we to rely upon some
     writing
Which was found quite by chance in your possession?   260
Trust testimony of some fugitives?
Forgive me, noble youth. Your tone and bearing
Are not those of a liar certainly;
But you could be *yourself* the one deceived.
The human heart can be forgiven its
Deception when stakes are so high. But what
Substantiation can you offer us?

DEMETRIUS: I can cite fifty attestations for
My oath, all from Piasts,[18] from freeborn Poles
Of unimpeachable nobility,   270
Who will confirm each point that I have claimed.
There sits the noble Prince of Sendomir,
The Castellan of Lublin at his side,
They will bear witness that I speak the truth.

THE ARCHBISHOP OF GNESEN: Now how do the illustrious
     estates
Opine? Before the joint force of so many
Witnesses all doubt must surely yield.
A furtive rumor has long circulated

[18]Piast — a native Pole of regal or ducal rank or a man of genuine
Polish descent, from the name of a legendary peasant from whom the
earliest Polish kings claimed descent.

That Dmitri, Ivan's son, is still alive;
By his fear Tsar Boris lends it support.
— A youth has here appeared, in age and form,
Down even to the very whims of Nature,
Exactly like the lost one being sought for,
But nob— *   deserving his high claim.
From monastery walls he wondrously,
Mysteriously emerged, with knightly virtue
Endowed, who was the pupil of mere monks;
He shows a jeweled cross which the Tsarevich
Himself once wore and never parted with;
A statement written by a pious hand   290
Supplies still further attestation of
His princely birth, while from his simple speech
And his pure brow truth makes a strong appeal.
Deception does not borrow traits like these;
It cloaks itself in fine grandiloquence
And in the ornaments of rhetoric.
Hence I no longer will deny to him
The name to which with good right he lays claim.
Invoking my prerogative of old
As Primate I cast the first vote for him.   300

THE ARCHBISHOP OF LEMBERG: And I vote with the Primate.
SEVERAL BISHOPS: With the Primate.
SEVERAL PALATINES: And I!
ODOWALSKY: And I!
DEPUTIES   (rapidly one after another):

                                            And all of us!
SAPIEHA: My Lords!
    Consider well. Let us not be too hasty.
    Do not allow this noble Diet to
    Be swept away *   *   *   *   *
ODOWALSKY: There's nothing
    To ponder. Everything has been considered.
    The proofs here speak incontrovertibly.

This is not Moscow. Here there is no terror
Of despots to choke up free souls. The truth
Is free to walk here with its head raised high.   310
I will not, noble lords, expect that here
In Cracow, in the Diet of the Poles,
The Tsar of Moscow has his purchased slaves.
 *   *   *   *   *   *   *   *

DEMETRIUS: Thank you, illustrious   *   *   *
For recognizing evidence of truth.
And if I truly am the person who
I claim to be, then do not tolerate
The usurpation of my heritage
By a bold thief and further blemish to
The scepter that is mine as true Tsarevich.   320
 *   *   *   *   *   *   *

So I may conquer my ancestral throne.
I have the righteous claim, *you* have the power.
It is the high concern of every state
And throne that justice shall be done and each
Man in the world shall have what is his own.
Where justice rules, there every man can safely
Enjoy his heritage and over every
Household and every throne the covenant
Will hover like a watch of cherubim.
But where   *   *   *   *   *   330
Unpunished holds another's heritage,
The firm and rockbound base of states will totter.
 *   *   *   *   *   * The universe's
Ingenious structure bears the name of Justice,
Where one holds all, and all holds one together,
Where with the one, the whole will fall in ruins.
 *   *   *   *   *   *   *   *

O look upon me, glorious Sigismund,
High and mighty King! Search in your heart
And see there your own destiny in mine.
You also have endured the blows of fate.   340

You were born in captivity, you came
Into the world amid a prison chamber,
Your first gaze fell upon a prison's walls,
You needed a deliverer and savior
To lift you from the prison to the throne.
You found him; you knew generosity;
O be now generous to me in turn!

*   *   *   *   *   *   *   *

And you, illustrious men of the Senate,
Reverend Bishops, pillars of the Church,
Much famed Palatines and Castellans,   350
Here is the opportunity   *   *   *   *
To reconcile two nations long at odds.
Gain for yourselves the fame of having Poland's
Power assign the Muscovites their Tsar,
And in the hostile neighbor that oppressed you
Gain for yourselves a grateful friend. And you
Provincial Deputies, *   *   *   *   *
Go bridle your swift horses and bestride them,
The golden gates of Fortune open for you.
I'll share the plunder of the foe with you.   360
Moscow is rich in treasure, untold wealth
Of gold and precious gems is in the Tsar's
Great hoard. I can and will reward my friends
In regal fashion. When as Tsar I enter
The Kremlin, then I swear that I will clothe
The poorest man among you who has followed
Me there in velvet and in sable furs,
And deck his harness with resplendent pearl,
And silver will be the least of the metals
That I will use to shoe his horse's hooves.   370

(*There is a great commotion among
the Provincial Deputies.*)

KORELA: *   *   *   *   *   *
ODOWALSKY: Shall we be robbed of fame and booty by

The Cossack? We have peace with Turkey and
The Tatars, nothing need be feared from Sweden.
Our valor has too long been dissipated
In * peace, our idle swords are rusting.
On, then! Let us attack the country of
The Tsar and gain a grateful friend and ally,
Thereby increasing Poland's might and power.

MANY DEPUTIES: War! War with Moscow!

OTHERS: Let it be declared!
Have them collect the votes!

SAPIEHA (*stands up*):   My Lord Crown Marshal!   380
Call for silence. I demand the floor.

A HOST OF VOICES: War! War with Moscow!

SAPIEHA: I demand the floor,
Lord Marshal! Do your duty!

(*Great din inside and outside the room.*)

THE GRAND MARSHAL: You can see
It's futile.

SAPIEHA: What! The Marshal too is bribed?
What! Is there then no freedom in this Diet?
Throw out your staff and order them to silence.
I so desire and order you.

(*The Grand Marshal throws his staff out into the
middle of the room, and the tumult dies down.*)

What are you thinking of? What are you doing?
Are we not at peace with the Tsar of Moscow?
I as your royal messenger myself   390
Arranged the twenty-year alliance. I
Raised my right hand aloft there in the Kremlin
And swore a solemn oath, and all this time
The Tsar has honestly held to his word.
What good is sworn good faith, what good are treaties
If any solemn Diet may break them at will?

DEMETRIUS: Prince Leo Sapieha! You say that
  You made a treaty with the Tsar at Moscow?
  That you did *not*, because *I* am that Tsar.
  In me is Moscow's majesty, I am   400
  The son of Tsar Ivan and his true heir.
  If Poland is to make a peace with Russia
  It must be done through me! Your treaty is
  Spurious and made with a spurious partner.

ODOWALSKY: What do we care about your treaty! At
  That time we wanted it, today we don't!
  Are we   *   *   *   *   *   *

SAPIEHA: So it has come to this! If no one will
  Rise to defend the right, then I will do so.
  This web of cunning I will rip apart,   410
  I will discover everything I know.
  — What, reverend Primate? Are you seriously
  So simple-minded, or pretending merely?
  Are you so credulous, you Senators?
  Are you so weak, O King? You do not know
  You are a plaything of the cunning Wojewoda[19]
  Of Sendomir who has set up this Tsar
  Whose measureless ambition has already
  Consumed the wealth of Moscow in his thoughts?
  Must *I* tell you that the alliance is
  Already made and sworn between the two
  Whereby he promised him his youngest daughter?
  And is this great Republic to plunge blindly
  Into the perils of a war in order
  To make the Wojewoda great and make
  A queen and a tsaritsa of his daughter?
  He has bribed everyone and bought them out;
  I know he means to dominate the Diet;
  I see his faction mighty in this hall;
  And it is not enough for him to lead   430

[19]Wojewoda — (Polish) "Palatine." (Schiller improperly drops the
final "a" when it suits his metrical purposes.)

The Seym Walny through the majority,
He has encircled the assembly with
Three thousand horse and flooded all of Cracow
With his own vassals. Even now they fill
The hallways of this house, and they intend
Coercion of our liberty of vote.
But no fear troubles my courageous heart.
As long as blood still courses in my veins
I will assert the freedom of my speech.
All men of good will will come to join me.   440
As long as I have life there will be no
Decision contrary to right and reason.
I made a peace with Moscow and I am
A man to see to it that it is kept.

ODOWALSKY: Pay no attention to him! Count the votes!

> (*The Bishops of Cracow and Vilna rise and go
> down, each to his own side, to collect the votes.*)

MANY: War! War with Moscow!

THE ARCHBISHOP OF GNESEN (*to Sapieha*): Yield, my noble Lord!
You see how the majority resists you.
Do not push things to an unhappy rift.

THE CROWN CHANCELLOR (*comes down from the throne to
Sapieha*):
The King requests you to give way, Lord Wojewoda,
And not to bring dissension to the Diet.   450

THE USHER (*privately to Odowalsky*):
Outside the door they send you word to hold
Out bravely. All of Cracow stands with you.

THE GRAND MARSHAL (*to Sapieha*):
Such good decisions have gone through this way.
Yield, then! For the sake of the other good
Things voted. Stand with the majority.

THE BISHOP OF CRACOW (*has collected the votes on his side*):
On this right bench it is unanimous.

SAPIEHA: Unanimous or not, I still say No!

I still say Veto, I dissolve the Diet.
— Let them proceed no further. Everything
Is null and canceled that has been decided.   460

>   (*General commotion. The King comes down
>   from the throne, the barriers are overrun, a tumul-
>   tuous din arises. Provincial Deputies draw their
>   swords and brandish them from left and right
>   against Sapieha. Bishops from both sides intervene
>   and protect him with their stoles.*)

Majority? Majority is nonsense.
Good sense is always with the few alone.
Who cares about the whole he does not have?
Does the beggar have his freedom or his choice?
For bread and shoes he has to sell his vote
To men of power who will pay him for them.
Votes should be weighed, not counted. Soon or late
The state will perish where majority
Wins and incomprehension makes decisions.

ODOWALSKY: Just hear the traitor!   470
PROVINCIAL DEPUTIES: Down with him! Death! Tear him to
>   pieces!
THE ARCHBISHOP OF GNESEN (*seizes the cross from his
>   chaplain's hand and steps between them*):
Shall blood of citizens flow in this Diet?
Prince Sapieha, hold your temper!
>   (*to the Bishops*) Take him
Away! And make your breasts a shield for him.
Remove him quietly through that side door
So that the mob does not tear him to pieces.

>   (*Sapieha, still with threatening looks, is led away
>   by force by the Bishops while the Archbishops of
>   Gnesen and Lemberg hold off the Deputies pressing
>   after him. Amid violent tumult and rattling of
>   swords the chamber is cleared, until only Demetrius,*

Mniszek, Odowalsky, and the Cossack Hetman are left.)

ODOWALSKY: It went against us   *   *   *
But you shall not lack help for all of that.
If the Republic keeps its peace with Moscow
We'll carry out our plan with our own strength.   480
KORELA: Who ever would have thought that he would have
Defied the entire Diet single-handed!
MNISZEK: Here comes the King.

(*Enter King Sigismund accompanied by the Crown Chancellor, the Grand Marshal, and several Bishops.*)

THE KING (*to Demetrius*): Let me embrace you, Prince.
The high Republic finally has done
You justice; my heart had done so long since.
Your destiny has deeply moved me, as
It surely must the heart of any king.
DEMETRIUS: I have forgotten all that I have suffered.
Upon your bosom I feel newly born.
THE KING: I do not like long speeches, but whatever   490
A king can do whose rule is over vassals
More wealthy than himself, I offer you.
I have beheld a   *   *   spectacle.
But think no worse now of the Polish kingdom
For this wild storm that tossed the ship of state.
MNISZEK: Amid the raging storm the helmsman guides
The vessel quietly to port and safety.
THE KING: The Diet is dissolved.
I cannot break our treaty with the Tsar,
But you have mighty friends. If my high nobles   500
Will take up arms for you at their own risk,
And if the Cossack tries the risks of war,
He is a free man and I cannot stop him.
MNISZEK: The entire Rokosz is still under arms.
If it so pleases you, Lord, that wild torrent

That rose against Your Highness can be turned
Quite harmlessly to pour itself on Moscow.
THE KING: Russia itself will give you your best weapons.
Your best protection is your people's hearts.
Russia by Russia only will be conquered.   510
Speak to the citizens in Moscow just
The way you spoke today before the Diet.
Acquire their hearts and you will be the ruler.
By foreign weapons no throne can be founded.
No nation yet with self-respect has ever
Against its will had rulers forced upon it.
I am the native-born King of the Swedes
And I ascended that throne peaceably,
I have   *   *   *   *   *   *
And still I lost the ancestral throne of my fathers   520
Because the people's sentiments opposed me.

[Enter Maryna.]

MNISZEK: Illustrious Highness, here before your feet
Maryna casts herself, my youngest daughter.
The Prince of Moscow   *   *   *   *
You are the high protector of our house
And from your royal hand alone it is
Befitting for her to receive her spouse.

(Maryna kneels before the King.)

THE KING: Well, Cousin, if it pleases you, I will
Assume the father's duty with the Tsar.

(to Demetrius, to whom he gives Maryna's hand)

Here I present you in this lovely pledge   530
The joyous goddess of Good Fortune.—May
My eyes live to behold this gracious pair
Seated upon the royal throne in Moscow.
MARYNA: Lord   *   *   *   *   *   *
I am your slave wherever I may be.
THE KING: Arise, Tsaritsa! Here is not the place

For you, not for the Tsar's affianced bride,
Not for the daughter of my chief Wojewoda.
You are the youngest of your sisters, but
Your mind flies on ahead of their attainments   540
And you with high will strive for things supreme.

DEMETRIUS: Be witness to my oath, exalted King.
As prince, I take it in a prince's hand.
I do accept this noble lady's hand
As a most gracious pledge of happiness.
As soon as I ascend my fathers' throne
I swear to take her solemnly to wife
As is befitting for a mighty queen.
The princedoms of Great Novgorod and of
Pleskov I will bestow upon my bride,   550
With all their cities and inhabitants,
With all their sovereign rights and privileges
In outright ownership perpetually.
And this bestowal I will then as Tsar
Confirm in Moscow in my capital.
And to the noble Wojewod I will pay
In reparation for his armaments
A million Polish-minted ducats.
So help me God and all His saints, I so
Vow honorably and I will keep my vow.   560

THE KING: You will do so, and you will never   *
Whatever you owe to the noble Wojewoda
Who risks his certain fortunes on your hopes
And on your hopes risks his beloved child.
So rare a friend is to be cherished dearly.
Therefore do not forget when you are happy
By what steps you ascended to the throne,
And with your garments do not change your heart.
Remember you first found yourself in Poland.
And love this country which bore you a second time.   570

DEMETRIUS: Not without *   *   *   *
Did I achieve *   *   *   *   *

I was brought up in lowliness, I had
To learn to reverence the gracious bond
That holds two human beings in affection.
THE KING: But you are entering a kingdom now
Where other manners and *   *   *   *   *
Here in the land of Poland freedom reigns.
The King himself, although supreme in splendor,
Must often be the servant of *   *   *   *   580
But there a *father's* sacred power rules,
The slave gives his obedience without
Demur, the master unaccounting bids.
DEMETRIUS: The lovely freedom I have *   *
I shall transplant *   *   *   *   *
Of slaves I will make *   * human beings,
For over souls of slaves I will not rule.
THE KING: Do not act rashly, learn to bide your time.
Prince, hear me.   *   *   *   *   *
Three precepts, Prince, I will *   *   *   590
Heed them with care when you come to your kingdom.
An old king who has much endured gives them
To you and your youth can well profit from them.
DEMETRIUS: Instruct me in your wisdom, O great King.
You are revered by a proud-hearted people;
What must I do to gain the same result?
THE KING: You come from outside,
The arms of foreign foes will bring you in.
You will need to make up for that first wrong.
Hence show yourself as a true son of Moscow   600
By paying due respect to its old customs.
Keep faith with Poland and   *   *   *
For once on your new throne you will need friends.
The arm that brought you in can work your fall.
Hold it on high but do not imitate it.
No alien ways can thrive in any land of
Ivan Vasilevich. No nation thrives,
It can bedeck itself in tatters of others' furs,

But living   *   *   *   *   *   must
For your country's   *   *   *   *   *   610
Whatever else you do, respect your mother.
For you will find a mother!

DEMETRIUS: O my King!
  *   *   *   *   *   *   *

THE KING: You have good cause to love her filially.
Revere her. She will stand between you and
Your people as a precious human bond.
The Tsar's might is free of all human laws,
No constitution limits the   *   *   ruler.
Except for Nature, there is nothing there
To dread; your people has no better pledge
Of your humaneness than your filial love.   620
But I will say no more. Much yet must come
About before you win the golden fleece.
Expect no easy victory.
Tsar Boris rules with might and with esteem,
You are not entering combat with a weakling.
Whoever mounts the throne deservingly
Will not be soon felled by opinion's winds.
  *   *   *   *   *   *   *   *

But he has deeds in place of ancestors.
—Farewell, and   *   *   *   *   *
To your good fortune I commit you now.   630
It rescued you out of the hands of murder,
It rescued you a second time from death,
And by a miarcle   *   *   *   *
It will complete its work and crown you Tsar.

SCENE 2

Maryna. Odowalsky.

ODOWALSKY: Well, have I carried out my orders well,

My Lady? Will you laud my zealousness?

MARYNA: It's well we are alone here, Odowalsky.
We have important matters to discuss
Of which the Prince must have no knowledge. Let
Him follow where the godlike call may lead him.   640
Let him believe himself: the world will then
Believe in him. Let *him* retain that darkness
Which is the mother of all great achievements ...
But we must see things *clearly,* we must *act.*
He will provide the name, the inspiration,
While we must do his thinking for him. Once
We have assured ourselves of our success
By skillful cunning, let him go on thinking
That it dropped from the sky into his lap.

ODOWALSKY: Command, my Lady. I live for your service   650
I utterly devote myself to you.
What do I care about this Muscovite?
It is for you, your grandeur and your splendor,
For whose sake I will risk my life and limb.
I was not able to possess you.
A propertyless vassal   *   *   *   *
I could not raise my hopes so high as you,
But I still want to earn your favor. Making
You great shall be my sole consideration.
Let someone else possess you: you belong   660
To me so long as you are my creation.

MARYNA: Therefore I trust my entire heart to you.
You are a man to carry out   *   *   *   *
The King is insincere, but I see through him.
A neat trick prearranged with Sapieha
    *   *   * It suits his purpose that
My father, whom he fears, should be made weak
By this large undertaking, and the nobles'
Alliance, which was terrifying to him,
Should spend its force in this campaign abroad   670
But he means to be neutral in the struggle.

The luck of battle   *   *   *   If we triumph,
He thinks   *   *   *   a weakened Moscow;
But if we lose, he will hope to impose
His yoke that much more easily on Poland.
We stand alone,   *   *   *   *   *
If he bides his advantage, we bide ours.
*   *   *   *   *   *   *   *

Escort the troops to Kiev. There have them
Swear loyalty to both the Prince and me.
To *me*, you hear? That is a prime precaution.   680
ODOWALSKY: To you! And it is your cause for which we fight.
I will engage them for your service.
MARYNA: I want your eye, not just your arm alone.
ODOWALSKY: Command, Queen.
MARYNA: You will escort the Tsarevich.
Protect him well and do not leave his side.
You will report to me his every step,
And who comes near him,   *   *   *   *
You will inform me of his inmost thoughts.
ODOWALSKY: Rely on me.
MARYNA: Do not let him out of
Your sight. Be his protector and his keeper.   690
Make him the victor,   *   *   *   but so
That he will always need us. You understand.
ODOWALSKY: Rely on me. He will need us forever.
MARYNA: No man is grateful. Once he is Tsar
He will be quick to cast his fetters off.
A good turn done becomes a grievous wrong
When it comes time to compensate it.
The Russians hate the Poles and cannot change;
There is no cordial bond to be forged there.
*   *   *   *   *   *   Whatever happens,   700
Good news or bad, inform me quickly of it.
I shall wait for your messengers in Kiev.
Station your messengers like milestones and
Despatch them any hour of the day.

Depopulate my army if you have to!

*   *   *   *   *   *   *   *

(*Enter numerous noblemen.*)

NOBLEMEN: Did we make our voices heard, Patroness? Did we
perform all right? Whom shall we kill? Make disposition
of our arms and sabres!

MARYNA: Who wants to go to war for me?

NOBLEMEN: We all will! All!

MARYNA: The mustering point is Kiev. There my father
Will march together with three thousand horse.   710
My brother-in-law will give two thousand. From
The Don auxiliary Cossacks are
Expected, who live down beyond the rapids.[1]

NOBLEMEN: First pay our debts if we are going to war.
Here we are stuck   *   *   *   *   *
The long assembly has used up our means.

OTHERS: Find money for us, Patroness, and we
Will go along. We'll make you Queen of Russia.

MARYNA: The Bishop of Kaminiek and of Kulm
Will lend you money on security   720
Of lands and vassals. Sell or pawn your farmsteads,
Coin all you own, invest in horse and armor.
War is the best of husbandmen: he makes
Gold out of iron. What you lose in Poland now
You will regain in Moscow ten times over.

ROKOL: There are two hundred more still in the taproom.
If you come down and drain a glass to their
Good health, they will be yours to the last man.

MARYNA: Wait for me, you shall be my escort down.

ALL: You shall be Czarina[2] or else we don't want to live!   730

OTHERS: You have new-clothed us and new-shod us and

(*Enter Opalinsky, Ossolinsky, Zamosky,
and numerous other nobles.*)

---

[1]The well-known Zaporozhny Cossacks.
[2]Polish "Czarina" — Russian "Tsaritsa."

We are your servants to our last heart's blood.

OPALINSKY: We want to come along. We will not stay
Behind alone!

ZAMOSKY: We're coming too. We want
Our portion of the spoils of Muscovy.

OSSOLINSKY: Patroness, take us with you. We will make you
Empress of Russia.

MARYNA: Who are these people? They are common riff-raff.

OSSOLINSKY: We're stable hands of the Starost[3] of   *

ZAMOSKY: I am the Castellan of Vilna's cook.   740

OPALINSKY: And I'm his coachman.

BIELSKY: I'm his turn-spit lad.

MARYNA: Fie, Odowalsky! These are really *too* base!

STABLE HANDS: We are Piasts and free-born Polish men.
Do not confuse us with low peasant trash,
We're men of quality, we have our rights!

ODOWALSKY: Yes, they receive their whippings on a carpet.[4]

ZAMOSKY: Do not despise us, we have noble hearts.

ODOWALSKY: Enlist them, give them boots and horses. They
Will fight their way through with the best of them.

MARYNA: *   *   *   *   *   * Go!   750
And come back when you look like human beings.
My steward will distribute clothing to you.

NOBLEMEN: You tend to that too? Nothing gets past you.
You were surely born to be a queen.

MARYNA: I know. Therefore I must become one.

OSSOLINSKY: Mount your white palfrey, take your warrior
weapons,
And like a second Wanda lead your hosts
Of valiant men to certain victory![5]

MARYNA: My spirit leads you. War is not for women.

[3] Starost — "Castellan."
[4] A detail which Schiller noted in one of his source works, Connor's
Description of the Kingdom of Poland.
[5] In Lauterbach's *Polnische Chronik* (1727) and in a Polish ballad
Schiller read of Wanda, the warrior maiden and daughter of Cracus,
the legendary founder of Cracow.

You pledge me faith, then?

ALL: *Juramus!* We swear![6]   760

(*They draw their sabres.*)

SEVERAL: *Vivat* Maryna!
OTHERS: *Russiae regina!*

SCENE 3

Mniszek. Maryna.

MARYNA: My father, why so grave when Fortune smiles
  On us *   *   *   *   *   *   *
  And every man draws weapons for our cause?
MNISZEK: Precisely that, my daughter. Everything
  Is being risked. Your father's entire strength
  Is being spent in this outlay for war.
  I have good reason to reflect upon it.
  Fortune is false, I fear the consequences.
MARYNA: But why *   *   *   *   *   770
MNISZEK: O dangerous girl, what have you brought me to?
  What weakling of a father am I not
  To have resisted your insistency!
  I am the wealthiest Wojewoda of
  The realm, next to the King... And should we not
  Have been content with that? Could we not have
  Enjoyed our blessings with contented souls?
  But you strove higher still, your modest lot
  Was not enough for *   *   *   *   *
  You wanted to attain the highest goal   780
  Of mortal beings and to wear a crown.
  And I, a father all too weak, was willing
  To heap the highest things on you, my darling.
  I let your pleading make a fool of me,

---

[6]Schiller deliberately made the word "júramus" in whimsical imitation of the notoriously wrong accents of Polish Latin.

I take up   *   *   *   *   *   *
And hazard certainty upon a chance!

MARYNA: Do you regret your kindness, then, my Father?
Who could be satisfied with lesser things
Above whose head supreme attainments hovered?

MNISZEK: None of your sisters wears a crown, however,   790
Yet they are high   *   *   *   *   *

MARYNA: What kind of fortune is it if I leave
My father's and the Wojewoda's house to go
Into my husband's house, the Palatine's?
What new gain would accrue from that exchange?
Can I rejoice in what the next day brings
If it brings nothing other than today?
O tasteless, flat recurrence of the old,
O dreary, empty sameness of existence!
What is the use of hoping and of striving?   800
It must be love or else it must be greatness,
All else is equal in its pointlessness.

MNISZEK: *   *   *   *   *   *   *

MARYNA: Dispel your frown, my   *   *   *
What is to   *   *   *   *   *   *
If we ourselves are first to lose our courage?
Let us trust to the tide that sweeps us on.
Do not think of the sacrifices made,
Think rather of the prize, the goal attained . . .
When you will see your daughter seated on
The throne of Moscow in an Empress' robes,   810
And when your grandsons will control this world.

MNISZEK: I think of nothing, I see nothing but
My daughter in the glory of her crown.
I yield to conquest, all my doubts recede.
You ask for this, I can deny you nothing.

MARYNA: One more petition still, beloved Father,
Allow me yet.

MNISZEK: What is your wish, my child?

MARYNA: Must I remain behind housed up in Sambor

With this unbridled yearning in my bosom?
Beyond the Dnepr my lot will be cast ...   820
Infinities of space divide me from it ...
Can I endure that? My impatient spirit
Will lie upon the rack of expectation
And measure out those monstrous distances
With anguish and with pulse-beats of the heart.

MNISZEK: What is it that you want?

MARYNA: Allow me to wait for success in Kiev.
There I can draw news up fresh from the source,
There on the border of the two dominions
Each new development   *   *   *   *   830
Will come to me post-haste, there I can catch
The tidings on the winds, there I can see
The Dnepr's waves that flow down from Smolensk,
There   *   *   *   *   *   *   *

MNISZEK: Your mind strains wildly. Check yourself, my child.

MARYNA: You will allow me, you will take me there.

MNISZEK: You will take *me! Must* I not do your will?

MARYNA: When I am Empress, Father dear, in Moscow,
Then Kiev will, you see, become *our* border.
Then Kiev must be mine, and you will rule it.   840
Just let me be the Empress once in Moscow
And mighty designs will ripen then.

MNISZEK: Girl, you are dreaming! Moscow is already
Too narrow for your mind. Already you
Want land gained at the detriment   *   *
Of your homeland.

MARYNA: Kiev ... *   *   *   *
The old Varangian princes once ruled there.
— I know the ancient chronicles ... It has
Been wrested from the empire of the Russians ...
I will return it to its ancient crown!   850

MNISZEK: Be still! The Wojewod must not hear such things.

                    (*Trumpets are heard.*)
They're starting out.

ACT Il

SCENE I

View of a Greek convent in a desolate winter landscape on the shores of White Lake.[1]

A procession of nuns in black habits and veils passes across the rear of the stage. Marfa in a white veil stands apart from the others, leaning against a gravestone. Olga steps out of the procession, stops for a moment to watch her, and then comes closer.

OLGA: Does your heart not urge you to come with us
 Into the freedom of new-wakened Nature?
 The sun has come, the tedious night retreats,
 The ice breaks in the streams; the sled becomes
 A floating barque, the migrant birds fly north.
 The world is opened up, and we are all
 Lured by new pleasure out of convent cells
 Into the open cheer of youthful meadows. 860
 And you alone, a prey to endless grief,
 Choose not to share the common merriment?
MARFA: Leave me alone and go on with your sisters.
 Let them delight in pleasure who can hope.
 The year that makes the whole world young can bring
 Me nothing. All things are things of the past
 For me; they lie behind me. They have been.
OLGA: Will you mourn for your son eternally
 And grieve for splendor you have lost forever?
 Time which pours balm in all wounds of the heart 870

[1]White Lake is located a hundred and fifty miles north of Moscow, but details remain in the scene from an earlier stage of composition when Schiller had misunderstood White *Sea*, near the Arctic port of Archangel, for White *Lake*.

32

Has lost its power over you alone?
You were the Empress of this mighty realm
And mother of a healthy, growing son;
A monstrous destiny robbed you of him
And you were thrust into this dismal convent
Here on the edges of the living world.
Yet sixteen times since that appalling day
The visage of the world has been made young.
Yours only do I always find unchanged,
An image of the grave, when everything   880
Around you lives. You are like that unmoving
Form which the sculptor fashions out of stone
To represent one thing forever changeless.

MARFA: Yes, time has set me up to be
A monument to a disastrous fate.
I do not want to be at peace, nor to
Forget. It is a coward soul that will
Accept its healing and its cure from time,
Replacing something irreplaceable.
Nothing shall buy my grief away from me. —   890
As heaven's arch walks always with the walker,
Surrounds him totally and endlessly
Wherever he directs his fleeing step,
So does my grief walk with me where I walk,
Surrounding me as with an endless sea;
My endless tears have not exhausted it.

OLGA: O let's see what the fisher lad has brought
Around whom eagerly our sisters press.
He has come from afar, from peopled regions,
He brings us news out of the lands of men.   900
The lake is open, roads are free again . . .
You have no curiosity to hear him?
For although we are dead to worldly things,
We do still like to hear about its changes,
And from the shore we may watch quietly
With wonderment the breaking of its waves.

(The nuns return with a fisher lad.)

XENIA: Come tell us all the news that you have brought!

ALEXIA: Tell us what's going on out in the world.

THE FISHER LAD: Give me a chance to speak first, holy ladies.

XENIA: Is there a war? Or peace?

ALEXIA: Who rules the world?   910

THE FISHER LAD: A ship has entered harbor at Archangel,
   Down from the North Pole where the world is frozen.

OLGA: How did a ship get into that wild sea?

THE FISHER LAD: It is an English trading vessel which
   Has found a new way of access to us.[2]

ALEXIA: What human beings will not do for gain!

XENIA: At least the world is nowhere closed entirely.

THE FISHER LAD: That is the least important of the news.
   Quite different undertakings stir the world.

ALEXIA: Tell us about it!

OLGA: Tell us what has happened!   920

THE FISHER LAD: The world is living through amazing things.
   Deceased men rise again and dead men live.

OLGA: Explain yourself.

THE FISHER LAD: Ivan's son, Prince Dimitri,
   Whom we have mourned as dead these sixteen years,
   He is alive, he came to life in Poland.

OLGA: Prince Dmitri lives!

MARFA *(starting up)*:   My son!

OLGA: Control yourself!
   Restrain your heart till we have heard him out.

ALEXIA: How can he still be living who was murdered
   At Uglich and who perished in the fire?

THE FISHER LAD: He got out safely from the fire's peril   930
   And found protection in a monastery.
   And there he grew to manhood in seclusion
   Until the time came to reveal himself.

---

[2]An English vessel, exploring Arctic seaways, found its way to the
port of Archangel in 1553, fifty years before the action of this play,
and a limited English-Russian commerce had developed.

OLGA (to Marfa):
  You tremble, Princess, and turn pale?
MARFA: I know
  That this is an illusion . . . but I am
  So little hardened yet to hope and fear
  That my heart falters in my bosom now.
OLGA: Why should it be illusion? Hear his story!
  How could such rumors spread without some basis?
THE FISHER LAD: Without some basis? All the Poles and all 940
  The Lithuanians are up in arms.
  The Grand Prince trembles in his capital!

*(Marfa, trembling in every limb, is forced to lean
for support on Olga and Alexia.)*

XENIA: O this is serious! Tell us everything!
ALEXIA: Tell us where you picked up this piece of news.
THE FISHER LAD: Where I picked up . . . ? A letter has been
    issued
  To all the lands of his dominion by
  The Tsar, and the Posadnik of our city
  Has read it in the general assembly.
  It says that they are trying to deceive us
  And we must not believe in their deception.   950
  For just that reason we believe it, for,
  If it were false, the Grand Prince would despise
  The lie.
MARFA: Is this the self-control I strove for?
  Does my heart still so cleave unto the world
  That a mere empty word can shake me to the core?
  I have mourned for my son these sixteen years
  And suddenly must think he is alive?
OLGA: You have mourned him as dead these sixteen years
  But you have never yet beheld his ashes!
  Nothing disproves the truth of this report.   960
  And Providence does keep its watch above
  The fates of peoples and the heads of princes.

— Open your heart to hope ... Unfathomed are *   *
*   *   Who can set the Almighty limits?

MARFA: Am I to turn my glances back toward life
On which I had pronounced farewell forever?
*   *   *   not in the grave?
Did all my hopes not dwell among the dead?
O tell me nothing more! Let my heart not
Cling thus to an illusion! Do not let   970
Me lose a second time the son I love!
My peace is gone, gone is my mind's repose.
I cannot trust this news, alas, and cannot
Expunge it permanently from my mind.
Alas, I have not lost my son till now,
For now I do not know if I should seek
For him among the dead or with the living.
I am delivered into endless doubt.

(A bell is heard.
Enter the Sister Porteress.)

OLGA: What does the bell mean, Sister Porteress?
THE PORTERESS: The Patriarch is here before our gates;   980
He comes from the great Tsar and asks a hearing.
OLGA: The Patriarch is here before our gates!
What unaccustomed matter brings him here?
The distant   *   *   *   *   *   *
XENIA: Come, let us all receive him fittingly.

(They are going toward the door when the
Patriarch steps in. They all genuflect before him.
He makes the Greek sign of the Cross over them.)

JOB: The kiss of peace I bring you in the name of
The Father and the Son and of the Spirit
Who proceedeth from the Father.
OLGA: Lord,
We kiss your hand in all humility.
What   *   *   *   Command your daughters.   990

JOB: My mission has to do with Sister Marfa.

OLGA: She stands right here awaiting your commandment.

[*The other nuns withdraw.*]

JOB: It is the Grand Prince who has sent me to you.
   *   *   *   *   *   he thinks of you,
  For as the sun with its high flaming eye
  Sheds plenitude and * through the world,
  Just so the sovereign's eye is everywhere.
  Out to the furthest borders of his realm
  His eye perceives and his concern is watchful.

MARFA: How far his arm can reach I have discovered.   1000

JOB: He knows the lofty spirit that is yours
  And hence he shares in anger the offense
  Now visited upon you by a scoundrel.

MARFA: *   *   *   *   *   *   *

JOB: An insolent impostor in the land
  Of Poland, a novice monk turned renegade,
  Abjuring vows and turning on his God,
  Is making misuse of your son's high name
  Whom death took from you in his infancy.
  This brazen mountebank boasts of your kinship
  And claims to be the son of Tsar Ivan.   1010
  *   *   *   *   *   *   [this]
  Pretender, whom he has himself created,
  Across our boundaries by force of arms.
  He is misleading loyal hearts of Russians,
  Enticing them to treason and revolt.
  *   *   *   *   *   *   *

  The Tsar to you in fatherly concern.
  — You hold your son's departed shade in honor,
  You will not have a bold adventurer
  Stealing his name from him out of the grave,
  Audaciously impinging on his rights.
  You will proclaim aloud before the world   1020
  That you *   *   *   this *   *   *

You will not foster alien bastard blood
Against your heart that beats so nobly, and
You will —the Tsar will so expect of you—
You will then controvert this shameless fraud
With all the righteous anger that it merits.

*(Marfa has been struggling with the most intense
emotions during this speech.)*

MARFA: What are you saying, Patriarch? Tell me!
  By virtue of what proofs and tokens does
  This insolent impostor show himself
  Son of Ivan whom we have mourned as dead?   1030
JOB: By superficial likeness to Ivan,
  By   *   *   *   *   *   *   *
  And by a precious ornament he wears,
  He fools the mob, who like to be deceived.
MARFA: What sort of ornament? O tell me that.
JOB: A golden cross set with nine emeralds,
  Which Knyaz Ivan Mstislavskoi, he claims,
  Once hung around his neck at baptism.
MARFA: What are you saying? He displays this cross?

(with forced composure)

—And how does he allege that he escaped?   1040
JOB: A faithful servant and d'yak, he claims,
  Then rescued him from murder and the fire
  And secretly took him off to Smolensk.
MARFA: But where could he have stayed ... Where does he say
  That he has been in hiding up till now?
JOB: In Cloister Chudov he says he grew up,
  A stranger to himself. From there he says
  He fled to Lithuania and Poland,
  Where he served with the Prince of Sendomir
  Until an accident revealed his status.   1050
MARFA: With such a fable he can muster friends
  Who will risk life and limb upon his luck?

JOB: Tsaritsa, Poles are treacherous of heart,
 They gaze with envy on our country's beauty.
       *   *   *   *   *   *   *   *

 To kindle fires of war within our borders!
MARFA: But can there be such trusting souls in Moscow
 As to be fooled by this *   *   *   * ?
JOB: The hearts of nations are unstable, Princess,
 They take delight in change, and they imagine
 That they will stand to gain by changing rulers.   1060
 The bold assurance of a lie intrigues them,
 The marvelous finds favor and belief.
 Therefore the Tsar wants you to break the people's
 Illusion by a *   *   *   *   *   *
 Yourself   *   *   *   *   *   *
 Who lies so brazenly as your own son.
 I am delighted to see you so moved.
 This bold deceit outrages you, I see,
 And noble anger gives your cheeks a color.
MARFA: And where—tell me—is he now to be found   1070
 Who has dared to declare himself our son?
JOB: Already he is moving toward Chernigov;
 He started out from Kiev, so we heard,
 Light cavalry of Poles in force behind him
 And with a force of Cossacks from the Don.
MARFA: Almighty God, I thank Thee, thank Thee, thank Thee,
 For sending me revenge at last and rescue!
JOB: What is this, Marfa? How am I to take this?
MARFA: O Heavenly Powers, guide him safely here,
 And all you angels, fly above his flags!   1080
JOB: Can it be possible? This villain could...
MARFA: He is my son. I know him by all of
 These tokens. By the Tsar's great fear I know him.
 He is alive and he is drawing near.
 Down from your throne, then, Tyrant! Tremble now!
 There lives a scion yet of Rurik's line,
 The true Tsar and the rightful heir is coming,

He will demand accounting for his own!

JOB: Mad woman, do you know what you are saying?

MARFA: The day of vengeance has arrived at last,   1090
The day of restitution. Heaven brings
Poor Innocence to light out of the grave,
*   *   *   *   * my mortal foe must
Come crawling to my feet and beg for mercy.
O my most ardent wishes are fulfilled!

JOB: Can hatred blind you to such high degree?

MARFA: Can terror blind your Tsar to such degree
That he hopes for deliverance from me —
From me, who was immeasurably offended?
That he sends you to me *   *   *   *   1100
*   *   *   to wrest   *   *   *
I should deny my son whom Heaven has
Called by a miracle up from his grave?
To please him, the assassin of my house,
Who has heaped woe unspeakable on me,
*   *   *   *   *   * I am
To thrust deliverance away which God
Has sent to me at last in my affliction?

JOB: *   *   *   *   *   *   *

MARFA: No, you will not escape me.
I have you and I will not let you go.   1110
At last I can relieve my bosom now,
At last I can pour out my grief and pain,
The long repressed resentment of my soul,
Can pour it right into my foeman's face.
Who thrust me down into this living grave
In all the force and freshness of my youth,
With all the warm impulses of my bosom?
Who tore my own beloved son away
And sent assassins out to cut him down?
No tongue can tell what torments I endured   1120
In those long nights all bright with stars when I
Kept vigil with my yearning unallayed

And kept the count of hours by my tears.
*   *   *   *   *   *   *   *

The day of vengeance and deliverance comes,
And I behold the mighty in my power.
Job: You think   *   *   *   *   *
Marfa: O he
Is in my power ... One word from my lips,
One single word can turn his destiny.
And that is why your ruler sends me visits.
Now all the Russians and the Poles are looking   1130
To me. If I acknowledge the Tsarevich
As being my son and son of Ivan,
*   *   *   *   *   *   *

If I deny him, he is wholly lost.
For who will credit that his actual mother,
The mother injured as I have been injured,
Will not acknowledge her heart's son, or that
She is in league with murderers of her house?
One word from me, and he will be deserted
By all as an impostor. —Is that not so?
This word from me is wanted ... This great service,   1140
Admit it, I can do for Godunov.
Job: You do it for the entire fatherland,
You save the country from the ravages
Of warfare if you honor truth. You have
No doubt yourself but that your son did die.
How could you testify against your conscience?
Marfa: For sixteen years I have been mourning for him
But I have never seen his ashes. I
Believed his death from my own grief and from
The common rumor. From the common rumor   1150
And my own hope I now believe his life.
It would be wicked to set limits to
The high Almighty's power by rash doubts.
But even if he were not my heart's son,
He still shall be the son of my revenge.

I shall accept him in lieu of a son
As born to me by Heaven for revenge.

JOB: (Unhappy woman, you defy the mighty
Man from whose arm you are not shielded even
Within the convent's holy sanctuary).[3]   1160

MARFA: O he can kill me, he can choke my voice
Within a grave or in a prison's darkness
So that it cannot echo through the world,
That he can do. But make me say what I
Will not, that he can never do. To that
He cannot bring me by *   *   *   *
  *   *   *   Of that goal he has failed!

JOB: Is this your final word? Consider well.
Shall I not bring the Tsar a better answer?

MARFA: Let him hope for Heaven if he dares,   1170
For the love of his people if he can.

JOB: Unhappy woman, you are bent on your destruction.
You lean on a weak reed that soon will break,
And with it you yourself shall fall.

                 (*Exit.*)

MARFA (*alone*):
He is my son. Of that I will not doubt.
The very tribes of the free wilderness
Take up their arms for him. That haughty Pole,
The Palatine, will stake his noble daughter
On the pure gold of his unblemished cause . . .
And I alone, his mother, should reject him?   1180
This storm of joy that catches up all hearts
In rapture and that has convulsed the earth,
Is it to blow for all save me alone?
He is my son. I *will* believe in him.
With eager confidence I will accept
The rescue that is sent to me by Heaven.
It *is* he. He has come with force of armies

[3]Lines in parentheses are added from an earlier draft of Schiller's.

To liberate me, to avenge my shame!
O hear his drums! His warrior trumpets! Hark!
You peoples, come from morning and from noon,   1190
Out of your steppes, out of your ancient forests,
With all your tongues, with all your costumes, come!
Bridle your horse, your reindeer, or your camel!
Pour countless as the billows of the sea
And throng about the banners of your king!
O why must I be hemmed in here, tied down,
Confined with infinite emotion here!
Eternal sun that moves about the globe
Of earth, be messenger to my desires!
O unrestricted circumambient air   1200
That swiftly finishes its furthest course,
Convey my eager, ardent longing to him!
Supplication and prayer are all I have,
I draw them up in flames out of my heart
And speed them winged to the heights of heaven,
I speed them toward you like a warrior host!

SCENE 2

*A height surrounded with trees. A broad and gladsome prospect
opens out. A pretty stream is seen flowing across the landscape which is vivid with the early green of planted fields.
Near at hand and further off the towers of several cities are
seen shining. Drums and martial music off stage.*

*Enter Odowalsky and other officers, directly after them De-
metrius.*

ODOWALSKY: Have the army move down past the woods;
Meanwhile we'll look around here on this height.

   (*Various ones withdraw. Enter Demetrius.*)

DEMETRIUS (*starting aback*):

Ah, what a view!

ODOWALSKY: Sir, you behold your realm
Spread out before you. That is Russian land.   1210

RAZIN: This pillar here bears Moscow's coat-of-arms,
Here ends the overlordship of the Poles.

DEMETRIUS: Is that the Dnepr that pours its tranquil stream
Across the meadows there?

ODOWALSKY: The Dnepr flows out there beyond Chernigov,
This is the Desna, Sir, which   *   *   *
And what you see is the soil of your realm.

RAZIN: And what gleams there against the distant sky,
Those are the domes of Seversk Novgorod.

DEMETRIUS: What a cheerful sight! What lovely fields!   1220

ODOWALSKY: The springtime has adorned them with its finery,
For this rich ground yields grain in plenitude.

DEMETRIUS: The eye roves on across immensity.

ODOWALSKY: And yet it is the mere beginning, Sir,
Of the great Russian realm that stretches out
Beyond the eye's reach toward the morning sun,
Nor has it any limits toward the north
Except the living earth's productive power.

RAZIN: See how our Tsar is wholly lost in thought.

DEMETRIUS: Across these lovely meadows peace still dwells, 1230
And here I come with the appalling gear
Of war to lay them waste in hostile spirit!

ODOWALSKY: Sir, things like that are thought of afterwards.

DEMETRIUS: You feel as a Pole, but I am Moscow's son;
This is the land that gave me birth and life!
Forgive me, precious soil, my homeland earth,
You sacred frontier pillar that I clasp
And whereupon my father graved his eagle,
Forgive your son for breaking in with alien
Weapons into the temple of your peace.   1240
I come here to reclaim my heritage
And my high patronymic which was stolen.
Here ruled my forebears, the Varangians,

For thirty generations in succession;
And I, the last one of their race, was wrested
By a divine fate from a murderous death.

(From Schiller's scenario:

Everything in this brief scene must be visually presented, and
when Demetrius has left, a procession must begin across the
stage, during which the scene change is made; march music
accompanies it.

Should this scene not also be used for some action? So much
must happen, there is so much to be shown.

Despatching of manifestoes and agents to the towns. —Condition of the Russian frontiers. This is learned by the return of
such an emissary. — Deputation of Cossacks, when does it occur?
— The good omen. — Disposition of the expeditionary force.—
The Desna is crossed. — One section of the army separates from
the other.)

SCENE 3

*A Russian village. Open square in front of the church. The
tocsin is heard. Gleb, Ilya, and Timoshka, armed with axes,
hurry onto the stage.*

GLEB   *(coming out of the house)*:
What are the people running for?
ILYA   *(from another house)*:   Who rang
The fire-bell?
TIMOSHKA: Neighbors! Come out everybody!

        *(Enter Oleg and Igor and many other peasants,
            women and children, carrying packs.)*

OLEG: Flee! Flee! Escape, who can!
GLEB: What is the matter?

Where do you come from with your wives and children? 1250
IGOR: Flee! Flee! The Poles have burst into the country
  At Moromesk. They're killing all they meet.
OLEG: Flee! Flee! Into the inner country, to
  Walled cities! We have set fire to our huts
  And started out, an entire village, fleeing
  Inland to the army of the Tsar.
TIMOSHKA: Here comes another troop of fugitives.

(*Ivanska and Petrushka and armed peasants
arrive at the opposite side.*)

IVANSKA: Long live the Tsar, long live Grand Prince Dmitri!
PETRUSHKA: Who * * * * is with you?
GLEB: What's this?
ILYA: Where are you hurrying to?
TIMOSHKA: Who are you? 1260
IVANSKA: *   *   *   *   *   *
TIMOSHKA: What's this now? Here's an entire village fleeing
  Inland *   *   *   *   *   *
  And you are heading right where they have fled from?
  You want to join our country's enemies?
PETRUSHKA: This is no enemy that's coming, but
  The people's friend, the nation's rightful heir.
  *   *   *   *   *   *   *   *

  But here comes the Posadnik!¹
POSADNIK (*enters with a scroll*):
  This is bad business, neighbors and fellow-councilors.
  God lead us out of our confusion! God give us light!
PEASANTS: What is it, Posadnik?   1270
POSADNIK: Here is a letter which has come from the Tsarevich,
  Who happens to be with the Polish army,
  In which we are *   *   *   *   *
  What shall we do?
PEASANTS: Read us the letter! Let us hear it!

¹Posadnik — mayor.

OTHERS: The letter! Read it!

POSADNIK: All right! Listen, then!
                "We, Dmitri Ivanovich,
by the grace of God Tsarevich of all Russia, Prince of Uglich,
Dmitrov, and other principalities, by my birth master and
heir of all Russian dominions, to all our royal subjects: Greeting!"

GLEB: That is the full title of our Tsars.

POSADNIK: "Tsar Ivan Vasilevich of glorious memory *   *
*   *   *   *   * to be loyal and devoted
to his children.

    "Now we, however, are the true and very son of this Tsar,
whose life Boris Godunov sought, but who was preserved by
divine destiny. We come now to take possession of our hereditary throne, the sword in our one hand and the olive branch
in the other, clemency to the loyal, destruction to the re-
fractory. Therefore we are mindful of your oath, we do exhort
you to abandon the party of Boris Godunov and to do homage
to us as your hereditary ruler and true Tsar. If you do so, we
shall rule over you clemently; if not, then may the spilt blood
fall upon your heads, for we shall not put the sword into its
sheath until we conquer the throne of our fathers."

TIMOSHKA: *   *   *   *   *   *

GLEB: Then how can we deny fidelity
    To our lord's son and shut the land against him?

ILYA: *   *   *   *   *   *   *

TIMOSHKA: Don't be so simple! Be more shrewd for once!
    How could he make up things like that, invent such lies! 1280
    If he were not the one, would he so state and claim?

GLEB: That's just what I think! Would the Poles take the field
    for a deceiver?

TIMOSHKA: And if he *is,* and there's no doubt he *is,*
    Then how can we deny fidelity
    To our lord's son and shut the land against him?

ILYA: But we have pledged allegiance and done homage
    To Boris Godunov as our true Tsar.

(From Schiller's scenario)

The purpose of this scene is to show how swiftly the fantastic finds reception among the common people and in what ways it works.

At first there are only men, and the greater weight seems to be on the side of Boris. Katinka arrives at the head of many women, all of whom are leading children by the hand. Women have heard the decision has been reached to set fire to the village and to flee inland. The question is: which side will be taken by the master of the village. They try to get weapons, they want to force the opposing party. . . . .

Nearness of the Polish army. Agents of Demetrius. Manifesto. Parties. Reasons *pro,* reasons *contra.* Sympathy with Demetrius. Hopes. Dissatisfaction with Boris. Fear of Demetrius' weapons. On the other side: hatred of the Poles. Fear of Boris. Scruples of conscience.)

(Continuation of Schiller's Scenario[1])

CAMP OF BORIS'S ARMY. It is a bad error that Boris is absent. . . . The commander is afraid the Cossacks will go over to where their fellow countrymen are fighting. [Dissension] among commanders.] Soltikov is inclined to faith in Demetrius' side. . . . The army of Boris occupies an important position which Demetrius dare not leave behind him.

SHUISKI			greedy for honor but devoted to Boris
SOLTIKOV	Generals	conscientious but devoted to Demetrius
DOLGORUKI	of Boris	honorable but weak
BASMANOV		treacherous
MAZEPPA, Hetman of Cossacks		unreliable

DEMETRIUS DEFEATED. Boris's army wins more or less *against* its will . . . Demetrius, who they think is already in their power, is allowed to escape. [He] wants to kill himself; Korela and Odowalsky have difficulty preventing him. . . . Soltikov declares for him . . . and prepares the defection of the whole army.

[1]Words in brackets are supplied by the translator.

ACT III

BORIS IN MOSCOW. Boris would gladly leave Moscow and go to the army, but he is afraid that, once he is gone, Moscow will immediately declare for Demetrius. Also, he is ashamed, as Tsar, to fight in person against the deceiver. His *Nordic* pride. The Patriarch Job can be about the Tsar.

Boris is, however, mortally wounded when he appears, and the Imperial grandeur still surrounding him is mere appearance and shadow. ... The fact that the very prince whom he had caused to be murdered must provide the pretender with an existence is in itself a fatality. He confesses the murder to the Patriarch ...:

> "Must I perish on account of this delusion? Must I actually? —Patriarch, it is driving me out of my senses. — It is true I did not gain the realm wholly innocently, but I have governed it well. What? Can a life of good actions not make good a crime? Can the good usage not excuse the reprehensible means?"

Graduation of misfortunes: 1. Desertion of the peasantry and the provincial cities, 2. inaction of the army, 3. desertion of a part of the army, 4. Moscow's uprisings, 5. Demetrius' advance, 6. Romanov's menacing arrival, 7. flight of the Boyars to Demetrius' camp, 8. desertion of the army, 9. insults of the mutineers. Demetrius is heard, as it were, approaching nearer and nearer, the *soulèvement* of the population must constantly grow and rise, so that this scene, although it is concerned with Boris, never loses sight of the principal hero.

Boris is touching as a father. He discloses his grief, his inmost conscience to his daughter. ... [She] is to hide herself in a convent. She is in love [with Romanov.]

49

... Boris is like a wounded tiger that no one dares go near. Bits of bad news have arrived which they *have not yet had the courage* to tell him, because he has already had one such unfortunate messenger *thrown from the tower.* Hence the worst is waiting for him.

Meanwhile Boris has gotten control of himself again and is ashamed of his vehemence. Thus he is *much more gentle* when he comes in than he has been described, and he has the worst things told. In fact, he *rewards the teller royally.* ... He thinks sooner than necessary of suicide. Scene with his physician; he provides himself with poison, he tests the point of a dagger. ... Boris is superstitious, but in the way a great man can be so. In his heart he has fixed a certain condition; when this is realized, it will be the voice of Fate. ... The report of Romanov's mysterious arrival completes his despair. This misfortune is worse than anything else to him, because he really has so much with which to reproach himself in respect to the Romanovs.[2]

Et nunc magna mei sub terras ibit imago.
Urbem praeclaram statui, mea moenia vidi.[3]

This situation also has something resembling Macbeth's situation at the end. Certain evil portents are fulfilled for him.

BORIS DIES. When Boris has heard what he believes to be his decisive misfortune he walks off without further explanation. In so doing he is calm and gentle like a man resigned. When he reappears he is in monk's habit. He dismisses his daughter from his final moment and takes the poison only when she is gone. When he has taken it, he withdraws to die in silence.

Between Boris's dying departure and Romanov's arrival something must occur so that this reversal of fortune will not be too abrupt. Should a loyal servant kill himself?

[2]Marya Pavlovna *Romanova* had married the Duke apparent of Weimar while this play was in composition, and Schiller forces history to pay compliments to the ruling house of Russia as well as to the family of his own Duke.

[3]*Aeneid* IV, 654-5 (in reverse order.)

Romanov and Axinia. Romanov can send a messenger
ahead to announce his submission to Boris. When the messenger
arrives Boris has already drunk the poison. Romanov follows
hard on his messenger and finds the Tsar dying. ... On the
corpse of the Tsar Romanov swears fealty to his son Fyodor, a
child, and makes the Boyars swear the same. ... We sense that
it will be *only* a futile attempt, for the overwhelming opponent
is already in Tula.

Romanov's love for Axinia is declared amid these unhappy
circumstances.

Romanov leaves Moscow to hasten to the army. ... In his
absence from Moscow the people of that city are roused to revolt
against Fyodor and Axinia; they storm the palace and capture
these two children of Boris. Romanov, deserted by the army and
by his own troops, proscribed and hounded by Demetrius' party,
comes as a fugitive to Moscow with the intention of rescuing
Axinia and the young Tsar.

Demetrius in Tula. The interest aroused by Romanov and
Axinia must not prejudice the high regard for Demetrius ...
[who] is kindly as the sun; ... no lust for revenge, no lust for
plunder, no overweening pride. And when he learns of Boris's
fall he displays a noble emotion: "He died a death worthy of
a king, but he robs me of the glory of magnanimity."

From here he sends for his mother and for Maryna. The
keys to the city are brought to him. ... In this scene in Tula
[Demetrius] stands at the pinnacle of fortune and favor.

Demetrius Discovers his Birth. ... Demetrius' whole becoming Tsar is founded on the testimony of a man who has not
been seen until now. He is an acquaintance from childhood
and earliest youth; since parting from him 14 or 15 years have
gone by. Amid the host of persons who throng to Demetrius
in Tula this man finally appears and is recognized by Demetrius.
Joy of the latter at this happy reunion. He sends all the others
out. When they are alone, Demetrius, with grateful heart, acknowledges he owes the whole lucky turn of his fate to him.

X[4] replies that Demetrius does indeed have a great obligation to him, and a greater one than he himself knows.

Demetrius urges him to disclose it to him and promises a royal gratitude.

A royal gift, replies the other, is surely worthy of a royal gratitude.

Yes, he readily admits that to his care alone he owes his restoration.

Not only that, he owes his very creation to him.

"How so?"

"I gave you what you never had. I do indeed deserve something from you. I gave you what you could never have hoped for, what your birth does not give you."

"How?"

"Everybody considers you, you consider yourself the son of Ivan. You are about to place the Tsar's crown on your head. You are not the son of Ivan! Your birth gives you no right to this crown. Ivan's son is in his grave, he will not dispute his name with you ..."

"I am not Ivan's son? Whose son am I then? Did you yourself not ... ?"

"I made you that, you are that through me, and you shall remain that too. Listen to how it came about, and if you find you owe me something, then ..."

"I am not Dmitri, Ivan's son?"

"Listen to me." (Now he relates to him the whole matter, and how he fled with him from Uglich, Boris's ingratitude, and his idea of avenging himself on him—his precautions to this end—even to the flight of Grishka and what ensued thereupon.)[5] ... "I could have kept it from you—maybe I should have kept it from you, but you had to know what you owed me, and ..."

While X is telling all this, a tremendous change comes over Demetrius, his silence is frightful and accompanied by a terrify-

[4]In a tentative list of characters in the play "X" is called Otrepev.
[5]A separate note indicates that Demetrius was the son of the real Dmitri's nurse.

ing expression. When Demetrius has mastered the first agitation, he gives play to cunning and sounds X out as to whether anyone else knows of this dangerous secret.

X reassures him on that score: all other accessories are dead.

... [Demetrius] seems suddenly to make his decision, and, partly in fury, partly with intention and premeditation, cuts the messenger down ...

"You have plunged a dagger through the heart of my life, you have torn from me my faith in myself. — Farewell, courage and hope. Farewell, you joyous confidence in myself! Joy! Trust and faith! — I am entangled in a lie, at odds with myself! I am an enemy of men, Truth and I are forever sundered! — What? Shall I wrest this nation and myself from its error? These great peoples believe in me. — Shall I plunge them in misery? In anarchy? Take their faith away from them? Shall I unmask myself as a betrayer? ... I must go forward. I must stand firm, and yet I can no longer do so through my own inner conviction. How shall I approach the Empress? How shall I enter Moscow amid the plaudits of the people with this lie in my heart?"

As people come in, they see the Tsar with the dagger and the dead man sprawled out, and they fall back with horror. ... "What?" they say, "Has the Tsar's purple so swiftly changed his spirit? Is it the new garments that have put him in this new frame of mind? The spirit of the Basilides[6] seems to have entered into him."

Directly from there he goes to his encounter with the Empress, his alleged mother, whose approach is announced to him. He issues commands concerning the manner of her reception.

MARFA MEETS DEMETRIUS. A large purple tent is set up, open in front, closed at the rear but so that with one pull it can be lifted. Marfa, now once again Marya, is waiting for Demetrius. Soltikov (or some other) has fetched her; Olga is with her. Imperial guards, who observe a restrained silence, surround the tent ...

She speaks of the impending meeting with more doubt and

---

[6]The Byzantine emperors.

fear than hope. Her faith in the person of Demetrius has almost entirely vanished, she trembles at the thought of the moment which was to have been her greatest bliss. Olga speaks to her, herself without faith. On the long journey both had had time to look at the obverse of circumstances and the initial exaltation had given way to reflection. . . .

As, anxiously waiting, she prepares herself for the ultimate, trumpets ring out; they pierce her heart. One hears the Tsar coming nearer and nearer by the drums. She trembles, uncertain as to whether she will go to meet him or collapse fainting. Finally Soltikov appears, swiftly opens the tent for the entering Tsar. Demetrius stands before his alleged mother, alone. . . .

The small remainder of hope in Marfa's heart vanishes totally at the sight of Demetrius. Something unidentifiable intervenes between the two, Nature does not speak, they are separated forever. The first moment was an attempt to approach each other. Marfa is the first to make a movement of retreat. As Demetrius notices this he stands *suspensus*. A momentary and supremely significant silence follows, which is broken by Marfa with the cry: "O, it is not he!"

Since Demetrius knows he is a deceiver, he would lose too much if he tried to counterfeit the emotions of Nature. Truth between him and her can elevate him. He behaves with dignity if he behaves as a prince and a statesman without showing himself a mountebank.

"Does your heart say nothing to you? Do you not recognize your own blood in me?".

Since she perseveres in her silence, he says: "Nature's voice is sacred and free. I wish neither to constrain it nor to counterfeit it. Had your heart spoken at sight of me, my own would have answered. You would have found a good son in me. . . . But if you do not feel for me as a mother, if you do not find your son in me, then think as a princess, summon self-control as a queen, and accede with wise choice to the inevitable. . . . I still rob your son of nothing; I did rob something from your enemy, but not from your son, and I will give you great things.

I have avenged you on your enemy, you and your blood-kindred;
I have brought you forth out of the tomb in which you were
buried alive and led you back to your princely throne. ... That
your destiny is fixed to mine, you quickly grasp; you stand with
me and with me you go down. I need say no more to you. You
know what you have to do. The nations are all looking at us. ...
I have not forged ahead as far as Moscow to lose the fruits of my
victory here, and you will not try to force me to fight in desperation for my existence. Therefore resign yourself. I trust you to
compose yourself and take your stand as a princess. ... Everyone is waiting to see the heartfelt meeting of the mother and
the son. Do not disappoint the general expectation. I detest
quackery, ... I really do feel a reverence for you, and this feeling, which bends my knees before you, is in earnest, ..."

MARFA: What shall I do? O Heaven, in what new, strange,
and confused state dost Thou plunge me?

DEMETRIUS: Take your stand and your distress will vanish.
Let your will's free action be what Nature and blood deny you.
I demand no hypocrisy, no lie, of you; I demand honest emotions.
Do not seem to be my mother, be her. Embrace me as a son!
... If I am not your son, I am still the Tsar. I have power.
I will treat you as a mother. You shall find a respectful son in
me. What more do you want? The one lying in his grave is
dust; *he has no heart to love you with,* he has no eyes with which
to smile at you, he will give you nothing; but I have given you
everything. Turn to the living one. ...

As she begins to burst into tears he finds the moment ripe
to show her to the people. "O these golden drops are welcome
to me. Let them flow! Show yourself *this* way to the people!"

"What do you seek from me?"

"Acknowledge me before the people. They are standing out
there with tense expectation. Follow me out to them. Give me
your blessing. Call me your son and everything will be decided.
I shall lead you into the Kremlin in Moscow."

"I am to [acknowledge] you who are a stranger to me,
who..."

At the close of this scene he drops the tent and shows his mother to the assemblage. ...

ENTRY INTO MOSCOW. [Schiller provides suggestions for the scene painters and the stage carpenters to create a spectacular perspective of the city of Moscow into which a gorgeous triumphal procession will move.] A pontoon bridge over the Moskva can appear, by means of which the procession can double back. Since the audience plays a role in this scene, more space can be assigned to it. ... [Demetrius] himself rescues Axinia from the bloodthirsty hands of the Cossacks or of the people, and he can even rescue Michael Romanov. Axinia displays a touching greatness in misfortune and thereby wins his heart. ...

ACT IV

DEMETRIUS AS TSAR IN THE KREMLIN. Demetrius is Tsar and the Russians do not like him. He cannot keep the Poles and Cossacks in order. ... He is in love with Axinia and would gladly forget and break his Polish engagement. He neglects the old Empress. He inspires mistrust in everyone because he finds himself a betrayer in his heart. Hence a highly sensitive pride which gives umbrage, and a moody despotism. He has no friend...

As he is planning disloyalty to Maryna, the latter appears in Moscow. He can discuss this question with Job. Job finds nothing simpler, he gives him a high idea of his Imperial might, of the totality of his power, of his will. (Job wants only to get rid of the Poles and then hopes to bring about Demetrius' fall the sooner.) Odowalsky, however, has his eye peeled for everything that is going on and notes Maryna's advantages. ... Soltikov bitterly reproaches himself for having betrayed his fatherland to Demetrius, but he does not wish to become a traitor for a second time... The arrival of the Polish fiancée is announced. He has to go to meet her. Shuiski comes to the [Russian] malcontents and incites them further. This scene is interrupted by the brutal intervention of the Poles... Romanov, unrecognizable and in disguise, comes to Moscow, seeking Axinia.

DEMETRIUS WITH MARYNA. False and cold reception, which she, however, is able to dissimulate superbly. She insists on a swift marriage. When the Tsar is gone, Maryna issues death commands and instructs her Poles. Raucous preparations for the festival.

AXINIA KILLED AT MARYNA'S BIDDING. She was close to becoming Empress and must go to her grave. Her beautiful death.

57

With joy she takes the poison cup from the hand of her enemy or from the latter's emissaries.

You bring me death? O welcome! I was afraid it was the Imperial crown!

Demetrius with broken heart has to follow Maryna to the marriage ceremony. She is a cold Fury.

Insolence of the Poles to the Russians and against the Tsar himself.

Conspiracy of Boyars.

Romanov in prison. He sees an apparition of Axinia and is summoned to the throne. He is to let Fate ripen quietly and not stain himself with bloodshed.

ACT V

DEMETRIUS AND MARYNA AFTER THE MARRIAGE AND CORONA-
TION. Maryna ... confesses she does not believe he is the Tsare-
vich and never did believe he was. Then she leaves him alone.
He remains alone and seeks to stupefy himself.

DEMETRIUS AND CASIMIR. [Demetrius recalls happier times
of youth at Sendomir and the tender friendship with Lodoiska.]
He asks Casimir, Lodoiska's brother, about that youth, i.e., about
himself, as if he were another person; he seems so unlike himself
and has gone through so much since then, that those days seem
to lie amid a twilight. ...

OUTBREAK OF THE CONSPIRACY. Fugitive Poles rush in, crying "Save yourself!" Demetrius escapes with his sword. Con-
spirators rush in, search for him. Lodoiska's brother alone sacrifices himself for him when all the others think only of their
escape.

MARFA AND DEMETRIUS. [Marfa] is in conversation with
some attendant ladies when Demetrius comes in. ... He tries
to inspire fear in her, fear of his desperation and fear of the
Russians who would not forgive her old deception; *she must
assert her first declaration or she is lost.. ....* He has only time
to express his reasons for these demands when the enemy rushes
into the room. Marfa has not yet had time to state her decision.

DEMETRIUS. THE REBELS. By his majesty and his boldness
Demetrius actually brings the furious rebels to silence for a few
minutes. In fact, he is on the point of disarming them as he
seeks to deliver the Poles to them. Actually it is more hatred
against the latter than against him that brought them to insur-
rection. ... Yet Marfa must not stand too idly by in this scene,
or else the scene would have to be very brief.

DEMETRIUS IS KILLED. When Demetrius is on the point of

bringing the rebels around, Shuiski forces his way in, followed by a more furious crowd. Priests are among them. He demands a categorical declaration from the Empress and makes her kiss the Cross in swearing that Demetrius is her son. Now she seems to have his fate in her hands. Everyone looks at her. But precisely this confidence in her honesty, this binding and religious thing, makes it impossible for her to speak contrary to her conscience. Both parties address her. Demetrius says she must not be afraid to acknowledge him. Shuiski says she must not be afraid to reject him, everybody knows she had recognized him only from being talked into it or from fear.

During this silence, which in itself is testimony enough, tension rises to the utmost. The palace is gradually filling up at the same time. Weapons are drawn against Demetrius' heart. Instead of answering, she walks away, or merely turns aside, or withdraws her hand that Demetrius is holding. One of those present observes quite rightly that her silence is already adequate condemnation of him. If she were his mother, if she so much as thought it were possible for her to be, she would surely offer him her own bosom as a shield. When she turns away, one of them cries out, "Ha! Betrayer! She is silent, she rejects you... Die, betrayer!"

ALL: Die, betrayer!

MARYNA SAVES HERSELF. END OF THE PLAY. Maryna is pursued by the Russians and also flees to Marfa, where she arrives just as Demetrius is murdered. With the raging enemy behind her, she rushes into Marfa's room, where she finds another crowd of raging enemies. ... She does not hesitate for a moment to renounce Demetrius and pretends to have been herself most miserably deceived by him. She makes common cause, as it were, with the Russians against him and seeks to rouse pity as an unfortunate victim of this deception. She does not rouse it, but the ransom which she promises for her life, the sacrifice of her jewels, the mentioned threat of Polish vengeance, etc. appease the rebels, who have been cooled off generally by the murder of Demetrius anyway. Shuiski says one victim is enough and commands the blood bath to be ended. His affair is now to mount the throne of Russia. ...

When everyone has gone, one of the mob can remain behind who has been able to get possession of the Imperial seal or who has come upon it accidentally. In this find he glimpses a means of playing the role of Demetrius. ...

[A] monologue of the second Demetrius can conclude the play, as he gives a glimpse into a new series of storms and, as it were, begins the old course anew. The man is a Cossack of reckless courage who has already appeared before.

THE BRIDE OF MESSINA, set in old Sicily, played to the chants of a unique double chorus in conflict with itself, unrolls a dramatic parable of the unequal struggle between man and the mystery of human destiny. Donna Isabella, her three sons, and all her house have been marked out by Fate, and Schiller catches them at the hour when doom engulfs them. Within a single revolution of the sun, blood ties and gentle breeding are slashed away by incest and murder. Weak and strong alike are stripped and tossed into annihilation. As in O'Neill's *Mourning Becomes Electra,* an almost romantically somber melancholy is crossed with classicism to produce a powerful effect of symbolic inevitability. Included as a preface to the text is Schiller's essay "On the Use of the Chorus in Tragedy."

WILLIAM TELL, a long play glorifying the legendary Swiss marksman, is an almost brass-band creation among Schiller's more symphonic plays. Against the magnificent backdrop of the Alps, the portrait of Tell shows a man of giant strength and singleness of purpose, who wished only to return to simple obscurity once he had destroyed the tyrant king. The themes of courage and freedom and the colorful cast of characters helped make this one of Schiller's most popular dramas.